GW00866285

SEASHORE MAN AND AFRIC/

and speculations about the origin of manki
6-8M years ago. The author's personal i   ...asoning knits
together the works of leading writers and ac   ....c papers in the relevant fields.

The principal role of the eastern African Indian Ocean littoral and seafood nutrition is central to his hypothesis. Also featured is the particular importance of seashores as endless highways for hominin migrations as ice-ages waxed and waned, thus making possible the spread of our ancestors around Eurasia, Australia and eventually into the Americas. The author's speculations about the mutational effects of cosmic radiation bursts, which he first investigated in 1991, have received attention.

The effects of cyclical ice-age glacial periods and regional climate changes creating environmental challenges, and sustained seafood nutrition over many millennia, were perhaps enhanced by radiation bursts in a complex of mutational triggers and feedback activities. It was this particular combination acting on our advanced primate ancestor in differing circumstances and intensities over five million years which may have resulted in the extraordinary being which is humanity today.

"SEASHORE MAN AND AFRICAN EVE is one of those ground-breaking books that only come along once a while, but when they do they overturn everything we know about who we are, where we came from, and what brought us here in the first place. Denis Montgomery has uncovered a remarkable secret of science by proposing that cosmic rays can and do effect evolutionary jumps and that our earliest ancestors taste for a better diet carried them ever further around the globe. Years ahead of its time, this book can now be appreciated for what it really is – a revelation in our knowledge of the past."

Andrew Collins - Author of *The Cygnus Mystery*

Denis Montgomery was born in 1934 in Natal, South Africa, and during his varied career he travelled widely in Africa and around the Indian Ocean rim. He lived and worked in Nigeria, South Africa, Mozambique, Brazil and England but whenever possible he travelled. It was tourism projects in the wilderness that spurred his early fascination with African pre-history and modern population and environmental impacts. Since the 1960s, these have been his abiding passions. He was elected a Fellow of The Royal Geographical Society in 1989.

Cover picture : "Seashore Men" at Tiwi Beach, Kenya in 1987. Photo by the author.

SEASHORE MAN AND AFRICAN EVE

An Exploration of Evolution in Africa

Third revised Edition

Denis Montgomery

What's past is prologue.
William Shakespeare

Other books by the same author
The Reflected Face of Africa, 1988
     Revised edition, 2006
Two Shores of the Ocean, 1992
Crest of the Wave, 2007
Mud, Sands & Seas, 2007
A beautiful Ivory Bangle, 2008
Closing the Circle, 2010
Hulett, 2014
etc

Third revised Edition, 2017
Produced with WordPerfect v 17 in Palatina Linotype.
All photographs are by the author unless noted.

Publishing history
Aquatic Ape and African Eve
1995 : Unpublished, deposited in the library of
the British Institute in Eastern Africa, Nairobi
1999 : Revised for the Internet
2003 : Revised for Lulu
2007 : Revision
Seashore Man and African Eve
2008 : Second revised Edition

African Insight
41, Majors Close, Chedburgh
Bury St.Edmunds, Suffolk. IP29 4UN
England
www.sondela.co.uk

Published by LULU in the United States of America
Lulu Enterprises Inc
Raleigh, NC. 27606
www.lulu.com
Lulu reference : 20598112

ISBN : 978-1-326-94714-9

CONTENTS

Contents continued:

ILLUSTRATIONS
Photographs are by the author except where indicated.

Climate graphs from the Internet were inserted where they seem appropriate.

'Seashore Men' at Tiwi Beach, Kenya south coast, August 1987.

One morning towards the end of our stay at Tiwi Beach, *I was sitting on the verandah as usual after breakfast nursing a mug of coffee. The tide was flowing and water was deepening over the reef. The thunder and roar of the waves breaking on the outer bastion was growing. A holidaying English family was coming home from an early morning exploration to their breakfast, picking their way carefully over the old coral, the children trailing behind the adults and chattering.*

Following the holiday makers were two dark figures, stopping here and there, moving confidently onwards, then pausing again. They were two local men whom I had seen many times and I idly followed them with my eyes, until a thought burst into my mind that astonished me with its simple and absolute obviousness. Those men went out onto the reef every day and on their return, they passed by our cottages peddling fresh fish and shellfish. I knew them by sight and they always greeted me whether I bought or not. Why had I not seen it? They were seashore men; there for any doubter to examine. It was not necessary to theorise at Tiwi Beach, intuitive observation provided me with proof.

I watched while they emerged from the sea and strolled up the lawn. Each young man was clad in a brief kikoyi cloth wrapped around his waist and they were burned obsidian black by the sun. Their curly Negro hair glistened with moisture. From a string around their waists was slung a handmade tool, a simple metal spike with a wooden handle that they used to pry shellfish from the rocks, and they carried a roughly barbed trident on the end of a long bamboo pole that they used to spear fish and octopus. A handmade sisal bag hung from their shoulders for shellfish and each had fish strung through their gills by a length of coconut frond. Remove the machine-woven cotton kikoyi and substitute bone, ivory or stone for iron and they were equipped as any seashore-living man would have been for a million years, since that last great evolutionary jump.

Adapted from *Two Shores of the Ocean* (1992) - Denis Montgomery.

AUTHOR'S NOTE TO THIS THIRD EDITION

The first edition was published on the Internet in the public domain in 1999. However, the first version was completed in 1995 and deposited in the library of the British Institute of Eastern Africa in Nairobi. This was revised several times as I learned and read more.

But my interest was fully sparked many years before, beginning with Robert Ardrey's *African Genesis* (1961) and Desmond Morris' *The Naked Ape* (1967). I was intrigued by their theses, and later extensions, but never convinced because I had intimate knowledge of African savannahs. I was a child of Africa with a fascination for its geography. I could not accept that habitual and irrevocable bipedalism and a naked skin would be an advantage to a hominin of four million years ago on the tropical savannahs. Indeed, I saw these changes leading straight to proven extinctions, so there had to be another path.

Elaine Morgan's *The Descent of Woman* (1972), with its obvious feminist slant, limited application and some easily recognised flaws, showed me the path. I was hooked. During the last fifty years there have been a vast number of books and papers published on the evolution of mankind, especially as landmark fossil discoveries in the Great Rift Valley and adjacent savannah were made. Many researchers have worked in associated fields of paleoclimate and paleobiology which provide interdisciplinary support for human evolution speculations.

Fossil evidence was understandably used to support a maturing savannah hypothesis. While Morgan published later books of greater scholastic rigour in support of a waterside alternative, she sustained personal attacks for her perceived lack of science and the waterside hypothesis was vilified by numerous commentators. Significantly, with a particular exception of Professor Phillip Tobias, prominent scientists in the field chose largely to ignore the waterside hypothesis and kept themselves clear of the often trivial and malicious controversy. Other scientists, not of the disciplines of palaeontology and palaeanthropology which were guided by the central African fossil discoveries, researching the development of brains and unique human abilities such as language and speech, were not so constrained. They were sympathetic to a seashore hypothesis and some have been ardent supporters.

I followed all the published material which came my way and developed my general hypothesis, which has no pretensions to academic science and is based on the science and speculative reasoning of others. I have interpreted these scientific speculations with my own reasoning and intuitive thinking during forty years and more. I have modified my interpretations as time passed, but I have always intended to present an inclusive discussion.

I published *Aquatic Ape and African Eve* with Lulu in the U.S.A. in 2003 with a supporting website. In 2008 I published a revised edition and changed the name to *Seashore Man and African Eve* because of the continuing barrage of criticism of a waterside and seashore hypothesis. I saw that the term, Aquatic Ape, was in any case outmoded and misleading. My hypothesis encompassed the whole period of human evolution until the African Late Stone Age of *Homo sapiens* and was not limited to the 'jump' from forest ape to bipedal *Australopithecus*.

In the last ten years the idea of a simplistic savannah locale for evolution has been gradually discarded with a greater understanding of the effects of Pleistocene climate changes on African vegetation zones. Intense study of fossils suggests that earliest bipedal hominins variously inhabited the savannah, forest fringes and even canopy forests. It has been remarked that : "there are savannahs and savannahs". Recognition that gorillas, chimps, baboons and other monkeys sometimes wade in freshwater on two legs adds to the complexity of opinion and speculation. However, the seashores of tropical Africa continued to be ignored or disparaged.

It appears to me that this is partly a product of criticism of the Aquatic Ape Theory of forty years ago, as prominently presented by layperson Elaine Morgan. The theory, at that time, could be interpreted by critics as proposing that early hominins evolved as semi-aquatic creatures, living much of the time in the sea. This was the source of much derision, but was not the intention of Morgan and her supporters. It is my belief that this misunderstanding, accidental or maybe deliberate in some cases, is the source of the decades-long confrontation between over-simplified savannah and seashore hypotheses. Arguments which could be applied forty and fifty years ago are long obsolete. The Savannah Hypothesis has undergone much revision, but so has the Seashore Hypothesis. Sadly, they are often still viewed as mutually exclusive, and I cannot understand why : they are both so obviously part of the same story.

It was incomprehensible to me how it was contended that *Australopithecines* and *Homo erectus* roamed the interior of Africa from the Sahara all the way down the Great Rift Valley and adjacent savannah, with their huge variation within mingling and merging habitats, during several glacial-interglacial climate cycles, to the South African Highveld and Kalahari fringes *for three million years*, but did not sojourn on the thousands of kilometres of hospitable tropical seashores of the Indian Ocean with abundant food from reefs, the sea and the perennial coastal monsoon forests. What was the logic?

Recently, I listened to Sir David Attenborough's BBC Radio 4 talk, *The Waterside Ape* in September 2016, and read two latest popular books by academics: Juval Noah Harari's *Sapiens* (2014) and John S. Compton's *Human Origins* (2016). This sparked my desire to update my own published material.

John Compton is a scientist at the University of Cape Town and his book is a masterpiece of detailed presentation of current knowledge for a general readership. It is clearly the result of many years of thought and study. He embraced the vital importance of seafoods as an ingredient in the development of brains and neural systems, but he applied this primarily to the South African Cape coast as the location for the transition from *Homo erectus* and their possible divergent variations to *Homo sapiens* during the last two hundred thousand years. He advocated seafood nutrition as an essential aid to this from evidence in recent archeological sites, but was hesitant in suggesting it during the previous two million years and more. He was beset by the problem of fossil evidence. Fossils of *Australopithecus* and earlier *Homo* species are found in the interior of Africa, but not on the tropical Indian Ocean shores.

There had also been new and significant paleaontological discoveries in South Africa by Lee Berger and associates at the University of the Witwatersrand. The focus had moved from East Africa, where there was something of a hiatus in new fossil discovery, to South Africa, but the general theme of the on-going revision of a modified Savannah Hypothesis remained. Arguments and speculations had been extended, but they were considering details and a seashore dimension previous to maybe 200,000 years ago was still excluded.

Here is the core of the problem. Since 1960 when Sir Alister Hardy, because of damaging exaggerations and derision in the popular press, needed to publish his thoughts on a possible semi-aquatic seashore solution to human evolution, there has been relentless opposition. A belligerent adversarial stance, most often by non-scientific commentators, has been maintained and has recently burgeoned with the expansion of the Internet and its 'social media'. I deplore the confrontational and adversarial treatment to which human evolution has been subjected.

The narrative of evolution has to be a combination of the two hypotheses. Quite simply, it has to be the interaction of the effects of long periods of residence in both complex and varied habitats over very long periods which has resulted in our evolution, and I see this to be an easy path to accept and describe. But it seems to have personal difficulty within the academic or professional scientific community. Who will break down this pattern of exclusion and controversy which has prevailed for over fifty years?

Attenborough made a gallant attempt but has been met by some of the usual spurious, even laughable, criticism together with personal attacks on his integrity. An example of the scientific establishment's reaction to Attenborough's radio programmes is this extract from the influential liberal *Guardian* newspaper of 16 September 2016 :

> Sir David Attenborough's Radio 4 series on the theory that human ancestors descended from the trees via an aquatic evolutionary phase has been dismissed as based on wishful thinking about an implausible theory by the anatomist and broadcaster Prof Alice Roberts.
>
> In an article for the Conversation, Roberts slammed Attenborough's decision to create a two-part radio series on the theory, known as the aquatic ape hypothesis, which she said lacks credible evidence to support it.
>
> "Occasionally in science there are theories that refuse to die despite the overwhelming evidence against them. The 'aquatic ape hypothesis' is one of these, now championed by Sir David Attenborough in his recent BBC Radio 4 series The Waterside Ape," she wrote in an article co-authored by Mark Maslin of University College, London.

The story of human evolution is one cohesive narrative, not two competing theories. I applaud the step forward towards the goal of an inclusive theory presented by Prof. John Compton's *Human Origins* (2016) and hope that he and other scientists will be able to expand the theme of seafood nutrition into wider time and space.

Denis Montgomery
Chedburgh
21 February 2017.

PREFACE TO THE SECOND EDITION IN 2008

This is a revised and abridged edition of my book published in 2003. Chapters not specifically relevant to the evolution of mankind were edited out and reworked into a new book, *A Beautiful Ivory Bangle,* published simultaneously.

There are additions resulting from new discoveries and publications. In March 2008, for instance, the journal, *Nature,* contained the defining paper on the discovery and analysis of a hominid jawbone in the Sierra Atapuerca in northern Spain, the first absolutely dated fossil of a member of the *Homo* genus in western Europe. And in April 2008 a new study of the genetic structures of Africans was published illustrating their evolution since the emergence of modern mankind 200,000 years ago. This has particular importance in defining divergence in Africa which I have endeavoured to unravel.

The hypothesis that humanity evolved from an ancestral ape through the influence and environment of the seashore has been current for more than forty five years. During enormous leaps in academic and popular knowledge, it has been generally known as the 'Aquatic Ape Theory', or AAT. This hypothesis is subject to continuous change reflecting advancing information, and both learned and sometimes acrimonious argument. Proponents of the hypothesis have been almost always laypersons (most notably Elaine Morgan) or, if academics, they have usually been of other disciplines than those directly concerned with palaeontology, palaeanthropology and archaeology. I believe that a barrier to serious international academic discussion of this seminal problem is that of the name itself. The 'Aquatic Ape Theory' has been treated without respect and derision for so long that it has acquired a crackpot image.

In any case, the name itself no longer has validity when considering the whole range of human evolution. The role of the ocean littoral and seafood nutrition may well be more important in considering the last two million years of *Homo* development than an aquatic stimulus to vertical stance and habitual bipedalism *per se.*

Continuing exploration of the African Middle Stone Age cave sites on the Cape coast and elsewhere in South Africa has become fashionable. There is a dawning acceptance that seafood nutrition has a principal role in the growth and increased complexity of human brains and neural systems at least during that era.

I have focussed on the themes explicitly concerning evolution which interested me, concentrate the scope of the book and therefore reduce its size.

Acknowledgments

I am grateful to everybody who has gone out of his or her way to help during my travels and researches. Without exception, many professionals and academics were welcoming. The debt owed to the books and papers which others have written is immeasurable. In the Bibliography I have listed not only those from which I directly culled information or opinion for my writing but also many others which have influenced my thinking and broadened my knowledge over the years.

I must record particular gratitude to busy people who critically commented on parts of my work, helped with discussion or gave me specific information : the late Dr Richard Wilding at the Fort Jesus Museum in Mombasa; Professor Tom Huffman of the University of the Witwatersrand; Dr Tim Maggs and Dr Gavin Whitelaw of the Natal Museum; Leonard van Schalkwyk previously of the KwaZulu-Natal Monuments Council; Professor L.B.Crossland of the University of Ghana; Prof. Jouke Wigboldus of the Wageningen Agricultural University; Prof. Felix Chami of the University of Dar-es-Salaam; Dr. Royden Yates of the South African Museum in Cape Town; Dr Tim Redfield of the Geological Survey of Norway; the late Prof. Phillip Tobias of the University of the Witwatersrand; Dr E Rohling of the School of Ocean and Earth Science of Southampton University; Dr Peter Jakubowski of the Naturics Foundation; Dr. Mark Maslin of University College, London; Richard Bailey of the University of KwaZulu-Natal, and especially Prof. Michael Crawford of the Institute of Brain Chemistry and Human Nutrition in London.

If I have to single out one of these, it has to be Phillip Tobias. I learned from him that we nearly met in July 1949 at the important Makapan's Valley palaeontological site. He was a student accompanying Raymond Dart, I was a teenager on an adventure holiday. At a meeting and in correspondence he advised and encouraged me to think and write. His breadth of knowledge of Africa, open mind and wisdom was a continual inspiration.

The Killie Campbell Memorial Library of the University of Natal provided valuable assistance on numerous occasions. I enjoyed a series of courses on European archaeology at Manchester University in the early 1990s and a brief course on latest issues with Saharan rock-art at Cambridge University in 2005.

I have always found my membership of the British Institute in Eastern Africa in Nairobi, Kenya, to be rewarding. This institute organised two unique and valuable conferences which I attended. Dr John Sutton is noted for the organisation of the conference on the Growth of Farming Communities in Africa South of the Equator at Cambridge, England, in July

1994, and Dr Paul Lane that on the Maritime Heritage of the Western Indian Ocean at Stone Town, Zanzibar, in July 2006.

The sadly defunct South-West Africa Scientific Society provided a unique service for research in its day and provided me with some unique opportunities.

The late Dr Lyall Watson suggested that I read Barrow & Tipler's *The Anthropic Cosmological Principle*. The late Elaine Morgan alerted me to the conference on the Aquatic Ape Theory at Valkenberg in August 1987. Her assiduous pursuit of the Aquatic Ape Theory for more than thirty years and her several books have informed and stimulated all who found conventional hypotheses unsatisfactory.

Professor Alan Collier expressed faith in my original project. I was indebted to Dr Patricia Collier and Dr Gregory Kerr who read entire texts, detected inconsistencies and omissions and identified poor argument. Gregory Kerr cheerfully undertook the tedious task of correcting my style which was not developed for the rigour of writing in this context. Miriam Vigar, besides being a staunch friend and a companion on many safaris, helped with revisions of the several texts and lent me her computer for weeks at a time when I was far from home. My friend Alan Fry devoted time and energy to instructing me in publishing on the Internet.

Following an article by Adrian Berry in *Astronomy Now* (March 2006) which mentioned my work, scientific author Andrew Collins was of great assistance in sharing his investigations and directing me towards latest research on bursts of cosmic radiation on the Earth, and the sources of these powerful agents for mutations in lifeforms. His extensive research on the prevailing influence that the study of astronomical bodies has had on mankind is described in *The Cygnus Mystery* (Watkins Publishing, 2006).

My companions on various safaris in Africa and around the Indian Ocean rim over some fifty years and more are "the very spice of life, that gives it all its flavour". I credit my friend, the late Tito Das Neves Larcher, with launching my lifelong fascination with the historical role of Indian Ocean shores. I am indebted to Harry Bourne and other email correspondents who provided information and lively inspiration.

My wife Sue is always the anchor about which my restless ship swings.

SEASHORE MAN AND AFRICAN EVE

An Exploration of Evolution in Africa

Third revised Edition

The chief said ... Man originated on the seashore, and many of the most primitive habits of humans, as well as their bodily differences from the apes, came from their early life there. Man pushed back from the salt water slowly.
- Frederick O'Brien in *Mystic Isles of the South Seas* [1921]

Beach tucker has the added advantage of remaining available when the savannah dries up during an ice-age.
- Stephen Oppenheimer in *Out of Eden* [2003]

... the point is that whatever the pressures experienced by our ancestors to develop a larger brain, no response would have been possible without the necessary nutritional resources. Diet is, in this model, an enabling factor, not a selective framework.
- John Parkington in *Shorelines, Strandlopers and Shell Middens* [2006]

We suggest that human evolution, like that of previous epochs, was substrate-driven. By using the land-water interface, Homo aquaticus *need have been neither wholly aquatic nor wholly land-based: he simply enjoyed the best of both.*
- Michael Crawford & David March in *The Driving Force* [1989]

Man with all his noble qualities ... still bears in his bodily frame the indelible stamp of his lowly origins.

*

I believe it is because we are always slow in admitting any great change of which we do not see the intermediate steps. The mind cannot grasp the full meaning of the term of a million or hundred million years, and cannot consequently add up and perceive the full effects of small successive variations accumulated during almost infinitely many generations.
- Charles Darwin [1809 - 1882]

Lake Kivu, the western arm of the Great Rift Valley   Author's photo, 1985

The forests and lakes where the ancient apes lived.

Tiwi Beach, Kenya   Author's photo, 2006

Tropical Indian Ocean seashores - abundant source of nutrients for the development of brains and neural systems.

Wilderness within Tsavo National Park, Kenya   Author's photo 1965

The great empty dry savannah plains of Africa.

Bamburi, Kenya   Author's photo, 2006

Tropical seashores - an endless safe highway for migrations.

19

CYCLICAL CLIMATE CHANGE DURING THE PLIOCENE AND PLEISTOCENE ERAS. DECISIVE DRIVER OF EVOLUTION

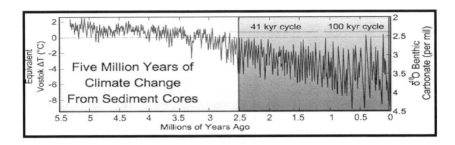

Diagram from the Internet, 2017 - Vostok ice-core proxy data.

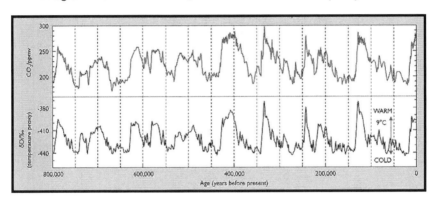

Diagram from the Internet, 2017 - Source : British Antarctic Survey.

The graphs are the result of analysis of ice-cores from the EPICA dome and Vostok in Antarctica. They show evidence of a consistently warmer climate during the Pliocene (when *Australopithecus* was evolving) and massive climate cycles during the later part of the Pleistocene, a critical period for human evolution. Cyclical climate changes dominate the narrative of human evolution. The diagrams will be repeated where appropriate.

Especially, note the close but not always exact, correlation of temperature and CO_2 concentration. CO_2 is also important to the evolution story because it is an essential ingredient of vegetation health and geographic spread.

20

During a warm interglacial, sea levels are high, global rainfall is at a peak, vegetation is at its greatest extent and habitable land area in the northern hemisphere is at its maximum. During the cold, glacial periods, the opposite applies. Mammal numbers, proliferation and genetic diversion is stimulated during interglacials; hardship, population reduction and extinctions occur during glacials. Natural selection at both ends of these climate cycles refines all species in this way.

During the last 10,000 years, the Holocene Era, during which humanity has developed agriculture, civilisation and metallurgy, cultural evolution has been extraordinary and exponential. The rate of change is bewildering and may be ascribed to the stable climate during this period. The small variations we discern, and which cause so much public and political comment at present, are minimal compared to the past record during which hominin evolution occurred. Obviously, there have been other periods of short-term stability like that which we are experiencing at present, and we can assume that there were 'jumps' in cultural evolution during those times.

However, although cultural evolution is proven to work fast, it is dependent on the platform of physical status. *Homo sapiens* will adopt new culture at very many grades faster than a chimp-like hominid. Genetic and anatomical evolution has to be much slower, of the order of major climate changes, as illustrated in the graphs. The relatively few, widely scattered fossils that have been found tell us about the forms of our distant ancestors, and the huge climatic swings during genetic and anatomical evolution clearly had a great impact on that evolution. There are clues in the climate record which may be used to understand particular 'jumps'. But there are undoubtedly other, more potent, short-term events which we still need to discover, understand and evaluate.

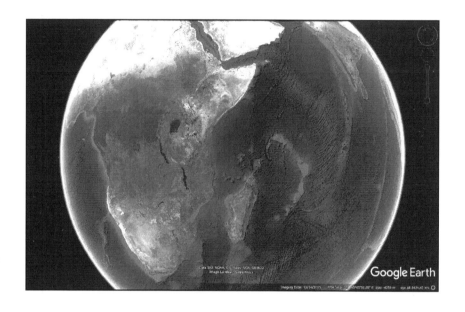

The world of ancient Seashore Man

INTRODUCTION
My fascination with a Seashore Hypothesis describing critical elements in the evolution and development of humanity.

In science the credit goes to the man who convinces the world, not to the man to whom the idea first occurs.

Sir Francis Darwin FRS [1848 - 1925], son of Charles Darwin.

For many years I had been baffled by the apparent indifference, often derision, with which scientists most concerned with human evolution had excluded discussion of the Seashore Hypothesis. I wondered if they were apprehensive because it was mostly non-academics who were the protagonists?

The logic, which thirty years ago still seemed somewhat tenuous, pointed at the simple common-sense of the particular environment of the tropical African shore. As circumstantial evidence accumulated from diverse sources, it fascinated me to watch a scenario, in which I had faith, grow to be unassailable.

I became heartened by the evidence provided by scientific disciplines other than palaeontology. I believed that palaeontologists had become trapped by their own speculative scenarios whose inconsistences some repeated as years passed. Alternative minor sketches within the general savannah hypothesis were devised and seemed to be tossed out without proper care for cohesiveness within the big picture. I wondered that people whose opinions I should regard with great respect seemed to have lost their way and were obdurate in disregarding a scenario which was so evident. Particularly, I was puzzled by the apparent absoluteness of scientific opinion : mankind either evolved on the savannah or at the seashore. Knowing East Africa intimately, I could not understand this. Several river-roads cross the dry savannah from proven hominin fossil sites to the Indian Ocean. If hominins could wander and settle interior Africa for millions of years, what prevented them from living at the seaside with its abundant foods, during many ice-age cycles?

In seeking answers to simple questions about the behaviour of animals in African wilderness, I had long become satisfied that the simplest answers were always the best. The most obvious questions loomed ever hugely in my thoughts. Why are we so addicted to seashores, especially in warm climates? Why do modern people with excesses of disposable income devote so much of it to seaside holidays in crowded and expensive resorts in warm climates? The usual explanations are unsatisfactory when you think about it with some depth and objectivity.

Why do we love to bathe in water and why are we such good swimmers, and especially divers; far better than other apes and almost all large land mammals? Why are babies naturally immediately at home in water? Especially, why do we love to bathe in seawater? We can't drink it! Why do we want to paddle about in canoes, ride on surf-boards, cruise about in sleek luxury yachts costing as much as a home, and 'mess about in boats' for hours and days of precious leisure time no matter how bad the weather.

Fishermen and traders have used the oceans to make an often precarious and dangerous living, requiring physical endurance and hardship far beyond any similar occupation on land, for many centuries. Surely these were ancient genetic imperatives since they apparently have no evolutionary or life-sustaining advantage?

In searching for our origins, we can recognize three distinct phases of development which fossils have been able to define. Much has been learned about these phases, but in the orthodox scenario there is a missing ingredient or driving force which should link them together. The three phases are : the jump from an early ancestral forest ape like a primitive chimpanzee to a two-legged upright walking hominin (the *Australopithecus* family), the jump from an upright walking hominin to a creature with a nearly-modern anatomy but a relatively small brain (*Homo erectus*), and the jump from *Homo erectus* to modern humans with a large brain (*Homo sapiens*).

How did these jumps occur? What drove the physiological and cultural changes? The institutional body of science has ideas, but mostly does not know. Individual scientists speculate, but there is no conventional consensus yet and certainly no proof of any speculation. There is no proof because there are no fossils clearly demonstrating transitions between them.

The Seashore Hypothesis connects these phases of human ancestry. The link is the Indian Ocean littoral environment and fossil evidence would open the door to enlightenment. But, no fossil evidence has been found and it is because no palaeontologist is looking where it may exist, which is along ancient seashores of tropical eastern Africa. They do not know where those ancient seashores may have been. It is a snake with its tail in its mouth!

The Aquatic Ape Theory (AAT) was opened for debate in 1960 by Sir Alister Hardy, a distinguished marine biologist, as the solution to the enigma of the jump from ape to upright walking ape-man or hominin. I believe there is over-sufficient evidence to promote wide scientific discourse on a presumption that an Indian Ocean littoral environment provided the driving force for all three jumps. It is where the core-population evolved, and from this core emigrant movements proceeded in favourable climatic periods during at least the last four million years. It is fossils of those emigres that have been found and the core-population is the missing link.

As the number and diverse locations of new fossil finds accumulates, the paleoanthropological leading to an understanding of human origins continually expands. What is fascinating, however, is that so far nothing negates the hypothesis that the jumps to our present state were stimulated by a seashore habitat for various long periods of time. And, so far, there is a continuing lack of acknowledgement in public statements or writing by many authorities on the power of a 'driving force' provided by long periods of uninterrupted concentrations of a seafood diet in tropical East African environments. It is through this research into seafood diet and its effect on mammal brains and neural systems that a body of scientists, not of the palaeontological or paleoanthropological disciplines, have had a positive leaning towards the seashore hypothesis for thirty years or more. Interestingly, I remember Phillip Tobias telling me that Raymond Dart had been intrigued but "did not have the time to look into it"! Dart died in 1988.

Research on seafood diet and the essential part that lipids play in the development of mammal brains and nervous systems continues to show the way. But at this time it is still the vital factor ignored in conventional hypotheses by most palaeontologists and anthropologists who, in public at least, reveal their adherence to an increasingly unsustainable unique savannah-origin. Irrefutable evidence that seafoods are the best possible nutritional regime for the development of brains has resulted in acceptance that *Homo sapiens* benefited from this during the last 150,000 years or more at the Cape of Good Hope. But, that it was more easily available in greater abundance along benign tropical seashores for the previous four million years continues to be ignored or denied.

I cannot understand the mind-set which assumes that a bipedal hominin (the ancestral human family) at various stages of millions of years of evolution, could roam Africa from the Sahara to the far southern Cape of Good Hope but not sojourn on the seashores of the tropical Indian Ocean. Perennial river-roads connect the Great Rift Valley to the sea, the seasonally arid savannah abuts the coastal forests and the coral reefs for thousands of kilometres.

New understanding of the effect of cosmic radiation provides another important theme which needs exploration. Very high-energy particles, undetected until recently, and bursts of electro-magnetic waves coming from supernovae, blazars and black holes are a puzzle and excite astro-physicists. Variations in our sun's output are being measured with greater accuracy, and interpretations of all this are being examined with new insights. Mutation in larger animals, especially complex mammals such as hominids, may be caused by exceptional bursts of high-energy cosmic radiation. Apart from negative effects in living animals which cause premature deaths from cancer and similar disease, and lead to extinctions, this may alter DNA resulting in benign changes in soft tissues. These changes would be honed by natural selection working in coincidental combination with all the other environmental factors, especially seafood nutrition.

One can imagine several feedback mechanisms acting in parallel and enhancing or influencing each other, and this is powerful activity. If changes in soft tissues and of behaviour then cause necessary skeletal adjustments these may not be widely detected in fossils until a great many generations have passed.

Recent study of cosmic radiation between 100,000 - 10,000 years ago may provide an additional clue to the solution of the cultural 'jump' into the African Late Stone Age, help to understand stimulation for the 'out of Africa' migrations and the birth of agriculture followed by urban civilisation. It is possible that similar activity occurred to force, aid or stimulate both cultural and anatomical 'jumps' at around 4M, 2M and possibly 500K years ago. There is unconfirmed evidence from sea-floor sediments for bursts of radiation at those important transition marks.

In 2004, an article in the *New York Times* quoted scientists proposing that a mutation to the gene controlling jaw muscles contributed to the enlargement of skulls in the emerging *Homo erectus* range of hominins. The date for this mutation was suggested at 2.4M years ago. It was beginning to come together.

Some professional scientists, confronted with the stubborn problems of the conventional theories, began to see solutions in a limited Seashore Hypothesis. In a BBC TV *Panorama* documentary in September 2005 it was stated that "some scientists" were recognising the possibility that the last great 'jump' from *Homo erectus* to *Homo sapiens* might have been precipitated by prolonged shoreside living and seafood diet. We were moving on, in a small way, at last. By 2008 an increasing number of archaeologists studying the cave sites and seashore shell middens of south-western Africa were persuaded that seafood, and its nutritional advantage in developing a large brain, played a critical part in the evolution of modern mankind. Professor John Parkington of the University of Cape Town, in particular, has published his conclusions in this context.

In 2016, Professor John Compton, a scientist at the University of Cape Town proposed that the evolution of *Homo sapiens* had occurred within predecessors along the Cape shores which had benefited from a seafood diet. Professor Christopher Henshilwood at the same university and leader of excavations at the Blombos cave site posted a video on Facebook which confirmed this belief.

There is, indeed, a shifting of opinion towards the unarguable effects of seafood nutrition, but this shift is towards the development of *Homo sapiens'* particularly spectacular behavioural changes in the last 160,000 years.

There is still a great quantity of intellectual inertia, and outright denial, regarding the contribution that seashore living made to human evolution over the enormous four million years it progressed. Professor James Lovelock, the author of the Gaia Theory, wrote in his book *The Revenge of Gaia* in 2006:

Science is a cosy, friendly club of specialists who follow their numerous different stars; it is proud and wonderfully productive but never certain and always hampered by the persistence of incomplete world views. ...

Science tries to be global and more than a loose collection of separate disciplines, but even those who take a systems-science approach would be the first to admit that our understanding of the Earth system is not much better than a nineteenth century physician's understanding of a patient.

Lovelock was referring to the inertia surrounding acceptance of the dire perils of artificial degradation of our planet's environment, but his remarks apply to all world views. African pre-history has often seemed to me to be particularly susceptible to the problem of specialists working in ivory towers far away from Africa, pursuing particular themes, without regard to the most obvious logic and supplementary evidence which either contradicts or should influence these themes.

This book, or series of articles, is my personal exploration of the problem of human evolution. There is no pretence at providing a continuous narrative of humankind's story. Particular themes have been chosen which I believe are critical to understanding, and which illustrate the more important phases of our descent from jungle to the dawn of urban civilisation.

Reflecting on the quotation at the beginning of this Introduction, I wonder who will have the credentials, charisma and the capacity for publicity which is needed for the inclusion and integration of the Seashore Hypothesis into a grand theory for it to gain widespread attention and, ultimately, acceptance.

MAKAPAN'S VALLEY - 1949

The Makapan's Valley *kloof*, looking west from the 'big krans'.
The Makapansgat cave is in the cliff on the left side in the
medium distance.

James Kitching was excavating the cave where hominin bones
had been found, under the direction of Raymond Dart

(Author's photo, 1949)

29

MAKAPAN'S
VALLEY

The author in 1949;
and at the observation
terrace above the
Makapansgat cave,
looking eastwards, in
2007.

(Photos : John van Riet
Lowe and Miriam Vigar)

ONE - *MAKAPANSPOORT, 1949*
Where it all started for me.

When I was fifteen years old I was invited by a school friend to spend the July holidays of 1949 at Makapanspoort in the Limpopo Province of South Africa. It was one of the more memorable adventures of my teenage years. Makapanspoort (now renamed Makapan's Valley) is where the momentous Makapansgat Limeworks 'ape-man' palaeontological site was then being worked.

My friend John was the son of Professor C. 'Peter' van Riet Lowe, a notable South African geographer and archaeologist, a colleague of the early giants of African palaeontology, Raymond Dart and Robert Broom, at the University of the Witwatersrand in Johannesburg. Professor van Riet Lowe was Director of the Archaeological Surveys in Uganda and South Africa during his distinguished career and attended the Nairobi conference in 1947 when Louis Leakey and Robert Broom dramatically revealed their post-war hominid discoveries in Africa. That conference acknowledged, for the first time, that mankind's origins were most probably in Africa. I remember Professor van Riet Lowe telling John and me something about the importance of that conference during an outing from school after he returned from Nairobi, and being particularly animated about it all. We were boys of thirteen or fourteen then, but my memory of the incident is sharp.

At Makapanspoort in 1949 we were to indulge ourselves to our heart's content, but there were three unbendable rules: we were not to shoot anything that moved, we were to obey without question the instructions of the adults with whom we were to stay and we were not to interfere with the diggings. From talking to John, I already knew that something important was happening there.

The excavations at Makapanspoort were being undertaken by the University of the Witwatersrand under the supervision of Raymond Dart and I was told something of what it was all about. Early Stone Age implements and ancient bones had already been found. I learned about the 'missing link', which is how a possible ape-man ancestor was popularly referred to in those days. John used to talk about Darwin and evolution, which fascinated him at the time, as much as 18th century British naval history was my passion.

From the web-site of Dr. Jeffrey McKee of Ohio State University in 2005:

> During mining operations in the 1920's, a local mathematics teacher, Wilfred Eitzman, first drew Raymond Dart's attention to the abundance of fossil bones being blasted out of the cave breccia by limeworkers. Dart published a short note on Makapansgat as an early human occupation site but did not investigate the site thoroughly until 1947, at which time he discovered that a sample of the vertebrate fossils contained free carbon, leading him to speculate that the bones had been intentionally burned by early hominins inhabiting the cave.
>
> In September 1947, one of Dart's researchers, James Kitching, discovered the occipital portion of an australopithecine skull on one of the limeworkers' dumps. Reasoning that this early hominin might have been responsible for some of the burned bones in the deposit, Dart named the new hominin *Australopithecus prometheus*.
>
> By the mid-1960s however, most workers concluded that the majority of australopithecine fossils previously described as *A. prometheus* and *Plesianthropus* (named for Broom's adult specimen discovered earlier at Sterkfontein) should be included in the single taxon, *Australopithecus africanus*
>
> Other important hominin discoveries were made at Makapansgat in 1948, including an adolescent mandible, an infant's right parietal bone, several craniofacial fragments and isolated teeth, and two fragments of an adolescent pelvis. The discovery of the pelvis was critical to paleoanthropological thinking at the time, since it proved conclusively that *A. africanus* was bipedal.
>
> At present [2005], 35 hominin specimens (representing about a dozen individuals) have been recovered from the Limeworks site. These included the recent discovery of two mandibular fragments found by the Makapansgat Field School.

I remember one evening sitting around the hissing paraffin lamp in the rough old farm cottage in Makapanspoort and asking James Kitching, the agreeable site foreman who was kindly to us boys, to explain what they were doing at the cave. He explained how they were clearing out the old lime quarry and looking for more really ancient fossil bones. It was hoped that when they got down far enough, evidence of the 'missing link' would be found in its original sites within the rock. He described stratigraphy and how they could make rough estimates of the age of fossils from the depth at which they were found contiguous to particular geological events or known extinctions. He talked about orders of a million years which was a concept of time I found impossible to imagine.

(Dr. James Kitching subsequently had a distinguished career as an internationally respected palaeontologist and was a professor at the University of the Witwatersrand. He died in 2003.)

Makapanspoort, or Makapan's Valley as it is now known, is a deep *kloof*, or gorge, running into a tableland with steep sides rimmed by vertical cliffs. The floor of the *kloof* and the slopes leading to the rock faces were scattered with acacia thorn trees, euphorbias, aloes and willow scrub. There were jumbled rocks that had fallen over the ages and a stream ran perennially down its length. Although there were no elephants sheltering there then, there were troops of baboons, rock-hyraxes, dangerous snakes, small antelopes and a wealth of bird life.

Early theories of human origins were unveiled by Raymond Dart. Discoveries at Makapanspoort were electrifying then, and it is still a most remarkable palaeontological site to-day. Remains of *Australopithecus africanus* hominins were discovered in the limeworks cave, together with fossil bones of extinct large mammals. Other sites within the *kloof* have provided evidence of much later occupation in the Middle and Late Stone Ages. *Australopithecus* (southern hominoid ape or ape-man) is not the missing link, but it was a family of species at the dawn of mankind more advanced than other apes of its time with greater ratio of brain to body weight than its cousins. Their uniqueness was that they habitually stood upright. Although the Makapansgat cave fossils cannot be absolutely dated they were 2 - 3,200,000 years old.

I have often thought of that holiday. We were free to ramble and hike in the deep *kloof* and scale the cliffs. We splashed about naked in icy rock pools and practised marksmanship with our rifles, played out imagined stories of hunting with Selous or finding the treasures of 'lost cities'. We ate well of the simple food cooked by James Kitching's young wife on a wood stove and nobody told us to bath or change our clothes! The effect of passing our days of teenage adventuring in wild country was occasionally shadowed by awe at the incomprehensible time-gulf that separated us from the 'missing link' who may have lived there. It was an extraordinary introduction for impressionable fifteen year-old boys to the immensity of the fourth dimension of time in Africa. It was the beginning of my lifetime fascination with our origins.

I accepted that early mankind evolved in Africa and Africa had always been home to our core-population. Whenever great natural disasters occurred in the northern hemisphere, notably the several ice-ages cycles of the two or more million years-long Pleistocene era leading to the present, a reservoir of people in tropical Africa was ready to expand again and fill the void after each long period of cold and glaciers.

Later, I became satisfied that the Indian Ocean seashore is the critical catalyst in the evolution of mankind. Without long time beside that ocean and adapting to a seashore life with a rich seafood diet we would never have become upright-walking creatures with big brains and extraordinary intellect.

During a period presently reckoned to be between six and eight million years ago, general climate change resulted in a refining of the primate groups of mammals. Many species which had proliferated in an eon of widespread lush rainforest became extinct. The great arboreal apes of tropical Africa became distinct in three ancestral families from which have descended three modern types: the chimpanzees, the gorillas and humans. Each of the three types have differences resulting from long residence in specific habitats. There are sub-species of chimpanzees and gorillas, and all three have divergent populations which used to be called races. Humanity, having spread the furthest and become adapted to all the varieties of Earth's geography, has the greatest number of these.

Latest fossil discoveries of the earliest hominids show that they lived in many places in Africa during the formative period of maybe 3-8 million years ago. Not surprisingly, they have been found near where water would have been at that time, because the great apes need to drink regularly. But, it has also been pointed out by Elaine Morgan and others that wading in a water-flooded environment has always been considered to be the first, principal stimulus and demand for upright, bipedal walking. Uprightness may not have been forced on hominid ancestors breaking away from the rainforest by living at the seashore; they may well have begun this precise transition anywhere where there was the need to forage for food in water for most of the time.

But it must have been for most of the time during many centuries to cause major skeletal changes to hips and backbone.

Professor Philip Tobias, doyen of African physical-palaeanthropology, in his autobiography, *Into the Past* (2005), described his student days under the tutelage of Raymond Dart. Dart dinned into his students the enormous 'jump' that apes had made to achieve upright walking. Tobias reminds us that the problem of skeletal changes is equalled by the enormous evolutionary effort required by the brain and nervous system. Especially this is applicable to the problem of easily maintaining balance in all the variety of activity that humans excel. Tobias wrote:

> Palaeontologists ... concentrate perforce on changes in the skeleton. Certainly these are impressive and must have been pivotal in the achieving of uprightness and bipedalism. ... We dare not, however, neglect the role of the nervous system, that is the brain, spinal cord and nerves. .... While a gorilla needs powerful muscle contraction to stand upright even for a short time, a modern man or woman requires only delicate muscular contractions to maintain upright stance even for long periods. It was this realisation that directed my attention to the subtlety of the information that the sensory nerves bring to the central nervous system, during such an apparently simple act as bipedal standing or walking in a relaxed fashion. ...
> ... We need much more evidence before these problems can be resolved. At this stage we have no ready answers to the question of whether and to what extent our success as bipeds, with gaze directed to the horizon, is to be laid at the door of the anatomical adjustments to the skeleton, and how much to a more exquisitely developed proprioceptive system [messages which reach the spinal cord and brain from 'anti-gravity' muscles, ligaments and joints].

Maybe uprightness began at any forest-fringe environment where flooding was usual; at the edge of lakes in the Great Rift Valley and the flat lands where ancient lakes spread about the modern position of Lake Chad in Central Africa and the Makgadikgadi system of the Kalahari in the south. But an ape which frequents freshwater to forage and over millennia of skeletal adaptation has somehow gained a permanent upright facility for wading has to have had a parallel and extensive change to its control of its limbs. Palaeontologists, concentrating on fossil bones, seem to ignore this imperative described by Tobias. From a Darwinian viewpoint, it may also be suggested that there is no need to evolve into a creature with all the other attributes of its *Homo* descendants, leading to ourselves. Where was the advantage?

If a water-oriented early ape, becoming familiar with wading and foraging in lakes and swamps dramatically evolved further, then other harsh demands or powerful stimuli were experienced. Following Tobias' remarks quoted above, there had to be conditions for a unique overhaul and advance in the brain and nervous system, breaking new grounds. Above all, the brain had to be enlarged relative to body size.

We must always keep in the forefront of our thinking that mankind's habitual and irrevocable bipedalism is unique in the mammal kingdom. It's uniqueness is possibly more strange and noteworthy than our extraordinary intelligence. Our intelligence is a matter of degree, depending on brain capacity and complexity, bipedalism is absolute.

The importance of the Indian Ocean and its effect on the climate of eastern Africa, and thence on evolution of higher mammals can be highlighted by recent research into monsoon systems. Studies of micro-organisms in sedimentary layers obtained from core-drilling in the ocean floor off East Africa show that the monsoons began about nine million years ago. At that time movements of tectonic plates northwards were creating the great Himalayan range and the high plateau of Tibet. Hot air rising over central Asia during the summer, exacerbated in the warm interglacial periods and lessened during glacial ice-ages, sucks in moist air from the Indian Ocean, which is the monsoon. The monsoons create the phenomenon of two rainy seasons in the highlands of East Africa along the Great Rift Valleys.

Not only did the rising of the Himalayas and the Tibetan plateau affect eastern African climate by the introduction of its two rainy seasons, but also the sucking away of air from interior Africa towards the northeast during the northern summer caused dry conditions during that time. Instead of a pleasantly uniform climate with general year-round rain in a tropical environment, resulting in the great forests where primates flourished, the eastern side of Africa dried out. Tectonic shifting caused the African Great Rift Valley to emerge with vulcanism and rising along its length. The volcanoes and highlands along the Rift caught moisture during the changing of the monsoons and resulted in the two rainy seasons. These coincidental manoeuvrings of the great tectonic plates caused first the drying of eastern Africa and then saved it from complete desertification by providing two rainy seasons.

It is noteworthy and of critical importance that this major change in tropical climate within the influence of the Indian Ocean occurred at about the time that the split between hominins and the African forest apes was taking place. This revolution in climate, with increased differentiation of general annual rainfall patterns, may have been one of several coincidental triggers for dramatic changes of evolutionary paths. For the last 9M years, the western Indian Ocean monsoon system, waxing and waning with global ice-age cycles, has dominated the eastern African environment.

Richard Leakey, in the 1980s, proposed that this unique climate was a major contribution to the emergence of diverse mammal species including the hominins. Mark Maslin and his colleagues, Martin Trauth and Beth Christensen, in an article in *Geotimes* in September 2005, based on detailed scientific work, supported this view and described the climate changes resulting from tectonic effects with particular changes 2 - 2.5M years ago and about 1M years ago. At about 2.5M years ago the closing of the Panama gap between North and South America, which strengthened the Gulf Stream, caused massive ice-sheets in the Arctic and probably contributed to, or emphasised, a cyclical cold-warm climatic regime. Dramatically lowered sea levels during glacial periods and effects on high air circulation systems intensified the Indian Ocean monsoons. About 1M years ago, the frequency and duration of glacial ice-ages and warm interglacials began to be more clearly defined.

These two periods of general global adjustment coincide remarkably with the jumps from the *Australopithecines* to the *Homos*, and then from the earlier *Homos* who remained in Africa to *Homo erectus* who migrated around the northern Indian Ocean rim to the eastern end of Asia and around the Mediterranean to the west of Europe.

The dramatic changes which affected the geography and climate of tropical Africa were pivotal for the emergence and later evolution of mankind. Upright walking seems to be an undoubted result of increasingly habitual wading and foraging in lakes and rivers. But I believe that a seashore habitat must have been the critical factor resulting in the final break between the great apes of the tropical African rainforest and the successful core-line of continually evolving species leading to ourselves.

The most natural locations for this critical occurrence are where the chain of lakes and rivers in the African Great Rift Valley meet the sea. These places are at the 'Afar Triangle' in Eritrea-Ethiopia, long proposed by Elaine Morgan, and the deltas of the Zambezi and Pungwe Rivers in Mozambique, suggested many years ago by Lyall Watson. Secondary locations are also obvious: the deltas of the major eastern African rivers that flow from the Rift Valley highlands to the Indian Ocean: the Tana, the Galana, the Rufiji and the Rovuma. These rivers were what I have termed 'river-roads' which connect the Rift Valley where most hominin fossils have been found and the ocean where undefined seashores have been subject to vast changes during ice age cycles.

During ancient wet periods during interglacials, the Great Rift Valley lakes were greatly enlarged and river systems linked the Lake Chad region to the central Great Rift, and the Makgadikgadi - Kalahari inland sea to its southern end. A vast chain of lakes and rivers, connected to the ocean shores and straddling the tropics, periodically covered the known locations of all hominin fossils previous to the emigration of *Homo erectus*. Martin H.Trauth and colleagues in their paper, *Late Cenozoic Moisture History of East Africa* (2005) further describe three particular humid periods at 2.7 to 2.5M years ago, 1.9 to 1.7M years ago and 1.1 to 0.9M years ago.

There had to be a surviving and evolving core-population of hominins. From this core, a number of species and sub-species branched out and eventually became extinct. I believe that the trunk of this evolutionary tree must have had its roots in the Indian Ocean shore where evolution continued unabated. From that core-population, fully-upright *Australopithecine*-type species periodically migrated back to riverine and lacustrine locations in Africa over a period of maybe two million years or more. Climate changes beyond their adaptability, vulnerability to predators and failure to obtain sufficient or appropriate nutrition extinguished them. Beside the ocean, the surviving core-populations prospered and evolved further, continually adapting to the seashore habitat and being fuelled by abundant seafoods.

At about 2.25M years ago, the new family of the *Homos* of which *Homo erectus* is the best known began to emerge. Their fossils have been found beside the Great Rift Valley lakes and in a wide swath across the tropical and temperate zones of Africa and Eurasia as far as China and Indonesia. *Homo erectus* had a large and powerful physique and many millennia of cultural evolution which enabled it to survive successfully in the interior of Africa and to migrate pulsatingly according to climate in increasing numbers along seashores. As their forebears had done in Africa, different populations of *Homo erectus* followed river-roads and found comfortable waterside habitats in further Eurasia.

As we know, the story did not end there. Repeating glacial ice-ages battered all mammals through the Pleistocene, and with each one there were extinctions of failed species or sub-species and distinct populations. Refined offshoots and mutated descendants filled the gaps during each next warm period. Hominins were subject to these fluctuations and no doubt there were failed subspecies which we have yet to identify. One recent example which we do know about was the Neanderthal group. Notwithstanding these trials of the millennia-long glacial periods with extinctions of species defined by fossils, one unbroken thread had to have held strong and continued to evolve with exponential increments in physical, intellectual and cultural capability.

It is the theme of this book that all of this was dependant, absolutely, on the effect of the particular eastern African seashore environment which constantly supported jumps in evolution during rigorous challenges of succeeding ice-age cycles, minor cyclical events and random-chance crises. The survival of our ancestral line was dependent always on the environment of waterside living and the powerful nutritional support of the Indian Ocean seashores where the core-people had their home-base for long periods of time.

Our most universal trait today, no matter how successfully we have colonised every environment on Earth, is our abiding love for the oceans and our particular ability to be at home beside them, and travel upon them. This trait was born with a supposed *Australopithecus aquaticus*, but it would long ago have been superseded and lost had our more immediate ancestors not been nurtured and refreshed by the benign Indian Ocean.

Within the Congo Basin rainforest in 1985 - A white-back gorilla in Kahuzi-Biega. (Photo : Katie Hale.

Charlie Hopkinson and Katie Hale are with a chimp orphan at the Epulu River.

TWO - *A BROAD BACKCLOTH*

The general conventional theory of our origins and the questions that were unanswered.

All people ponder their origins and there is no society that does not have its creation legend. We do not know when people first began devising stories to account for their existence and place in the Universe. It probably occurred during the emergence of language capable of communicating abstract thought. There is controversy about when this happened, but it probably began more than 500,000 years ago. According to the present fossil record, Early Stone Age people then inhabited most of Africa from the Cape to the Mediterranean Sea, southern Europe, the Middle East, India, China and Indonesia.

In one way or another, whether in oral mythology of tribal societies or dogmatic religion and philosophical systems in civilisations, early evolution theories were based on some form of divine creation. The Universe was beyond the understanding of anybody, thus a concept of God was born. In later civilised societies, philosophical argument about evolution was mainly between those who proposed that the world was created in all its finest details by a Master Designer and those who saw that God ordered the principles and laws of the Universe. Subsequently, through development by other mystical spiritual forces, often personified in a pantheon of lesser gods, God's will resulted in the world as they knew it. In the monotheistic Jewish, Christian and Islamic religions, the Book of Genesis was the foundation of the creation story.

In Europe, during the 18th and 19th centuries, when scientists were exploring increasingly complicated and detailed strands of physics, discovering the nature of electricity and magnetism, developing Newtonian concepts of gravity and cosmology and, in the case of Darwin, tackling the giant problems of evolution, these stories faltered on the hazy dividing line between the secular and the spiritual.

At the beginning of the 20th century, growing awareness of the unique role of chemistry in the existence of life provoked continued argument. Without the seemingly miraculous properties of hydrogen, oxygen, carbon and nitrogen, and the simple compound water, the variety and marvels of life could not exist. Carbon formed in the decay of stars and expelled in their red-giant phases is the ultimate key to life as we know it and carbon-based organic compounds provide the basis for a universal biochemistry with almost limitless flexibility. From these facts an axiom emerged which became known as the Anthropic Principle: that mankind or some similar warm-blooded reasoning animal was inevitable and part of a Universal Design.

Professor John Gray in his book *Straw Dogs* (2002) reviews the reasoning of the several philosophers and writers of the Enlightenment and in the 20th century, from Schopenhauer through Kant, Nietzsche and the others to Wittgenstein and Shaw. Very broadly, he asserts that following the effect scientific discovery had on the religious belief of divine origins, philosophers wrestling with the problem proposed personal forms of religion to account for the role of humans on Earth. Humanity was 'different', if not superior, to the rest of animal life because of our abstract reasoning and creative abilities. We are rational and have free will or the ability to control our destinies; the rest have not. In his Foreword, Gray writes:

> *Straw Dogs* is an attack on the unthinking beliefs of thinking people. Today liberal humanism has the pervasive power that was once possessed by revealed religion. Humanists like to think they have a rational view of the world; but their core belief in progress is superstition, further from the truth about the human animal than any of the world's religions.

Having observed many animals in the wild behaving rationally, I have long rejected the concept that humans have some mental or psychic ability denied to other species. As Gray points out in different contexts, our particular ability lies in our extended use of complex language both in communication over time with writing and within our own psyches in thinking. I have no doubt at all that other species 'think', our special ability lies in the anatomical evolution of larynx and breath control which enabled the development of greatly extended articulated language. Complex language enhances logical and exploratory thinking, and the use of imagined models. This is a theme I explored in relation to the Seashore Hypothesis.

The conflict between some form of divine or supernatural intervention and Darwinian evolution does not go away. This is certainly a problem besetting the study of all evolutionary transitions and specifically to mankind's evolution from ape to *Homo sapiens*. But whereas creationists following whatever dogma cannot see another course than to believe in a supernatural force, I am sure that the lack of fossils either shows that transitions occurred through very rapid extinction and mutation at the time of a catastrophic cosmic event or because the transitions occurred in locations either unsuitable for the formation of fossils, were unavailable to palaeontologists or where they have not got around to looking. Fossils are found where they are relatively easy to find and where it is sensible to look for them. This is a theme which is central to the Seashore Hypothesis. Is it possible to look for fossils along really ancient seashores of the Indian Ocean? Where are these seashores? Nobody knows.

Professor Eric Axelson, an authority in his day on European exploration of southern Africa, was investigating the mouth of the Quelimane river in central Mozambique, at the southern end of the Great Rift Valley, searching for a medieval Portuguese monument. He found evidence of recent dramatic changes in the shoreline. He wrote in an academic pamphlet published in 1957:

> At the lighthouse I met a Portuguese naval officer, who was doing a new survey of the coast. He said that the sea was indeed swallowing up the land, over half a mile had disappeared since 1910, and it was quite possible that da Gama's cross was five miles out to sea.

In 1505 a stone fortress was built on firm land at Sofala, again not far from the southern end of the Great Rift Valley. It was still standing and in use as a government building in 1900 but was destroyed in a cyclone shortly thereafter. I visited Sofala looking for the ruins in 1973 and the fort was a sad pile of stone in the middle of a wide sandbank covered by the tide. The town of Sofala beside the fort had disappeared together with a substantial tree-covered offshore island which was shown in old maritime charts.

I have studied the Bay of Inhambane on the Mozambique coast at the Tropic of Capricorn and the coast northward towards Sofala in some detail in relation to maritime history of the past millennium. In that short time, the seashore has been altered quite substantially because of tropical cyclones. On the Kenya coast remains of many ancient coral reefs can be seen inland from the present seashore and there are lines of those under water away from the present live reef. Ancient coral has been quarried for building construction since the Middle Ages and recently for cement manufacture.

The ancient sandy shorelines and coral reefs of eastern Africa, during the past four million years, have waxed and waned with tectonic movement, large changes of 100 metres and more in seashore levels from cyclic ice-ages, great floods of silt from rivers and the onslaught of thousands of cyclones.

*   *

There has been a general understanding that behaviour is influenced more by learning and experience than by genetic inheritance. Of course, all animals learn the detailed particularities of their environments, but the structures of their minds and bodies, and therefore the manner of their learning and application of knowledge, are decided by their genes. If the environment is sufficiently alien or different to that for which they are adapted by inheritance, no amount of learning will enable survival. Frequently, attempts to adapt to an environment which conflicts with genetic inheritance leads to failure. We may seem to be masters of the Earth, but there are warning signals in the increase in metabolic and mental disease experienced by people living in modern technical civilisation at the beginning of the 21st century.

Recent research into epigenetics shows that nutrition in all its forms, and stresses experienced by recent ancestors, modify the transference of genes to offspring by the switching off of certain genes without changing the genes themselves. The research is primarily focussed on the transference of vulnerability to genetic disorders and disease such as cancer, for which funding is available.

44

The effects of stresses and consumption of harmful substances such as recreational drugs in parents and ancestors further back can cause defects in later generations resulting in disease. However, if epigenetic effects can transfer malign possibilities rapidly to descendants, it follows that benign effects and useful adaptations to abrupt changes to environment and nutrition are also transferred. This has important relevance to the whole problem of evolution.

Personal communications from Prof. Michael Crawford in August 2006 emphasised the importance of epigenetic processes in enabling rapid changes in immediate descendants without altering the underlying DNA. Recent research in several institutions in Europe confirm earlier indications and this mechanism must now be seen as an essential tool or function in evolution.

*   *

Within our galaxy, our solar system moves relative to others and to intergalactic gas clouds which we sweep up. Within our solar system, the sun is converting matter in an atomic furnace to release the energy that drives us. That process has variations. The form of the planets depends on their size, composition and location. Each planet is different and none has ceased evolving. Our Earth has a fluid centre and the continental plates ponderously move about the surface, causing volcanic activity and earthquakes along the fault zones.

The planet Earth's relative stability, achieved after four billion years, is jolted from time to time by random and cyclical events both external to our solar system and within it. Swirling forces within the rotating disc of our galaxy buffet our solar system, causing subtle shifts in the planetary orbits. Those orbits are all eccentric to a degree; none are perfectly circular, and the planets moving on their differing orbits interact with each other. Powerful galactic sources bombard us with cosmic rays. The close approach of comets and asteroids to Earth causes minute wobbles and there are occasional collisions, some of which are so catastrophic that major extinction of life occur.

There are recurring cycles which seem to govern the catastrophic events which cause these mass extinctions. Scientists perceive these cycles at more than one level, like storm swells on an ocean, with giant cycles recurring at enormous intervals of 295 million years and subsidiary waves reaching their peaks at 24 million years and 2 million years. When the solar system moves through the plane of our parent galaxy we are not only subject to a peak of gravitational effects but we encounter moving molecular dust and particle clouds. This cyclical event is reckoned to occur every 35 - 40 million years. In the short term there are minor wobbles and the sun has strange cyclical surges of energy. These result in the cyclical ice-ages. Presently we are 10,000 years into a warm interglacial period and could be due to enter a freezing glacial period. This would most severely damage our present civilisation and we humans would need hugely comprehensive cultural evolution.

Between thirty and maybe ten million years ago, during the period known as the Miocene epoch, all mammals proliferated and apes evolved separately from monkeys. Asiatic apes, ancestors of the orang-utans and gibbons, split away as tectonic drift separated tropical Asia from tropical Africa. In Africa, several species from that epoch have now been identified. A particular genus of ancient apes, *Ramapithecus*, who lived 12-10 million years ago in Africa and western Asia, was considered one of several possible candidates for our direct ancestors.

At the end of the Miocene epoch (approximately ten million years ago, also coincident to the beginning of the Indian Ocean monsoon system) general cooling of the Earth reduced rainfall and the tropical forests began to shrink. Much of eastern and southern African vegetation changed to scattered woodland (the so-called mosaic savannah), grassy savannah and dry grassland. At about eight million years ago (as the monsoon system consolidated) this process became acute and many forest species, including apes, disappeared in a minor mass-extinction. Surviving forest animals, forced to adapt to plains and woodland, diversified and were refined; primates, elephants, antelopes and buffaloes spread genetically and geographically, and their predators followed. The baboon and savannah monkey families became the principal primates in the drier zones.

Within these great cycles, shorter waves of change occurred, and they have become clearly definable in the last two million years (the Pleistocene) with alternating cool and warm periods. Some of these cooler periods have been punctuated by sharp drops in global temperatures. During cool periods, the glacials, much of Europe and

North America were covered by glaciers and ice sheets and sea levels dropped by up to 120 metres.

There were extinctions and retreats during glacials and re-dispersions when the climate was amenable during warm interglacials. Ancestors of hominids and other mammals adapted and were forced along evolutionary paths by the rigours of dramatically changing climate. Tracing the ape line in Africa, there was a major divergence some time between 6-8 million years ago. During that immense span of time, the lines of some African forest apes split into two distinct mainstreams of evolution; ancestors of gorillas and chimpanzees in one stream, and ancestors of upright-walking hominins in the other.

Fossils from the past six million years illustrate evolutionary progress and there is now quite a respectable record. The remains of dozens of ancient creatures have been dug up and assembled from the famous South African complex of Sterkfontein, Swartkrans, Kromdraai and Makapansgat, all along the East African Rift Valley from Lake Malawi to Olduvai in Tanzania to Lake Turkana in Kenya and onwards into Ethiopia and Eritrea. Discoveries in Chad show that eastern and southern Africa do not have a monopoly.

The general classification for the early fully-upright, bipedal hominin, *Australopithecus*, was coined by Raymond Dart in South Africa in 1925 to define the first true hominin skull identified, the Taung child. By 1997, *Australopithecine* fossils had been classified into seven separate species and as scientists delve ever more deeply into the detail of differences between relics in various places more species are defined and redefined.

When most new fossils are discovered new taxonomic names are created. The layperson inevitably becomes confused by this, but it illustrates the proliferation of these creatures seeking survival in a changing world and expiring after failing to adapt. The *Australopithecines* now have forebears, some of whom may also have lived in parallel for a while, with genus names such as *Ardipethicus*, *Orrorin* and *Sahelanthropus*. There will be more of these ancient, lost species when their fossils are found. But it is the *Australopithecus* group which is important to us, for they survived in a series of closed related species or subspecies over most of Africa for up to three million years. They existed in parallel with the first divergences into the *Homo* line.

Recently, genetic scientists studying the human and chimpanzee genomes have concluded that this very early period of diversion between the ape and hominin lines was not clear-cut. There was not some sudden abrupt cleavage and the speciation hovered in the balance for maybe as long as one or two million years. Hybridization occurred until a sufficiently large population of hominins had been geographically separated from the forest apes for clear speciation to have occurred. This conforms precisely with my intuitive thinking following the discovery of the large variety of hominin or hominid fossils with dates varying from seven to four million years ago.

I am satisfied that a genetic path was set with the move to habitual upright stature, no doubt precipitated by adaptation to finding food in lakes and rivers. But this was a perilous evolutionary path with frequent losses of isolated populations and emerging species. Small numbers survived until the adaptation was sure and a firm genetic platform emerged. This is a factor favouring a possible isolated seashore habitat; speciation occurred when hominins were isolated from forest or forest-fringe apes by sojourn on the Indian Ocean coast.

*   *

At this point, some further clarification of names and species identification is necessary. Until recently, all the early hominins (creatures in the direct ancestry of humans since the split from apes) whose fossils had been discovered were classified within the *Australopithecus* genus. New species names were introduced, usually by the discoverers of the fossils, as described above.

Two species, *robustus* and *boisei* identified by Robert Broom in South Africa and Louis Leakey in East Africa, were always considered to be different from the 'gracile' species known usually as *Australopithecus africanus*. They had jaws and teeth most suited to a diet of tough roots and nuts with a stronger skull to support powerful chewing muscles, and a generally more thickset skeleton, the result of a mainly vegetarian diet. When a fair quantity of fossils of the whole range of hominins had been discovered and dated, it seemed that the 'gracile' *A. africanus* became extinct at the beginning of the Pleistocene, about 2M years ago, while the two 'robust' species survived for several hundred thousand years longer in South

Africa and the Great Rift Valley. It also became clear that the 'gracile' species had been omnivorous, like baboons, while the 'robust' pair had been vegetarian, with a diet more like gorillas. It could be assumed that the 'graciles' lived on the savannahs and the 'robusts' survived longer within the protection of forests in the margin between high rainforests and open savannah.

When Dr Robert Broom identified the first fossil of the *robustus* species from Kromdraai in 1938 he named it *Paranthropus robustus*, believing it was sufficiently different to Raymond Dart's *Australopithecus africanus* to have its own genus. With the proliferation of *Australopithecines* and the application of new family names to fossils from earlier times, Broom's name has been revitalised. The 'robust' *Australopithecines* are now generally known by the genus *Paranthropus* and I have endeavoured to use this nomenclature throughout without creating too much confusion. Those who are not academics or professionals engaged in the regular study of hominin fossils will find all this difficult. In keeping my writing both clear and up-to-date I also have difficulty and have tried to limit the use of species names in my narrative.

Way back in 1972, Richard Leakey wrote :

> In answering this [the question of different types of early hominin] we run smack into one of the most thorny problems that has bedevilled human prehistory ever since the science got underway. During past years fossil finders frequently attached labels to their discoveries on the flimsiest of anatomical nuances. New species and genera were created with little regard to the inevitable variations between individuals. ...

The problem of identifying each fossil find without an even greater cluttering of the range of genus and species names has not eased since 1972. There is presently controversy about the proliferation of *Homo* species and subspecies which have been named because of the variation in fossil skull shapes during the past two million years. There are differences in skull shape and size, stature, appearance and genetic inheritance within the range of modern people, but we are not categorised in subspecies.

*   *

There are fundamental questions. How and why did a small, omnivorous ancestral forest ape pass through an evolutionary jump to *Australopithecus*, a habitually vertically-walking, bipedal hominin? If changing climate caused the rainforests to decline, leaving the ancestral ape to survive in fringe woodland and savannah, why didn't it evolve simply into an ape in parallel with the African baboon? Within the rainforest, evolution resulted in gorillas and chimpanzees, and their ancestors had evolved alongside a large number of monkey species.

In the 1960s and 70s, it was proposed that a *Ramapithecus*-type ape, or possibly a more specific relative, a *Kenyapithecus*-type, lived in the trees of the declining rain-forests and was forced to evolve by natural selection into a savannah ape. Unable to survive on the savannah by eating fruit, the ape changed to exploit the possibilities of scavenging and hunting. According to the hypotheses of that time, the upright stance was the result of the need to stand higher to seek prey and avoid the big cats, bipedal locomotion enabled them to chase antelopes while carrying weapons, improved hands enabled them to become tool and weapons makers, bigger brains were necessary for using weapons and coordinating hunting teams. Team-work in toolmaking and hunting required language and bigger brains still. The division of labour between hunting males and child-rearing females stimulated pair-bonding with sophisticated socialising and greatly increased sexual activity which led to monogamy.

One of the main distinguishing features of mankind, the loss of hair or fur, was a feature of Desmond Morris' book, *The Naked Ape* (1967). Hominins, it was suggested, lost their fur because of the need to cool themselves by perspiring in the heat of the hunt. This nakedness was more advanced in females because it played a dual role by increasing sexual attraction for pair-bonding, which also led to the evolution of prominent breasts and buttocks. In 2004, Morris in *The Naked Woman* continued to follow this time-worn path, ignoring the crucial fact that massive sweating without frequent drinking in the dry savannah leads to a quick death.

Robert Ardrey devoted massive research and writing to the hunting hypothesis and he made a plausible case. He expanded his theories to explain aggression and warfare through a genetic territorial imperative developed during this early savannah period. But there were a number of gross errors which became obvious as the result of studies of San-Bushman hunter-gathering nomads in southern Africa and various species of predators.

Hunting is not carried on by running about in a specialised vertical stance with much verbal discussion, but by crawling and dodging about silently in cover. Four-legged running is much faster and easier than two-legged. Evidence from observation of surviving African nomadic hunter-gatherers is that they were not aggressive socially and did not fight for territory. Those modern hunter-gatherers whose natural aggressive nature had been extensively observed and reported are those who were constrained by their environment in tight territorial pockets. It is the natives of the dense rainforest in Papua-New Guinea mountains and parts of the Amazon basin who are quoted as being violently territorial with head-hunting rituals; whereas the San-Bushmen of the Kalahari were especially noted for their peaceful society.

Robert Ardrey's hunting hypothesis and its violently aggressive offshoot, the territorial imperative, were discredited and a gentler scenario was generally accepted as the convention. Richard Leakey wrote in *Origins* (1977):

> Meat eating was important in propelling our ancestors along the road to humanity, but only as part of a package of socially-oriented changes involving the gathering of plant foods and sharing the spoils.

It was proposed that tool-making developed hands and brains, vertical stance was needed for surveillance and especially to carry weapons, tools and possessions while food-gathering or hunting. As gathering and hunting became more successful and complex, social organisation developed, and communal food sharing and preparation took place, enhancing the need for language and more brain power. Positive feed-back promoted greater variety and sophistication of all these facets of behaviour, particularly the complexity of social manners as children matured more slowly with the advent of larger brains.

Chris Stringer and Robin McKie in their masterly summary, *African Exodus* (1996), presented what I found to be one of the more interesting scenarios for a savannah origin.

> For many millions of years, in an era we call the Miocene, the primate group to which we belong - the apes - had

been thriving across the warmer parts of Africa, Europe and Asia. These large-bodied tail-less, relatively large-brained animals were a highly successful, widespread and diverse group. Then they began to die out, losing a battle for resources with monkeys, who tend to be smaller-brained and smaller-bodied, but who nevertheless began to take over the forest of the Old World ... about ten million years ago. The reasons for this shift in the primate power axis are not clear, though anthropologists believe that climate change probably played a key role, since the Earth began to get cooler and drier then. In addition some scientists point to the ability of monkeys to digest relatively unripe fruit, a power that would have allowed them to pick off less mature produce ahead of their ape competitors...

... some scientists believe the rise and spread of the monkey ... played critical roles in our own evolution. Faced with creatures that displayed greater flexibility in diet and environmental tolerance, some apes began to adapt to life on the level. Our ape ancestors were forced down from the trees, and once on the ground, evolved upright gait and later the large brains and tool technology that are the distinctive hallmarks of hominid intellect.

This speculative suggestion is that those apes forced from the trees to the east of the African Great Rift Valley, on the emerging savannahs, became hominins and those to the west, within surviving rainforests, became the chimpanzees and gorillas. This was the so-called 'eastside hypothesis'.

Thus, there were more benign hypotheses than Ardrey's picture of the emergence of vicious gangs of snarling cat-men. But there were a number of awkward, unanswered questions and I detected circular arguments. In any case, the discovery of early hominin fossils in west-central and South Africa tends to negate the simple eastside concept. If hominins developed on the savannahs to escape competition from forest monkeys, how could they survive amongst the more agile, omnivorous savannah baboons and prolific vervet monkeys and the big cats, hyenas and packs of African hunting-dogs? Within the rainforest, how did the ancestors of chimps and gorillas survive this same competition from forest monkeys?

Did our ancestors really have to habitually walk around vertically? *Australopithecus* walked vertically four million years ago and how did it benefit them? They were not tool-makers and did not carry kits around with them, so what had tools or carry-bags to do with promoting vertical stance? Leakey's explanation was flawed.

If *Australopithecus* evolved from tree-dwelling forest apes, they did not need to stand to pluck fruits, as some anthropologists have suggested. They were only about four feet tall, anyway, much the same height as a vertically-stretched male modern baboon which runs fast with four limbs on the ground and climbs around in trees with great facility. Human boys in our own 21st century want to climb trees if their parents will let them and children's playgrounds have jungle-gyms. We still climb trees to gather fruit, but we can't run fast enough to escape cats and dogs with only two limbs.

Why are we naked? Furlessness in the tropics is a great disadvantage for it leaves the skin vulnerable to insect bites, parasites and the weather. At higher altitudes or interior plains in South and East Africa people in today's warm interglacial period need clothing and fire to combat cold. During glacial cool periods of hundreds of thousands of years, with average world temperatures up to ten degrees Celsius lower, this would be an insurmountable problem for a furless *Australopithecus*. Yet it is claimed that a colder drier climate, resulting in declining tropical rainforests, was the essential spur to the evolution to hominins.

Why do we have a layer of fat under our skin? No other tropical savannah or forest primate is encumbered with this. If we had to develop a fatty layer coincidentally to compensate for losing our fur, there had to be some great imperative at work.

Why do we sweat such a lot, if we evolved in response to a dry environment in which heavy salty sweating without frequent drinking kills very quickly? There seems to be no reason for natural selection to have led to nakedness and sweating on the savannah plains of Africa; indeed it would have been counter-productive and rapidly have led to extinction.

Why did we complicate our drinking and breathing mechanisms? Other mammals drink and breathe at the same time when exposed to predators at vulnerable watering places, but we cannot.

Later, was it necessary to develop language and massive brains? Baboons and vervet monkeys are excellent riverine and associated savannah woodland gatherers with disciplined clan societies. Gorillas and chimpanzees are efficient forest gatherers and have complex family groups. Chimpanzees are occasional cooperative hunters and meat eaters. Wild dogs, lions and hyenas are superb cooperative hunters. None of them needed to develop big brains and complicated spoken language. Big brains create problems in giving birth and rearing children with many years of immaturity.

How did we develop our massive brains together with increased bodily stature when it has been shown that a largely vegetarian diet, or one short of specific nutrients only found abundantly in fish and shellfish, results in diminished brain to body ratio as size increases?

Why did we need to visualise and make a wide range of tools and habitually use them? Presumably not to survive, since none of our primate cousins need them.

Nor did *Australopithecus*!

THREE : *THE 'AQUATIC APE'*

Physiological changes resulting from a waterside stimulus for the jump to early hominins.

Sir Alister Hardy stated as long ago as 1960:

Many animals can swim at the surface if they are forced to, but few terrestrial animals can swim below the surface as man can, or can gracefully turn this way and that to pick up what he is looking for.

And Elaine Morgan wrote in 1982:

It has been discovered that human babies are able to swim not merely before they are able to walk, but before they are able to crawl. The mistake made in the past has been not in introducing them to the water too soon, but in delaying it too long.

The Niger River delta in West Africa was a vast region of flat country still covered with rich virginal rain forest sixty years ago, before logging decimated it and an unfettered petroleum industry wounded it. Threading the forest, streams and rivers spread like a system of veins in a leaf: draining the land, joining each other, flowing into tributaries of the giant artery of the Niger River, which itself split and spread like a fan to meander through a growing network to the ocean. I knew the Delta well, then.

There was a place where a clearing in the forest overlooked a tranquil section of the Ethiope River within the Niger delta system where a pure pool was clear right down to the bottom, maybe twenty five feet deep. While picnicking there in 1957, I was surprised by half a dozen boys aged between about nine and thirteen coming down the track. They pulled off their ragged shirts and shorts and dived in to swim and play in the serene waters of the deep pool.

They were like sleek brown dolphins flashing through the pale green. They would come up for a quick breath then lazily roll and pull themselves down with strong kicking and slow sweeps of their arms before holding them to their sides. Their heads were held up and eyes watched where they were going in the clear water. They propelled themselves with their legs, like frogs, or by kicking them together up-and-down so that their whole bodies rocked rhythmically. They climbed out onto the bank and dived back in, legs together and feet pointed, arms clasped to their sides; naked brown torpedoes. With little planing movements of their hands they steered in a graceful, varying curve down to the bottom, along it and up to the surface. Deep in the pool again, they paddled strongly with practised strokes, twisted and turned their bodies, jack-knifed and changed direction gracefully, like three-dimensional ballet dancers.

Another time I was waiting for a canoe-man to paddle me across the river at Sapele where the Ethiope and Benin rivers meet. A woman was feeding a plump naked child, chatting to friends and when the child ceased its sucking and began to wriggle in her arms she picked her up and dropped her into the river. The child bobbed in the water, on her back with arms and legs waving. The woman, still gossiping with friends, looked at her off and on and even pushed her under to wash her face with a casual touch. It was all so natural. The child's face surfaced from time to time as she squirmed in the water and made happy gurgling sounds.

In 1957 I was not at all conscious of the wider significance of what I had seen in the tropical rainforest, but those images imprinted themselves vividly in my mind.

*   *

Descent of Woman (1972) was written by Elaine Morgan seemingly in protest at the overpoweringly macho masculine tone of Robert Ardrey's series of books commencing with *African Genesis* (1961) and Desmond Morris' *The Naked Ape* (1967). These speculative studies, which gathered a vast popular readership, assumed that the evolution of mankind occurred primarily because of the massive thrust of males going out to hunt and the imperative of behavioural and genetic changes that this generated. Elaine Morgan was a professional writer and a layperson and I enjoyed reading her book for its witty and competent feminist refutation of Ardrey's hunting hypothesis. But I was also immediately struck by her logic and the exciting alternatives which she proposed. Ten years later she wrote *The Aquatic Ape* (1982), more scholarly and up to date. Later, she published *The Scars of Evolution* (1990).

Morgan more-or-less wound up her arguments in, *The Aquatic Ape Hypothesis* (1997). This scholarly work summarised refutation of the several competing conventional hypotheses for that seminal break between the arboreal apes and the hominin line. She reinforced over and again the need for the Aquatic Hypothesis to be given its correct standing as a logical and sensible scenario. The particular anatomical differences between the hominins and the apes were dissected thoroughly. She showed how continued growth in our information base of the anatomy and culture of early hominins indicated that conventional hypotheses, however refined with time and increasing information, did not stand against the aquatic objections, and that the aquatic hypothesis remained staunch.

Elaine Morgan pioneered the development of an idea originally suggested by the respected marine biologist Sir Alister Hardy in a lecture in March 1960 and an article in *The New Scientist* in April that year. The argument, reduced to simplicity, was that our ancestral apes who lived in the rainforests were trapped by the climatic changes of the cool dry Pliocene epoch. As the forests retreated, rather than struggle for existence on the expanding dry savannahs in eastern Africa they exploited the richness of the tropical sea coasts. They became 'aquatic apes' and the particular challenges of living in and around the littoral led, by natural selection, to all the dramatic changes observed in *Australopithecus*.

Bipedalism is now usually considered to be the major attribute distinguishing *Australopithecus* and related hominin families from forest apes. It was seen by Sir Alister Hardy as the principal difference when he first suggested an aquatic solution. Almost all larger animals can swim, and quadrupedal mammals swim much as they walk or run, paddling with all four legs. It is not necessary to make drastic changes to the pelvis and thigh bones to enable creatures to swim. It is the practice of spending long periods wading in surging sea water that demands an upright and steady stance.

Apes and monkeys, mongooses and squirrels can stand on their hind legs and frequently do so in order to see over obstructions and long grass to look for their companions or predators. Goats and browsing antelopes such as the gerenuk stand on hind legs to get at succulent leaves on bushes or trees. Chimps have often been seen and filmed shambling on two legs when dragging or carrying in the wild. Gorillas have been observed and spectactularly filmed wading on two legs to forage in waist-deep water in the Congo and there are several monkey species which spend some time in the water.

I have been charmed by watching a wild-life TV documentary film of baboons wading in flooded grassland plains in Africa to forage for fresh growth. Baboons are close to us in regard to environmental adaptation; they live wherever humans live in Africa and are omnivorous and gregarious. Baboons will wade in flooded flat lands and will do this, unsteadily, on their hind legs if they have to. There can be no doubt that baboons have been doing this for as long as the conditions exist. The same applies to bears who fish in rivers for seasonal salmon and can shamble along on two legs; and all the other examples of dryland mammals which opportunistically take to the water or stand and move occasionally on two legs.

There are vast areas of flat plains in Africa, notably in the Makgadikgadi-Okavango-Chobe-Zambezi zone in the south and around Lake Chad in the north where grassland and forest were perennially flooded in wetter times. It must be in those places, and all along the chain of the Great Rift Valley where the first 'steps' were taken in habitual bipedalism by hominids. Not surprisingly, it is where early hominin fossils have been found. And, always, it must be remembered that in the millions of years of changing climate in Africa no other family of species became bipedal, irrevocably chained to an upright stance.

It has been stated so often with an assumed and assured authority by scientists and writers that the earliest hominins 'learned' to habitually walk upright and hunt large prey-animals on the African savannah because they were forced to do so to survive. To me, it seems incredible that for fifty years many scientists or science writers have proposed that a primitive ancestor of the forest apes could have visualised a concept such as upright walking as being a superior method of being agile in what was to them an alien savannah environment. Is it remotely feasible that an ancestor of the chimpanzees and gorillas noticed that their forest environment was declining over a period of tens of thousands of years and began 'learning' to habitually stand and walk upright, in order to run and hunt large and dangerous herbivores in the open landscapes, in competition with cats and dogs? In any case, the Darwinian mechanism of survival of the fittest would not have taken them past the first tentative steps towards such extraordinary and doomed behaviour. The only possible introductory path to bipedalism has to be wading in lake margins or shallow rivers, searching for vegetable food and small freshwater prey such as frogs and crabs which they could catch with their hands.

The alteration was whole-hearted and went all the way. *Australopithecus* did not just stand tall more easily, they could *only* stand and move naturally on two legs. And it must have happened in an environment where they were not extinguished during the transition. An in-between ape whose anatomy was suited to neither four-legged nor two-legged standing and running would have been especially vulnerable to predators on the ground and could not have had any advantages for acquiring conventional forest or savannah foods. Surely the several earlier hominid species, such as *Orrorin tugenensis*, so-called 'Millennium Man', which appeared before the *Australopithecines*, and whose fossils have been found and named, suffered this fate.

For me, this is the final nail in the coffin of an exclusive Savannah Hypothesis. The mosaic woodland concept, a proposed variation of the savannah grassland environment, is equally flawed. It is hardly surprising that fossils of the transition period are proving difficult to find. Where fossils are being sought, transition species could not survive.

That our ancestral apes began their transition to bipedalism beside lakes, slow-running rivers in the forests and the vast open flood-plains of tropical Africa is perfectly feasible, but I am confronted by problems for the later development and consolidation of genetic divergences over the next several million years: a very long time spanning many dramatic climatic changes and evolutionary 'jumps' in the *Homo* line. The mystery of what happened in the extraordinary long time between the appearance of apes showing evidence of bipedalism about seven million years ago and the clear-cut emergence of *Australopithecus* between four and five million years ago is a puzzle.

Ever-wider research into the human genome shows with some certainty that the diversion of the hominin and ape species did not occur until six million years ago and maybe as late as 5.4 M years ago. But, there are possible proto-hominin fossils which have been dated to at least seven million years ago and they may be described as transitional, but their fossils are very rare and they did not survive. Presumably, they either evolved to the early *Australopithecine* group, or became extinct.

Further genetic research comes to our aid. *Science* Magazine in May 2006 had an article by Elizabeth Pennisi summarising recent published material in the journals, *Nature* and *Molecular Biology and Evolution*. These quotes are relevant:

> Early hominids interbred with their chimp cousins, says David Reich, a geneticist at Harvard Medical School in Boston. This hybridization helped make the human genome a mosaic of DNA with varying degrees of similarity to the chimp genome.

This would provide a bridge and a survival mechanism for hominid genes when groups became impoverished, and were forced back into the forest where they mingled with their closest ape cousins. But was this possible? The article continues:

> By comparing discrete sections of the primate genomes, Reich's team was able to calculate at least a 4-million-year difference in the ages of the oldest and youngest parts of the human genome. The X chromosome's age was most surprising. Chimp and human X chromosomes are much more similar than are the rest of their chromosomes, says Reich. Based on this congruency, he and his colleagues calculate that the X chromosomes became species-specific 1.2 million years after the rest of the genomes. To explain

this oddity, Reich proposes that after evolving their separate ways for an unknown length of time, the earliest hominids and chimps hybridized. To be fertile, the hybrids had to have compatible X chromosomes, and thus there was intense selection to weed out any differences on that chromosome. Only after hybridization ceased did the X chromosome evolve into two different ones again.

And when did this hybridisation cease, and the hominin line become both fully independent and virile? In my view this happened when adventurous, or lucky, groups of proto-*Australopithecines* found their way down those East African rivers and settled beside the ocean. It was the separation of populations into those who lived along the line of the Great Rift Valley and those who lived on the seashore, for sufficient time, that made possible the independent *Australopithecine* line of descent.

I am particularly emphatic that a major objection to a permanent anatomical change to upright bipedalism in a savannah environment is the danger from predators for a primitive bipedal hominin. The argument that upright walking and running is some kind of an advantage in surviving predators seems quite ludicrous.

A warm-water ocean shore environment with its rim of littoral forest was a special niche where the most dangerous predators seldom penetrate. Big cats and packs of hyenas and dogs have natural prey well away from littoral forest, sandy beaches and rough salty water. Cooperative large cats and dogs do not hunt in forest; they are open savannah creatures. Leopards hunt baboons and would have hunted *Australopithecines,* but they are solitary and territorial and their numbers were relatively few. Baboons have survived the leopard's predation for millions of years and so would *Australopithecines.*

Beside the sea where there were coastal forests watered by the monsoons and local streams providing fresh water was a safe haven for that crucial final transition to sustained bipedalism to take place. It was also an environmental vacuum waiting to be filled; a particular and special niche which suited them well, where their established diet which was already partially water-oriented and included freshwater crustaceans could be indulged by a new and familiar cornucopia.

Any emerging bipedal ape which was becoming habituated to wading had a great western-curving crescent of interconnected habitat to roam which extended from Lake Chad (presently at about 15ºN. latitude), via the Chari and Congo basin systems, through both western and central arms of the Great Rift Valley to the Makgadikgadi (presently at about 20ºS. latitude). Joining this western crescent, and superimposed on it, there was another crescent, eastern-curving, which ran southward along the Great Rift Valley from the Red Sea and Gulf of Aden, through the eastern Rift Valley lakes to the Indian Ocean at the mouth of the Zambezi. This eastern-curving crescent was also connected to the ocean by the major perennial river-roads draining the Rift Valley highlands eastwards: Tana, Galana, Rufiji and Rovuma. The Pangani rises at the Kilimanjaro massif. Seasonal today but full-flowing during wetter periods, the Ewaso Ng'iru/Lak Dera, Jubba and Shebelle are roads from the northern Kenyan Rift and Ethiopian Highlands. There a number of rivers connecting the highlands alongside Lake Malawi to the ocean such as the Lurio, and south of the great Zambezi are the perennial Save, Limpopo, Komati and Crocodile Rivers running down from the southern African Highveld with its famous fossil sites. The ancient lake of the Makgadikgadi in the Kalahari was linked to the Chobe-Zambezi and Limpopo.

Recent work, published by Trauth, Maslin, Delno and Strecker in *Late Cenezoic Moisture History of East Africa* (Science v.309, 2005), shows that there were particular periods of high lake levels at 2.7 - 2.5 M years ago, 1.9 - 1.7 M years ago and 1.1 - 0.9 M years ago. (Earlier evidence of high water levels is unavailable because vulcanism and tectonic movements disturbed lake bottoms.) They state: "These periods of deep lakes correlate with important global climate changes".

Elsewhere, Maslin and his colleagues, Trauth and Christensen, have pointed out that these high rainfall and high lake level periods coincide with hominin transitions. They also suggest that transitions between high and low rainfall and lake level periods occurred rapidly within thousands of years, resulting in relatively rapid change between rainforest and dry savannah bush in the Great Rift Valley region. They speculate that it was these major environmental challenges that caused hominin evolution in what I call 'jumps'.

During these high rainfall periods when my suggested 'two crescents' were interconnected, it may be assumed that there was a rapid expansion of hominin numbers, and presumably most opportunity for population and species deviations in the extended geographical ranges. Movement between the forests and the ocean shores and back would have been best facilitated. Between those high rainfall periods there were long dry ages when many lakes dried completely and savannah and semi-desert spread. During these inter-pluvial ages, the glacial periods, which severely reduced hominin and other species, survival-of-the-fittest effects dominated and a refuge was most advantageously available along balmy tropical ocean shores, bathed by the monsoons.

Survivors retreated, in a natural migration, downstream to the ocean. It was then that the seashore environment was most likely to enhance the evolution of the core-populations inhabiting the seashores. The survivors from upcountry, arriving in trickles over many centuries, provided an infusion of evolved genes and refined culture. When populations recovered in this benign regime and climate swung again, the natural route of territorial expansion was back up the river-roads. Hominins and other large mammals were honed by natural selection in the more challenging interior. They flourished with improved behaviours, or became extinct.

This must have been a recurring pulsing activity of contraction, recovery by the seaside, expansion to lacustrine mosaic savannah to be tested once again by a tougher environment inhabited by predators. This pulsing happened how many times during two million years ? How many failed divergent variations of the hominin line resulted? We have only found a relatively few of their fossil relics, scattered far apart all the way down the Great Rift Valley.

Locked into our intellectual vision of time in a nominal lifespan of seventy years, how can we properly imagine two million years and the activity possible by a dynamically evolving ancestral hominin line. A hundred thousand generations, perhaps? A possible 10,000 pulsations?

No other primate had these drastic evolutionary experiences because they remained anchored to the environment to which they were best adapted. Climate cycles affected their environments too, of course, and their numbers and condition fluctuated with the climate. Fossil relics of quite astonishing variants of elephants and baboons, antelopes and zebras, have been found often in the same places as hominins. But these other species, and the chimps, gorillas and monkeys of the forests, remained remarkably stable. They did not experience the periodic and powerful driving force of seafood during those sojourns beside the ocean.

When most of the species with early aquatic adaptations to freshwater systems finally died as their habitats became too small or disappeared, it is not difficult to visualise a retreat of remnant populations down to the sea along the main river-roads. As lakes and the upper reaches of rivers dried and the forests around them thinned and were desiccated, apes who depended on them moved naturally downstream. Those who could survive that experience were the toughest and most adventurous that natural selection created during the pruning of rigorous climate changes. When they reached the sea there were challenges, but they were not as ill-equipped by then as they would have been had they moved directly from deep rainforest.

Chimps and gorillas, remaining in the central rainforest zone had an environment that never disappeared, however much it waxed and waned, but those transitional species, moving towards bipedalism, and adapting to a lacustrine existence were not so sheltered.

Where the forest fringing their safe-havens by lake and river succumbed, so did they if they had no escape route. Their fossils have been found in places like the Chad desert and contiguous to parts of the Great Rift Valley, notably in Ethiopia and close to modern Lake Turkana. It is hardly coincidence that Lakes Chad and Turkana have massively grown and shrunk many times as ice-ages waxed and waned during the last 5-6 million years.

I have no doubt at all that similar evidence of extinct early hominins awaits discovery on the ancient southern edges of the rainforest zone, probably in Botswana, Namibia, Zambia or Angola, where the ancient Makgadikgadi Lake in the Kalahari provided conditions similar to that of Chad.

The problems of massive change to permanent vertical stance with its vulnerability and lack of advantage, especially in the transition stages, is the discussion needing more study by conventional science. Freshwater foraging in inland waterways in the 'mosaic' of forest fringe cannot be sufficient incentive for such a fundamental anatomical revolution in that potentially dangerous environment. Cats and dogs haunt water because they need to drink regularly themselves and it is where they can always find prey. Watching nervous antelopes at water tells how seriously they take the threat of predators, and they have four legs and drink without a break for breathing. Buffalo herds have wise old lookouts and so do agile baboons and monkeys which scamper fast on four legs. Elephants will chase lions away from a waterhole when they have babies with them.

Apart from anything else, there were crocodiles in fresh water everywhere in Africa. It is argued that crocodiles' principal prey is fish, and that is true. I have watched a group of modern people throw stones at basking crocodiles before confidently wading through water into which they have slithered. But, basking crocodiles are at ease and not hunting. Hunting crocodiles cruise in the water and will take any prey when it suits them. It suits them to take land animals at the water's edge when fish are scarce. There are innumerable stories and photographs of crocodiles grabbing all sizes of mammals up to baboons, people, antelopes and domestic cattle. Crocodiles can move like lightning out of the water onto land and are unpredictable. I have watched many crocodiles over the years and have waded a wide river in which there were crocodiles that have seized people in the same locality.

For an ape had to go completely bipedal over many generations, the only place I can imagine it could have happened safely was beside the sea, which is where there was a vacant niche and there were strong food-gathering incentives. If they were at the brink of extinction, the seashore was their only opportunity for survival. The anatomical change could have been driven relatively fast by uninterrupted and rigorous natural selection. Phillip Tobias' requirement of massive change to neural systems for muscle control was enabled by the seafood diet. Wading in pools with surging surf or clambering about on tidal reefs needs a high and firm stance with agile bipedal mobility. An imperative for a semi-upright ape with freshwater food-gathering experience is to wade on tidal sea reefs and have free hands to get at a regular supply of highly desirable protein- and mineral- rich food. In fact, a seashore with reefs provided a bonanza far outstripping all freshwater sources.

The problem of abundant sweating, so significant in the savannah hypothesis, is explained by a seashore environment. Abundant salty sweating from the eccrine glands and tears from the eyes help to rid the body of excess salt. From where comes an accumulation of excess salt in a central African lacustrine or savannah environment? Those salt lakes of the Great Rift Valley are alkaline and poisonous; no mammal drinks from them. Apocrine glands excrete oils which create distinctive odours when broken down by bacteria and provide distinctive odours for identification. Horses, antelopes and furry animals sweat from apocrine glands, but not from eccrine which produce abundant salty liquid. Humans also have apocrine glands which excrete oils and wax which protect ears and eyes from salt water and are found in residual hairy places like armpits and groin. Crying is another strange and unique attribute of humans and oceanic aquatic mammals.

A fatty layer under the skin coincidentally evolved to act as insulation during prolonged bouts in the sea, females having more fat because they performed less active roles. This fatty layer was also a valued anatomical addition to combat cold in the interior savannah or highlands when fur or hair was discarded. It was not exclusively of use at the seashore; it evolved coincidental to nakedness in all climates and environments. Nakedness was the obvious driver, but nakedness was most likely an advantage at the seashore as it has no sensible advantage on the savannah or Rift Valley highlands. It is difficult to seriously imagine a reason for a thoroughly unique selection for nakedness on the African savannah or its fringes. Chimps and gorillas, secure in their tropical forests and clothed in their hairy fur, are not burdened by this human attribute which is causing such concern nowadays with our sedentary and affluent lifestyle. Baboons, other monkeys, cats and dogs who live on the savannah have not discarded their fur.

A simple reason for improved manipulation of fingers and hands easily leads to consideration of habitual crude tool-using to prise shellfish off the reefs and to break open crayfish, lobsters, crabs, and mussels, and to spearing fish and octopus with simple wooden shafts. Chimps famously use straws to seek ants and grubs in their holes and a number of animals use stones in different ways to break nuts or shells, but they never progressed further because there was no selective advantage; it was not necessary.

Another earlier conventional argument for the change to bipedalism is that vertical walking allowed the freeing of hands to carry tools, bags and children. Free hands more naturally apply to more efficient gathering of seafood and to keeping children safe from the waves. There was no advantage or imperative for a forest or savannah hominid ape to habitually use tools or carry children. Neither chimps nor baboons need to carry tools about and their babies cling to their fur. Children cannot cling to naked skin, of course, but that returns us to the problem of nakedness.

At the seashore, males, unencumbered by children, became expert fishermen and brought back surpluses. Swimming and diving became a part of their repertoire. Cooperation at a communal campsite in a gradually more sophisticated social system developed naturally because shellfish have to be prepared before eating and a man can easily catch or spear more fish than he can eat. This is one of the few characteristics where the seashore and hunting hypotheses superficially coincide, but it can be easily argued that the amicable sharing of butchered meat by later *Homo* species was learned during seaside phases.

Females could gather sea-birds' eggs, insects, fruits, herbs, roots and vegetables in the coastal forests; adding turtle eggs and the cornucopia of shellfish on low-tide reefs. It was an easy division of labour. Males specialised in fishing and used their growing expertise to improve their ability as hunters of birds, small mammals, reptiles or rodents in the coastal forests when sea conditions were unfavourable, or the community felt like a change in diet. Honey and other stored insect foods and larvae became important as dexterity and intelligence made them accessible. Most females stayed in shallow water with their children, harvesting shellfish, went gathering in the forests and fostered the home base.

A greater variety of vocal sounds began to develop because survival was improved by individuals being able to communicate with different barks and shrieks against a background roar of waves while they were scattered over reefs and in rough water. Arm signals and gestures by hominins swimming and splashing about, or running on a beach, cannot be meaningful in those conditions and simple barks are vague in the thunder of surf. Females needed a greater vocabulary of barks and calls to control and guide children in a dangerous environment.

Controlled breathing is necessary for diving and spending time underwater, holding in air or letting it out slowly, or making quick and economic inhalations. Such command is also required for voice control. The position of the larynx and the opening to the lungs is critical. Humans can easily block off the breathing passage and do it both unconsciously and consciously, thus preventing water entering the lungs while diving or working and playing in the ocean surf. Other land mammals cannot do this as efficiently. It has its disadvantages, however, because we cannot drink and breathe simultaneously as baboons or antelopes do.

Significantly, human babies can drink and breath at the same time but they cannot articulate efficiently. Their language is like that of apes or monkeys. When children's larynxes and throats develop to the stage at which they cannot breath and drink together without choking, they are suddenly able to control sounds and begin to form words. *Australopithecines* were not able to talk with language but there is no reason to suggest that they were not developing and improving the breathing mechanism necessary for seashore living, which was also exploited for an extending variety of calls and shrieks.

A specific enlarged node in the brain is one of the earlier signs of a more sophisticated communication system. It evolved before speech was perfected during the final changes to the larynx in the later *Homo* range of hominids. During the *Homo* phases, the development of language was easy because changes in the throat and the breathing mechanism in the brain were already in place to control breath for diving.

Stephen Oppenheimer in *Out of Eden* (2003) engages this problem of speech relative to brain development. He points out that studies have shown that *Homo erectus* had what is described as a 'lopsided brain', one side larger than the other, which is thought to be associated with the ability to use complex abstract language. *Homo habilis*, a precursor of *Homo erectus*, has evidence of an enlarged portion of the brain known as Broca's area which is associated with speech. Other authorities I have noted have also referred to this differentiation from the *Australopithecus - Paranthropus* group who lacked these changes in skull shape before the jump to the *Homo* line. Oppenheimer uses this evidence to speculate that it was the need for speech for survival on the dry savannah that may have promoted exceptional brain growth. Maybe his argument makes some sense if the other essentials for speech are ignored. The development of breath control necessary for articulate speech clearly results from the seashore environment, not from a long sojourn on dry and dangerous savannahs.

In August 2006, a documentary on British Channel 4 TV, *What Makes us Human?*, reported that a genetic mutation which enables speech with language had been discovered which occurred in early humans and not in chimps. The link between speech, language and creative abstract thought was noted though not explored extensively.

The particular fascinating physical changes and mental abilities for breath control, and therefore speech, are not duplicated in other primates and are some of the most convincing connections between a seashore environment and humanity. There seems no reason at all why these complimentary developments should have ever taken place in an inland environment whatever the pressures. If there was no survival imperative for savannah baboons and forest apes to talk in complex language, a change which would make drinking at a savannah waterhole or riverside more difficult and dangerous, why then would it be necessary to alter the breathing apparatus?

Stephen Oppenheimer makes this remark in another context, but it reflects an awareness of this particular problem amongst scientists.

> As far as language is concerned, chimps are obviously hampered by lack of vocal control. ...

Others have pointed out that some land mammals, such as dogs, which have a repertoire of sounds, have a degree of breath control and a complex larynx. Dogs, for example, can whimper, bark and howl. Our ape and other primate cousins have a quite wide range of articulated sounds requiring a moveable larynx. But none of these other higher land mammals are developed to the degree that we are. And none can remain under water, controlling the desperate imperative of the breathing reflex until lack of oxygen causes a blackout of consciousness.

Relevant to this complexity is another physical anomaly. It is the hyoid bone, which is exclusive to the *Homos*. Apart from the particular ability to override the breathing reflex, thus enabling an extraordinary range of breath control, we can articulate clear and complex speech with very precise and rapid muscular controls of tongue and larynx, a unique human ability. The hyoid bone lies at the upper side of the throat, supporting the tongue, and is not attached or connected to the skeleton. Its function is to enhance our ability to control the muscles around the tongue and the larynx.

I suggest that the appearance of the hyoid bone coincided with the emergence of all those complexities of our throats which enable breath control, which are integrated with the seashore hypotheses. There had to be a powerful evolutionary need to have this strange bone to aid muscular activity in this region and I doubt that this was the result of a growing desire to talk. Talking followed long after the need to control breathing. There was a highly complex matrix or array of interrelated factors at work in our mouths and throats which was not experienced by our primate cousins.

Interestingly, the existence of the hyoid bone both in early *Homo sapiens* and in *Homo neanderthalis*, goes a long way to providing additional proof that the common ancestors of both Neanderthals and our main branch, *Homo erectus*, had developed the ability to articulate complex sounds, as in a language, similarly to *Homo sapiens*. The development of language, and therefore abstract thought and creativity, we can be reasonably certain began before divergence within the main line of *Homo*, presumably well before 500,000 years ago. *Australopithecines* could not talk, but their evolutionary experience at the seashore was the beginning.

*   *

All of these anomalous anatomical changes, difficult to explain or inadequately rationalized by the Savannah Hypotheses, occurred over the whole period of evolution from ape to modern human, over maybe as long as six million years. It is intermediate stages which are illustrated in the fossil record. There were jumps in that record, and it is evident that the extinction of earlier species and families of species along the ancestral line of descent happened because the next refinement had not yet been accomplished. The continuous core-line of descent has yet to be established, and it is presumed to be along the missing ancient seashores.

But there is more background to consider.

In her masterly work *The Aquatic Ape Hypothesis* (1997), Elaine Morgan showed that earliest changes to ancestral hominid skeletons may have resulted from a wading lifestyle in any kind of watery homeland and successfully reiterated the several answers to questions about sweating, breathing mechanisms, fatty layers beneath the skin and nakedness. She was up-to-date with latest detailed information. Comparison with oceanic species of mammals was clearly set out once again. However, my own view is that her thesis was still mainly concerned with the particular jump from arboreal ape to *Australopithecus*. Necessarily, the later developments in the *Homo* line, such as massive brain size and language, is part of this thesis, but the separation of the evolutionary stages of a missing core-population is not considered. There are 'missing links' between each jump in anatomical and behavioural change.

Scientists labouring with human evolution are increasingly forced to be specialists in compartments. Studies of the human genome or paleo-climate, for example, have become complex branches of scientific research which hardly existed a few decades ago. Scientists may agree with much of the seashore hypothesis, but they cannot present it formally within their particular discipline.

Professor Phillip Tobias is notable for admitting that the old ideas must be revised. He attended the meeting at the Royal Zoological Society in September 2001, which included Prof. Michael Crawford and Dr. Chris Stringer, during which he is quoted as stating: "We were profoundly and unutterably wrong" about the Savannah Hypothesis.

Later in this book, the role of nutrition is shown to be crucial. The importance of seafood is now fully accepted and John Compton in *Human Origins* (2016) describes in detail the archaeological and other evidence proving the role of seafood in the evolution and development of *Homo sapiens* on the Cape coast of South Africa. More than a decade earlier Stephen Oppenheimer wrote in 2003:

> For most of their first 2 million years on Earth, Homos were roaming the savannah as hunter gatherers . .... As the major glaciations of 130,000 to 190,000 years ago began to reduce their savannah range, someone had the idea of foraging and eating shellfish and other marine products .... It is always possible that beachcombing started even earlier, but since the beaches are now under water, we will never know ....
>
> Beach tucker has the added advantage of remaining available when the savannah dries up during an ice-age.

I have to remark that Oppenheimer could have as easily referred to many major cold periods in the preceding two million years and more. The same could have been said of *Australopithecus* or the earliest *Homos*. And in this statement, Oppenheimer reveals the problem that scientists have with the Seashore Hypothesis. As he seems to be saying maybe despairingly: "we will never know".

71

But, many of the most exciting and profound discoveries in science have been made by chance, or by that elusive magic, good luck.

In April 2005 a friend who was retired from head of the tidal authority of the South African Hydrographic Service gave me a copy of a paper published by the *South African Journal of Sciences* in May/June 2001 which he had come across when clearing his desk. It is entitled: *Discovery in Table Bay of the oldest handaxes yet found underwater demonstrates preservation of hominid artefacts on the continental shelf* by B.E.J.S.Werz of the Southern African Institute of Marine Archaeology and N.C.Fleming of the Southampton Oceanography Centre in England. The paper describes in detail three handaxes and their discovery by Werz during excavation of the 1697 wrecks of the Dutch East Indiamen, *Waddingxveen* and *Oosterland* in Table Bay. The finds were made in 1995. The authors wrote:

> Two Acheulian handaxes and a bifacial handaxe-like artefact found in the sea at a depth of 7-8 metres in Table Bay, Cape Town, demonstrates that hominids occupied the near shore continental shelf in this region between 300,000 and possibly 1.4 million years ago, and that artefacts deposited on the continental shelf can survive *in situ* during successive, glacially controlled transgressions and regressions of sea level.

This find is no surprise since ice-age cycles produce large variations in sea level, but it is a rare report. We will have to wait until knowledgeable divers or professional marine archaeologists with keen eyes find similar stone tools together with fossilised skeletal remains at various depths along the eastern African coast.

Author's photo, 1985

The modern African baboon, *Papio cynocephalus* : similar in size to earliest hominins and inhabiting similar environment with similar diet. But with the agility which goes with four-legged running and essential fur to keep insects at bay.

African savannah baboons have been much neglected in conventional consideration of human evolution. They are omnivorous primates who have also proceeded though evolutionary stages, need to drink water regularly, live in disciplined social groups, and have survived with great success until today. Their omnivorous savannah diet has not promoted a huge brain. And they do not walk dangerously on two legs.

Photo by the author, 2008

Dolphins and humans - the two extraordinarily intelligent 'naked' mammals. Entertaining the crowd together in Durban, South Africa
.

When watching humans and dolphins together, as in this photograph, I experience a strange and powerfully warm emotion. Is it remotely possible that any other land mammal could have this extraordinary physical resemblance and psychic rapport?

Image from the Internet, source not known..

74

FOUR : *'THE NAKED APE'*
The specific problem of our loss of hair or fur.

The only large modern mammal which approximates humans in brain capacity relative to body weight is the dolphin. Dolphins eat only seafoods and they have an extended verbal communication system, not fully explored. There are many stories during all of historical time of friendly, intelligent encounters between wild dolphins and people. Many have suggested that there is greater psychic rapport between dolphins and people than between chimps and people.

Furry animals with humanoid hands and feet, especially pandas, koala bears and monkeys are admired with affection because they are cuddly and probably reflect an ancient common origin with our ape cousins. We even have special affection for pussycats with their soft fur as substitutes for pet monkeys.

Our unique attraction to dolphins is rather more complex. Dolphins are quite naked, having become aquatic millions of years before our far ancestors' presumed sojourn beside the Indian Ocean. Maybe this shared sleek nakedness is a factor in our special rapport despite the enormous difference in our everyday habitats? Swimming with dolphins and physical contact with them has become an established therapy for treating speech and personality difficulties in children.

*   *

In December 1991, a book appeared which debated the Seashore Hypothesis. *The Aquatic Ape: Fact or Fiction?* It contains twenty-two papers following a conference held in 1987 at Valkenburg in the Netherlands. After Elaine Morgan launched herself into the controversy in 1972, I waited for the lively debate that should surely follow. As years passed, I became accustomed to the inertia. It is extraordinary how long it takes innovative and unorthodox argument to become respectable.

The editors wrote in their Preface to *Aquatic Ape: Fact or Fiction* (1991):

> In accordance with the rule that the human mind is inclined to select from new facts only those which fit into the pattern of concepts already shaped, and with our resistance to new, strongly deviating facts, the idea that hominid speciation was initiated during a (semi-) aquatic period has been ignored or played down. This occurred despite the fact that this new idea gave rise to various quite reasonable explanations, some more acceptable than those that have arisen from the Savannah Theory.

Graham Richards, in his essay within the book, wrote:

> Between 1972, when Elaine Morgan's reformulation of Sir Alister Hardy's Aquatic Ape Theory (AAT) first appeared in her best-selling book *The Descent of Woman*, and the convening of the Valkenburg meeting in 1987, the hypothesis received no serious academic attention. The references to it in the academic literature were at best patronising ... and at worst contemptuous....

Having read this collection of papers, I feared that these remarks still applied partially to some of the contributors. In my opinion, there was a prevalence of a Eurocentric view of a tropical African problem. There was much logical argument based on facts applicable to various aquatic species in certain specific habitats or circumstances from which general conclusions were drawn. It is tempting to undertake a detailed critique of all the statements and conclusions I believe to be somewhat erroneous or irrelevant, but I will tackle only one about which there has been widespread general interest since the publication of Desmond Morris' *The Naked Ape* in 1967.

Vertical stance and nakedness are probably the two most obvious and contentious issues raised in the confrontation between the Savannah and Seashore hypotheses. How bipedalism first appeared is somewhat resolved by both hypotheses accepting some kind of freshwater environment resulting in having a strong evolutionary process. The solution to problems of bipedalism, however, is still unresolved. I maintain that during the transition period, if it occurred within the range of predators, bipedalism was

76

a huge disadvantage leading to extinction. The Savannah Hypothesis ignores the problem, proposing that organised groups of hominins with weapons can outwit lions and dogs. Of course they can, but early hominins, *Australopithecines*, were small and had no weapons. *Homo erectus* were as large as we are, had the wit and the weapons, but they evolved two million years after bipedalism was fully established.

How did earliest hominins, small and slow-moving and especially those most clumsy species in transition, survive predators and defend themselves? It would seem that in the interior of Africa they must have remained close to riverine and lacustrine forests where they could more easily escape the predators of the open savannahs, and did not attempt to compete for meat or carrion. Indeed, they behaved as baboons do today. If we search for an example of *Australopithecine* behaviour it is a good idea to consider baboons.

*   *

Climate change

Australopithecines and related species of early hominins evolved during the Pliocene (about 5M to 2.5M years ago). It was consistently warmer during the Pliocene (as can be seen) and global climate cycles, though significant, were less extreme than in the Pleistocene which ushered in dramatic, large ice-age climate cycles. These became most marked during the last one million years. These graphs from the Internet which follow are aids to understanding the enormously long history of climate changes.

77

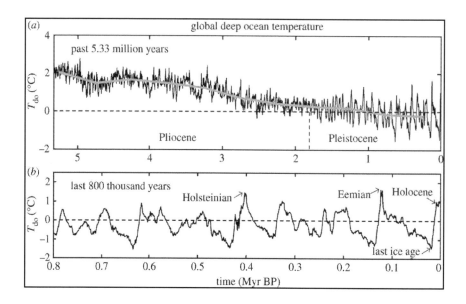

Climate Change graphs - the upper indicates the fluctuations over the whole period of hominin evolution, and the lower shows the critical period of the later Pleistocene when they became greatly increased.

*   *

The naked ape.

Another central argument around the Aquatic Ape Theory which was explored exhaustively at the Valkenberg Conference, was the emotive problem of nakedness. Argument concerning nakedness centred then around the usefulness or otherwise of body hair in an aquatic or semi-aquatic environment. Much discussion in *The Aquatic Ape: Fact or Fiction?* seems to be about an ape which spent most of its time carrying out one specific aquatic activity whilst living on the land. Discussion often proceeded at length about either wading and swimming in shallow water or swimming and diving in deep water. Comparisons were made with other hairy or furry aquatic mammals like seals. These comparisons are often irrelevant because these aquatic mammals inhabit the temperate or frigid zones where specialised fur has been retained to support fatty

78

insulation when spending time out of the water in very cold and windy conditions.

Seashore hominins and their *Homo* successors on the tropical eastern African littoral would have been engaged in frequently varying activities depending on changing circumstances of food needs, season, locality and tide. Rarely would they engage in one activity for more than an hour or two before resting, warming in the sun, feeding, socialising and changing to another activity. Any modern beachcomber on the tropical littoral wades, clambers and gathers on sharp coral and rock at different states of the tide; sturdily swims channels, ploughs through muddy mangroves, walks, squats and lies about on sandy beaches. I have watched all of these activities thoughtfully. Seashore hominins would do any number of other regular activities including sleeping, socialising, grooming, sexual mating, minding children and watching for the occasional intrusion of predators, in and out of the water.

On land they were active in shellfish preparation, dividing big fish, gathering roots and fruits and hunting for insects and small animals in the littoral forest or scrub bush, establishing roosts or nest-making. If one can imagine shifting the area of a chimpanzee troop's home territorial range from the forest until it straddles a slice of the tropical littoral, or the whole of a small island and its surrounding reef, then one has a picture of the lifestyle of an East African seashore-living ape and a speculative *Australopithecus aquaticus*. Later, their *Homo* descendants made tools, considerably refined swimming and diving technique together with further evolution of physiological changes to breathing controls, ranged to collect tool-making materials and hunted for skins and meat.

It is no hardship for modern Africans to spend long periods in the tropical sea, alternating with warming in the blazing sun. What would be a constant nuisance would be a thick mat of body hair constantly getting wet and drying off, being suffused with sand and seaweed, during those rapidly varying activities of seashore hunter-gathering. Seals which have been slaughtered to make fur-coats, have had to compromise in the colder climates and oceans they inhabit. Their land-bases, colonies, are often uncomfortable rocky areas and islands where they are able to avoid excessive contact with sand. Where fur-seal colonies have been long-established, rocks are worn smooth by the constant movement of their bodies. It is significant that, where practical, they prefer uncomfortable rocky places to sandy beaches. Contrarily, sea elephants and walruses, which lack hair to the same extent as humans (with a compensating thick blubber layer like whales), do not mind sandy beaches.

I believe that early hominid ancestors probably had thick furry hair somewhat like chimps or baboons. All over, it would have required much daily grooming to manage matting with seagrass and weed, crumbled shells and sand in order to keep their skins healthy and to attract mates. Natural selection could quite simply have resulted in nakedness and provides a clear explanation without having to resort to a matrix of complex and convoluted argument.

Loss of this thick hair aided diving and swimming by making the body more streamlined, providing a coincidental and powerful stimulus for natural selection. It has been universally noted often enough that modern humans' residual body hair is aligned as if it developed in conditions of aquatic movement.

There has never been any doubt in my mind that the absence of a full covering of hair or fur on an African hominid living on the savannahs or in woodlands was a great sacrifice. Losing hair without growing a thick skin is a dangerous and unpleasant thing to do, because either abundant hair or a thick skin is essential to combat parasitical flying insects. Modern humans have neither.

The other common naked African land mammals, elephant, rhino, and hippo, are all water oriented. Despite tough skins, they suffer when they cannot bathe or wallow adequately during droughts in country with many flies. If rhinos and elephants cannot wallow, they take sand or dust baths which are a less efficient substitute. Sometimes, fly populations expand in sudden explosions and become life-threatening. In the dry season I have observed rhinos with their thick, tough skin penetrated and diseased where parasites have made their home. The early physical evolution of ancestral naked African elephants and rhinos, and possibly warthogs, also needs proper attention and may provide obvious and important insights. Why did they become naked, need to wallow, and now inhabit hot dry environments?

Modern 'white' Eurasians are hairier than all the tropical peoples and the 'yellow' people of the East. An easy assumption has been that this is because of the colder climate. This may be a factor, but probably the more important one is that biting and stinging flies are more prevalent and active in the brief northern summer than in the tropics, as camping parties in Scotland, Canada or Scandinavia are well aware. Natural selection would promote a reversion to hairiness in modern out-of-Africa migrants into Eurasia during recent millennia.

I have not read any statement by exponents of the Savannah Hypothesis that nakedness makes a mammal vulnerable to insects. It is not the nuisance and discomfort of stings and bites, it is because these are life-threatening.

The need for abundant sweating in humans in order to cool their bodies during long periods of running in a warm tropical environment is still assumed conventionally to be the reason for nakedness, and the trait evolved with *Homo erectus* when hunting began. As an example, John Compton in *Human Origins* (2016) is quite specific :

> All primates can sweat and generally do so in amounts that relate mostly to how active they are during the day. Because *H.erectus* was especially active under a full sun in habitats with few shade trees, they were probably able, like us, to sweat profusely. ...
> ... With the control of fire to keep them warm at night, our larger bodies burning more calories during the heat of the day placed the emphasis on cooling our bodies down rather than keeping them warm. As a result, our ancestors became less hairy as they developed a greater capacity to sweat.

There are obvious problems with this concept. The assumption is that nakedness was specifically selected by *Homo erectus* who had to travel great distances daily in open grassland savannah to survive. This assumes that their principal occupation was hunting in competition with cats and dogs. Compton and others go further by stating in support that *Homos* needed to be 'marathon runners' to follow wounded prey, and that was not possible without abundant sweating. Apart from the fact that humans mostly sweat from eccrine glands which excrete much salt, which is scarce on the grassland plains, the quantities are large, somewhere between one and four litres an hour. Without frequent drinking when engaged on a 'marathon' hunting chase, this level of exercise is not sustainable.

As always, the problem is complex. For a species to undergo natural selection for such a major and unique change there has to be a powerful reason, and the reason had to be existent for a long time in stable circumstances. If the circumstances changed or varied, natural selection worked in ways to meet those changes, or the species expired. As always, it also has to be remembered that in the case of human evolution we are dealing with two or more millions of years broken down into glacial-interglacial cycles, and, in the case of *Homo erectus*, with dispersion of the species from the tropics to the tundra edges of the northern ice-sheets. *Homo erectus* migrated throughout Africa and Eurasia wherever the environment was supportive, not only on the warm, dry savannah plains of tropical Africa.

*

I review the problem in its simplest outline, once again.

The transition from a forest ape in tropical Africa within the Miocene to a habitually bipedal hominin at the beginning of the Pliocene appears to be rather roughly explained, transition having occurred through wading in shallow freshwater. Having regard to the need for long time to enable skeletal evolution there have to be issues which are not yet resolved. There is the critical matter of particular danger from predators to a clumsy, transitional bipedal form.

The ancestors of gorillas, chimps and humans deviated into the lines of descent leading to ourselves: chimps today are divided into at least two species, or subspecies, are largely omnivorous and their survivors live in both the dense forest zones and on their fringes. They are closest to us genetically, but are not bipedal and are not naked. Gorillas are large-bodied because they have remained vegetarian, their remnants live in the dense forests and they are neither bipedal or naked. Chimps and gorillas have not migrated out of their original habitats and have not dramatically evolved.

Australopithecines were similar in stature to chimps and baboons, lived in the forest-savannah fringes and watersides and migrated throughout sub-Saharan Africa. They were omnivorous and freshwater animals were part of their diet. They were irrevocably bipedal but maybe not naked. *Australopithecines* evolved to be *Homo erectus* : naked and tall, bipedal tool-makers, inhabiting all parts of temperate Eurasia, with increasing brain size and unique attributes of increasing intelligence and cultural complexity.

The conventional Savannah Hypothesis assumes that *Homo erectus* became meat-eaters because they joined the hyenas, jackals and vultures as scavengers of antelopes killed by large cats, hyenas themselves, and dogs. Meat-eating forced the evolution of bigger brains and increased intelligence. Having invented tools and weapons, *Homo erectus* became hunters of large mammals, and to be successful they had to select for marathon running which required heavy salty eccrine sweating and therefore nakedness.

It seems to be simple!

Earlier, I questioned the ability of transitional hominins and *Australopithecines* to survive the predation of lions and dogs. But this simple scenario depends almost entirely on the assumption that they not only survived being prey but were able to adopted carrion-eating, sharing predator's kills, as habitual for long enough in a stable environment to develop taller skeletons, bigger brains, and the intelligence necessary to imagine tool-making and successful hunting tactics with spears. There are too many inconsistencies; too great reliance on sufficient time for a particular population in a particular environment to undergo this unique and doubtful evolutionary process.

The fossil evidence itself casts doubts. *Australopithecine* relics have been found from the vicinity of the Red Sea, all along the Great Rift Valley to Makapan's Valley in South Africa. This environment is also native to baboons and neither *Australopithecus* nor baboons evolved to be naked hunters during the early Pliocene of two million years of climate cycles during a generally warmer era than the Pleistocene.

Coincidentally, and this is important, *Paranthropus* hominins were living in parallel with *Australopithecus*, and their fossil-proven habitat also stretched down the Great Rift to South Africa. *Paranthropus* did not evolve into the 'gracile' omnivorous *Australopithecines* and remained largely vegetarian and heavy-bodied. They survived in the fossil record for several hundred thousand years longer. Thus, the early hominins separated into two main families of species. Why, in two million years, did one group deviate so strongly into scavenging meat, if that is what drove evolution to the *Homo* family, while the other did not? Living side-by-side, how did they remain discrete for two million years? That is extraordinary. Scavenging is the deviant behaviour, and has severe practical problems. In the next chapter, I describe *Paranthropus* in more detail and their story is the more natural path of evolution in the tropical savannah.

*   *

Heavy sweating results in fast dehydration and unless there is frequent drinking death follows. Sweating, according to the Seashore Hypothesis, is required to cleanse the body of excess salt ingested while in the sea. A proper salt balance has become specially important to our species. In the tropics today, people need not only to drink water as often as possible if they are active, but to include salt in their diets. Wars have been fought over salt. Without a salty seashore phase, how would our bodies have developed a metabolism which needs salt, and the expulsion of excess through sweating, if it is life-threatening?

I had been astonished to read in Stringer and McKie's book, *African Exodus* (1996), that they dismissed the hairlessness of hominins in one brief paragraph. Stringer and McKie (1996) :

> The rest [of the body] is nakedness, the remainder of our primate hair having thinned dramatically because our ancestors evolved in hot, unshaded ground on the savannah plains of Africa. In extreme heat, the body is capable of sweating off a maximum of twenty-eight litres of water in a day. Thick hair would have reduced the effects of that cooling and would also have allowed salt, and other wastes to build up in our fur or hair.

In 2016 academic inertia continued. Compton in *Human Origins* (2016) was saying much the same, (quoted earlier.)

Contradictions and inconsistences are obvious. If the hot treeless grasslands were life-threatening, what was *Australopithecus* doing there? There was no food for them, baboons don't live there. Their natural habitat was lacustrine and riverine mosaic forest where they had become bipedal through freshwater wading. Is that not the accepted theory? If they were out on the treeless grasslands because their principal food was hunted meat, the necessary traits of marathon-running capacity and weapons-making abilities did not appear until the emergence of *Homo erectus* two million years later during the

Pleistocene. Dogmatic adherence to a savannah-only hypothesis keeps running into buffers and its own contradictions.

*   *

Turning to the important matter of insects, it is easier to consider modern human behaviour and experience then to speculate about naked hominins two million years ago.

Carefully selecting sites for camps, and later for homesteads and villages, is an obvious learned procedure by modern humans. Sites were chosen for many conveniences, the most important being the health of the occupiers. The way sites were maintained reflected learned necessity to keep insects and vermin at bay. The contrast between native and European settler homesteads in twentieth century colonial tropical Africa was stark. One sat in a neat area which was bare of all vegetation apart from selected trees, and scrupulously swept clean daily. The other was closely surrounded by a luxuriant cultivated garden of lawns, flowers and shrubs, and the house was furnished with fly-screens and mosquito-nets.

Africans living in traditional iron-age conditions spent much time around smoky fires. Fires were often lit inside huts. When people in a homestead suffered from disease or there were too many insects about, the huts were burned and the group moved. African people smeared animal fat or vegetable oils on their bodies, especially faces, whenever they had a surplus, usually mixed with mineral or vegetable powders. Some daubed themselves periodically with powdered ochre, clays or other washes, especially as part of rituals. One of the earliest signals of the emergence of later stone-age cultures in *Homo sapiens* has been shown to be the widespread use of ochre. Great efforts were made to acquire this mineral and trading in ochre may be one of the earliest exchange customs, following trade in suitable stone for tool-making and the tools themselves.

Not surprisingly, it has recently been discovered scientifically that smoke from dry cow dung is a powerful deterrent to mosquitoes. Cow dung has long been used as a fuel or fuel supplement in many parts of Africa, particularly amongst nomadic herders. Interestingly, it has been discovered that malaria which is such a terrible scourge today only became an endemic disease with the appearance of agriculture and fixed settlements and towns in the last 12,000 years. When modern humans were nomadic and practised simple methods of keeping flying pests at bay, the malaria parasite had not mutated to cause illness in our species.

Europeans and Africans used to complain about each other's different body odours before the universal promotion of laundry detergents and toilet soap. Africans sweat differently from Europeans and their smell, with regional variations, was compounded by smoke from their fires and diet. When I travelled in the African wilderness I never used soap for washing, apart from my hands, and I was seldom troubled by insects. Many Europeans do not have natural antihistamines as Africans do and suffer severely from itching stings which become dangerous ulcers if scratched and infected.

On the eastern African littoral beaches where the core-populations of *Homo* must have sojourned, with constant monsoon breezes, insects are less of a problem unless you choose to live in a sheltered house near rubbish tips or stagnant water. Modern shantytowns are excellent examples of where not to live. Tropical islands were often completely free of many insect pests until they were introduced by modern travellers.

Early European colonial observers were often more perceptive than current non-African 'experts'. As one of many examples, Augusta Uitenhage de Mist, a travelling gentlewoman, wrote of the indigenous Khoisan people in her *Diary of a Journey to the Cape of Good Hope and the Interior of Africa in 1802 and 1803*:

> Their sole covering is a layer of sheep-fat mixed with earth, with which they besmear themselves from head to toe. This unattractive garb has, however, the advantage firstly of protecting them against the stings of insects, and in addition, it gives them the colour of the mountains they inhabit. ...

Our nakedness is much discussed relative to massive sweating, cooling and marathon-running on the hot savannah plains, whether it is an aid or hindrance in the sea and whether it is sexy or decorative. But nobody seems to have reflected on the critical matter of an insect barrier and the widespread use of animal fat- and vegetable oil- based smears and mineral washes, especially red-ochre and ash from fires, by nomadic, modern 'tribal' Africans of every part of the continent. Today, we spend huge quantities of money on cosmetics, oily skin unguents and insect deterrents. The only sure way of avoiding malaria at the beginning of the 21st century is to evade mosquitoes. Various aid organisations distributed mosquito nets to

Africans in an attempt to save lives. I see enormous irony in this situation.

A random note.

In 2003 the BBC commissioned a massive poll of 20,000 people in Britain, asking what were the most desirable events they would like to accomplish during the rest of their lives. Among a great number of various replies the two most favoured by far were swimming with dolphins and scuba diving on the Great Barrier Reef.

Ancient coral reefs - top : a corral rock quarry, some distance from the sea, and an old reef at the shore. Ancient reefs can extend for several kilometres from undersea to inland over the range of climate-induced shorelines.

FIVE : *THERE HAD TO BE A TRIGGER !*
What provoked the next jump?

In 1985, when forced by an injury to my knee and repairs to our vehicle to lie about idling in a simple village in the depths of the Congo rainforest, I ran a number of strings of thought around in my mind. I was fascinated by the observed fact that after the departure of Belgian colonists the native people had not then, with a few exceptions, occupied the abandoned colonial houses, farmsteads or commercial buildings. This led me into several conclusions about native African people in general and the gulf of cultures between the two very different societies which had been cohabiting for nearly a century. Doubtless, my thinking roamed around the theme of Conrad's *Heart of Darkness* and other questioning commentators' and anthropologists' writings I had come across. The breadth of my own thinking and understanding was enhanced.

One of the themes I mentally explored was the question of the progress of evolution. It had been common to assume some kind of gradual, linear progress. Darwin's theories of 'survival of the fittest' and 'natural selection' were established and accepted as powerful and inexorable forces at work. The existence of ice-ages cycles in the past was known but their extent and the mechanisms were not then clear to me. There were scientists and science scholars exploring these themes and data and evidence from specialist disciplines were being accumulated but were not always properly associated. The problem of compartmentalised research seemed prominent.

One of the conclusions I came to, while languishing in our camp in the Congo high rainforest, was that there had to be a series of evolutionary jumps followed by plateaus of consolidation. I was no pioneer in this thinking, but neither was I an academic or scientist in touch with the work and opinions of colleagues and peers. I could not see some endless and static ladder of change on which mankind, and other animals, labouriously climbed. There had to be shocks and sudden change in environments as well as long periods of great inertia and stability. Populations had to face near extinction and also severe overcrowding. In travelling throughout Africa in those years I was observing both factors at first hand as it affected various large mammal species and different communities of my fellow humans.

When writing the early versions of this book, this was a central theme that I followed. It is an acceptable doctrine and I was interested to find later the following neat summary in Dr. Paul LaViolette's book, *Earth Under Fire* (revised in 2005) :

> If extinctions occur at times when cosmic ray fluctuations and genetic mutation is very high, one would expect to find these extinctions coinciding with sudden evolutionary jumps. This is exactly what is found. The geological record indicates that evolutionary changes occur in bursts, with a majority of changes in a species occurring over just a few generations followed by long periods of little change. This view of evolution, first proposed in 1942 by Ernst Mayr, is termed *quantum speciation*. Often these evolutionary quantum jumps occur at times when the population of the parent species has become decimated to the point that all that remain are one or more localized populations, a situation termed *catastrophic selection*. This evidence weighs against Darwin's theory of natural selection which instead suggests that major evolutionary changes should occur at times of overpopulation when the forces of competition and survival of the fittest are particularly acute. Darwinian selection also has difficulty accounting for the phenomenon of adaptive radiation, wherein a single ancestral group surviving at an extinction boundary may rapidly proliferate to spawn many new kinds of animals. This is because adaptive radiation usually takes place in isolated habitats where Darwinian competition and predation would be minimal.

This is a theme that I have always espoused and is most important when thoughtfully examining the Seashore and Savannah Hypotheses and their subsidiary and interacting paths to the present through long time.

Once the essential genetic and behavioural changes to an ancestral hominin, a presumed *Australopithecine* species, had been well-established in the rich and forested seashore environment, it can be assumed there was evolutionary stability while numbers grew and they migrated along the whole eastern African littoral, filling this special environmental niche.

At different times and at different stages of evolution or change, they also moved up the few perennial rivers and colonised the inland valleys and lake shores of the Great Rift Valley. There, they met their close hominin cousins, the *Paranthropus* family, branches on the ancestral tree who had remained behind in the freshwater interfaces of the mosaic forests. Migration progressed as far as the highveld in South Africa following the Great Rift Valley southwards, or using the Zambezi and Limpopo rivers directly from the seashore, which led towards the fluctuating shallow inland sea of the Makgadikgadi. It is in these places that omnivorous gracile *Australopithecus africanus* fossils have been found. The *Australopithecus* stage was achieved and the evolutionary march to mankind had begun through extinctions and diversification into the *Homo* range.

The classical selective mechanism of survival of the fittest was at work and some of the oceanic aquatic traits were refined or subordinated in the savannah or forest-fringe environments. Raymond Dart named his South African Taung child *Australopithecus africanus* which was the slender gracile form also found at Sterkfontein and Makapansgat. In Louis Leakey's time, other distinct species were defined : the strongly built *robustus* from Swartkrans and Kromdraai and the *boisei* from Olduvai with its heavy nutcracker skull. These cousins of the gracile, omnivorous *Australopithecus* have their own family name: *Paranthropus*.

Donald Johanson's *Australopithecus afarensis*, which he nicknamed 'Lucy' and discovered in 1974 in the northern end of the Great Rift Valley in Ethiopia, is probably the variation from *A. Africanus* best known by many people. A fossil pelvis indistinguishable from that of 'Lucy' has been found amongst an unnamed parcel dug up at Sterkfontein suggesting the enormous range of particular *Australopithecus* and *Paranthropus*. More have been named, some to be discarded later as irrelevant, and there will undoubtedly be more to come as each new fossil is discovered.

Maeve Leakey, Richard's wife, took up the continuing task to push back the frontier. In an article for *National Geographic* in September 1995 she described the discovery and evaluation of the earliest true hominin fossils at that time. Two hominins were identified from sites at Lothagam and Kanapoi in the Kenyan Rift Valley, provisionally dated to about 4.4 and 4.1 million years ago. A species name was coined for them: *Australopithecus ramidus*. Maeve Leakey continued to seek but wrote:

> Comparing differences in the genes and blood proteins of humans, chimps and gorillas, molecular biologists estimate that the hominid line split off from other African apes between five and seven million years ago, a time poorly known in the African fossil record.
>
> I knew a site in the Turkana Basin called Lothagam that held sediments of exactly this age. ....
>
> Unfortunately, in five years of collecting abundant animal fossils we found only two possible hominid teeth. I had to conclude that our ancestors between five and seven million years ago preferred a more forested environment.

Fossils of a hominid named *Ardipithecus ramidus* were found by Tim White, of the University of California, and his associates in Ethiopia with a probable date of more than 4M years ago. It was proposed that this species was a possible ancestor of *Australopithecus*. White believed that his discovery was close to the transition phase because it had more ape-like features than *Australopithecus* and a smaller brain, but had vertical bipedal stance. It may well have been one of many doomed very early forms.

Maeve Leakey in 1999 discovered another distinct variant and in 2001 revealed it with the species name *Kenyanthropus platiops*, 'flat faced ape-man'. When describing her find in a TV programme she pointed out the principal facial differences between her flat-faced skull and skulls of hominins with protruding cheeks and nose like Johanson's famous Lucy of the same date, about 3.5M years ago.

In 2000 Martin Pickford and Brigitte Senut of the National Museum of Natural History in Paris announced the fossils of a presumed transitional hominid which were found by their exploration team in the Tugen Hills immediately to the west of Lake Baringo in the eastern Great Rift Valley of Kenya. No skull has been found, but there were teeth, part of a thigh with the vital clue of the head of the femur and part of the humerus. The teeth showed that the ape was omnivorous. The humerus suggested that it was used to climbing in trees, but the thigh bone strongly indicated bipedalism. Here was a hominid which may have lived within a rainforest canopy in process of adapting to spending more time on the ground. Lucky circumstances of two lava flows enclosing the sediments in which the fossils were found enabled fairly precise dating, which was supported by examination of the magnetic properties of rock in the sedimentary layer. The date was between 5.8 and 6.1 million years ago.

The 'Millennium Man' fossils, as they were named, show that there was an arboreal platform on which could be built a lasting bipedal evolution. Martin Pickford when commenting on their Millennium Man discovery in a TV documentary was definite in his opinion that the savannah hypothesis for bipedalism was now quite obsolete. It seemed to me that from the arboreal orang-utan type of a Millennium Man transition ape, there could have been two main descending branches with their sub-branches; one which survived in the lacustrine forests of the Rift Valley and a riverine forested environment along the length of Africa as far as South Africa until it eventually became extinct, (*Paranthropus*) and the other which successfully bourgeoned on the lush littoral of the Indian Ocean before spreading widely and evolving further (*Australopithecus*). This idea encompasses both Savannah and Seashore Hypotheses.

In 2002, it was announced in *Nature* that Michel Brunet of the University of Poitiers had been rewarded for years of searching in the Chad Desert by fossils of a 7M years old hominid which was named *Sahelanthropus tchadensis* with the nickname 'Toumai'. Here was an example of a failed offshoot of the earliest transitional hominids living in the Lake Chad lacustrine and flood plain zone.

Michel Brunet and his collaborators declared in *Nature* (2002):

> The search for the earliest fossil evidence of the human lineage has been concentrated in East Africa. Here we report the discovery of six hominid specimens from Chad, central Africa, 2,500 km from the East African Rift Valley. The fossils include a nearly complete cranium and fragmentary lower jaws. The associated fauna suggest the fossils are between 6 and 7 million years old. The fossils display a unique mosaic of primitive and derived characters, and constitute a new genus and species of hominid. The distance from the Rift Valley, and the great antiquity of the fossils, suggest that the earliest members of the hominid clade were more widely distributed than has been thought, and that the divergence between the human and chimpanzee lineages was earlier than indicated by most molecular studies.

Bernard Wood, of George Washington university, writing in the same journal in 2002 had this to say regarding the Chad announcement by Brunet and his colleagues :

There are two current hypotheses about human origins and the early stages of hominid evolution. According to the linear, or 'tidy', model the distinctive hominid anatomy evolved only once, and was followed by a ladder-like ancestor - descendant series. In this model there is no branching (cladogenesis) until well after 3 million years ago. The bushy, or 'untidy', model sees hominid evolution as a series of successive adaptive radiations - evolutionary diversification in response to new or changed circumstances - in which anatomical features are 'mixed and matched' in ways that we are only beginning to comprehend. This model, to which I subscribe, predicts that because of the independent acquisition of similar shared characters (homoplasy), key hominid adaptations such as bipedalism, manual dexterity and a large brain are likely to have evolved more than once. So the evidence of one, or even a few, of the presumed distinguishing features of hominids might not be enough to link a new species with later hominids, let alone to identify it as the direct ancestor of modern humans.

What is remarkable about the chimp-sized cranium TM 266-01-060-1 discovered by Brunet *et al.* is its mosaic nature. Put simply, from the back it looks like a chimpanzee, whereas from the front it could pass for a 1.75-million-year-old advanced australopith. ...

... if it is accepted as a stem hominid, under the tidy model the principle of parsimony dictates that all creatures with more primitive faces (and that is a very long list) would, perforce, have to be excluded from the ancestry of modern humans. ...

... In contrast, the untidy model would predict that at 6 - 7 million years ago we are likely to find evidence of creatures with hitherto unknown combinations of hominid, chimp and even novel features. ...

My prediction is that *S. tchadensis* is just the tip of an iceberg of taxonomic diversity during hominid evolution 5 - 7 million years ago. Its potentially close relationship with our own, hominid, twig of the tree of life is surely important. More notably, however, I think it will prove to be telling evidence of the adaptive radiation of fossil ape-like

94

creatures that included the common ancestor of modern humans and chimpanzees.

Fossils keep being discovered and detailed analysis and review must continue. In 2004, for example, Yohannes Haile-Selassie and his team from the Cleveland Museum of Natural History, publishing in *Science*, were reporting on hominid teeth discovered in the Awash Valley of Ethiopia. These teeth were dated to 5.8 - 5.2 Mya and were sufficiently different for them to propose another possible new species, *Ardipithicus kadabba*.

A more recent example is that of Lee Berger and associate's find in Malapa Cave near the Sterkfontein complex outside Johannesburg. The *New York Times* of 8 April 2010 reported:

> [In a report published] in the journal *Science* [Science 328, 195-204], Dr. Berger, 44, and a team of scientists said the fossils from the boy and a woman were a surprising and distinctive mixture of primitive and advanced anatomy and thus qualified as a new species of hominid, the ancestors and other close relatives of humans. It has been named *Australopithecus sediba*.
>
> The species sediba, which means fountain or wellspring in Sotho, strode upright on long legs, with human-shaped hips and pelvis, but still climbed through trees on apelike arms. It had the small teeth and more modern face of *Homo*, the genus that includes modern humans, but the relatively primitive feet and tiny brain of *Australopithecus*, Dr. Berger said. Geologists estimated that the individuals lived 1.78 million to 1.95 million years ago, probably closer to the older date, when australopithecines and early species of *Homo* were contemporaries.
>
> The team said that the new species probably descended from *Australopithecus africanus*. At a teleconference on Wednesday, he described the species as a possible ancestor of *Homo erectus*, an immediate predecessor to *Homo sapiens*, or a close side branch that did not lead to modern humans.

Having accepted that there were any number of 'trial' evolutionary branches in response to the challenges of changing environments, and natural selection had caused their extinction, there had to have been a core-population somewhere where continuity was maintained and where the jumps in evolution to the *Homo* range occurred. The 'radiation' of forms, suggested by Bernard Wood, and given a range of genus and species identities by the scientists who found the fossils, had to be radiating from some core line at the end of which we exist.

Palaeontologists will no doubt continue to find the fossils of those species which had expired. Based on what laypeople might consider to be a natural variation in populations, new genus and species identities may continue to be allocated. However, it should be constantly born in mind that considering the time span, the number of fossils, which have been found on which to base any final conclusions, is quite small.

*   *

It has been established that *Australopithecus* and *Paranthropus* were probably no more intelligent or culturally advanced than modern chimpanzees who have themselves evolved from an ancestral form. If these early hominins had a greater brain to body ratio than modern chimps, I would suggest that this was directly related to the need for greater brain and neural strength to enable bipedalism, as described by Phillip Tobias. Later on down the evolutionary trail when *Homo erectus* had emerged, although their bodies were larger and strongly developed, the brain related to body weight ratio remained about the same. Brains grew while bodies grew, but the ratio remained somewhat constant. Further on, modern *Homo sapiens* retained a similar body size to *Homo erectus*, but a much larger brain had developed. It was the brain to body weight ratio which increased substantially.

When relative brain capacity merely kept pace with body development, the several species concerned eventually, and apparently inevitably, became extinct. Each evolutionary jump onward permitted the new species to survive longer or to migrate further to find suitable habitats. But when climate changed during major cold-warm cycles, their numbers, in scattered populations were severely reduced, if not extinguished. They were faced with an 'extinction evolution' phase as described above : they evolved fast or expired. *Australopithecus* and *Paranthropus* eventually could not keep pace and they faded away during the course of the cyclical ice-ages of the Pleistocene epoch, *Australopithecus* first at about 1.8M years ago (*A.sediba*) and *Paranthropus* about 1.2M.

It was not until the new *Homo* group of species became established with larger, taller bodies and corresponding brains, accomplished with markedly advanced technology and social structures, and control of fire, that our ancestors were able to combat and survive all the deeper climatic shocks of the Pleistocene.

What triggered the jump from *Australopithecus* or *Paranthropus* to *Homo*? There was some factor still missing from all the conventional evolutionary theories.

There were questions in my mind. Was it increasing brain size that was the leader? Did brains develop to control a growing body; or did the body grow under the stimulus of a developing brain? Did increasing brain capacity, and therefore intelligence, promote general development of the body by widening the cultural platform, extending nutritional regimes and varied lifestyles? If so, would it in turn expand consciousness in a developing brain? Feedback, 'natural selection', that fastest of evolutionary processes, was at work. But, what was the trigger? What was the chicken, or the egg? Why our hominin line, what was unique to us?

In 1987 I was travelling on the coast of East Africa visiting numerous medieval ruins, gathering material for a book on pre-European Indian Ocean trading systems. My travelling companion, a nephew, and I decided to take a week off at Tiwi Beach. During lazy days at the seashore where the great eastern African barrier reef shelters the white coral-sand beaches, I was preoccupied with the conflicting arguments about a seashore-living ape. I reviewed Elaine Morgan's arguments and my own interpretations and enlargements and tried them out on my nephew. There, in the precise environment where the enormous evolutionary jump may have occurred it was suddenly so obvious and natural. My doubts were finally assuaged. I described the revelation in my book, *Two Shores of the Ocean* (1992), which I quote again for its immediacy:

> *One morning towards the end of our stay at Tiwi Beach, I was sitting on the verandah as usual after breakfast nursing a mug of coffee. The tide was flowing and water was deepening over the reef. The thunder and roar of the waves breaking on the outer bastion was growing. A holidaying English family was coming home from an early morning*

exploration to their breakfast, picking their way carefully over the old coral, the children trailing behind the adults and chattering. ...

Following the holidaymakers were two dark figures, stopping here and there, moving confidently onwards, then pausing again. They were two local men whom I had seen many times and I idly followed them with my eyes, until a thought burst into my mind that astonished me with its simple and absolute obviousness. Those men went out onto the reef every day and on their return, they passed by our cottage peddling fresh fish and shellfish. I knew them by sight and they always greeted me whether I bought or not. Why had I not seen it? They were aquatic men; there for any doubter to examine. It was not necessary to theorise at Tiwi Beach, intuitive observation provided me with proof.

I watched while they emerged from the sea and strolled up the lawn. Each young man was clad in a brief kikoyi cloth wrapped around his waist and they were burned obsidian black by the sun. Their curly Negro hair glistened with moisture. From a string around their waists was slung a handmade tool, a simple metal spike with a wooden handle that they used to pry shellfish from the rocks, and they carried a roughly barbed trident on the end of a long bamboo pole that they used to spear fish and octopus. A handmade sisal bag hung from their shoulders for shellfish and each had fish strung through their gills by a length of coconut frond. Remove the machine-woven cotton kikoyi and substitute bone or ivory for iron and they were equipped as any aquatic man would have been for a million years, since that last great evolutionary jump.

Later that same year I was travelling in northern KwaZulu-Natal in South Africa and spent three days resting beside the shores of the lagoons of Kosi Bay. I was with an archaeologist friend who was concerned with relatively modern fossils, pottery and other relics of the African Early Iron Age. There are three lakes or lagoons joined to each other which debouche into the Indian Ocean, where inshore rock and outlying coral reefs have created a break in the seemingly endless high dunes of that coastline. While Leonard wrote his field notes, I pottered about and continued to argue the merits of the finer points of the Seashore Hypothesis in my mind.

We were fascinated that modern people at Kosi Bay with access to nearby supermarkets still practised methods unchanged in the two thousand years of the Iron Age. In the shallow waters of the lagoons, local men laid out fish traps made from mangrove poles and the women of the community went out onto the reefs at low spring tides to gather shellfish. I admired this long and successful continuity of seafood hunting and gathering. Modern technology and machines could not improve on the harvests the people obtained.

As at Tiwi Beach a few months before, I was struck that the methods used there were not much different to methods that early ancestral seashore dwellers may have used. It was another boost to my faith in a Seashore Hypothesis.

But, despite these convictions, I had questions. I saw that ancestral chimpanzee-like hominid apes, Millennium Men perhaps, could have survived successfully in the littoral habitat without suffering a dramatic sea-change and developed those large brains. Alongside the tropical Indian Ocean there was always forest somewhere similar to the Central African forests. As long as the ocean currents were warm and the monsoon systems operated, with whatever variations there may have been during the glacial ice-ages, the tropical shoreline was lush. The littoral forests may have moved north or south as climate changed, but hominins at whatever level of evolution could easily follow them as they gradually migrated.

An ancestral Millennium Man would have been at home beside the sea living on fruits, roots and other vegetation and catching small animals. Without going out into surging water, at low spring tides they might have occasionally gathered shellfish. If otters can manage shellfish, then *Australopithecus* would have done. Their development could have stopped at that level, which is precisely what did happen in the central rainforests. There has never been a Tarzan.

As I have pointed out often enough, irrevocable bipedalism is no advantage to a hominid ape that had to live in savannah or forest. It is a fatal disadvantage, as shown by all those extinctions. They would not have had to develop larger brains, even if there had been the opportunity. What triggered the advance to the next jump to the *Homos*? If the concept of seashore phases succeeded where the savannah hypothesis had failed, then some irresistible imperative must have promoted it. The conventional idea, first proposed popularly by Ardrey so long ago now, that somehow behavioural dynamics required for survival on the savannah (or forest fringe) promoted larger brains made no sense. There are too many modern primates around whose ancestors successfully faced similar problems of survival without growing bigger brains. We are unique and there had to have been a unique reason.

Despite all the convincing physiological and behavioural arguments, rigorous thought about the changing geography and its effects, and comparisons with our nearest forest-ape cousins and the savannah baboons, there was a particular gap in the logical progression. I feared that the Seashore Hypothesis skated over a similar failing which I saw in the outmoded conventional savannah explanations.

But, there had always been the recurring theme in front of my eyes which continually tormented me. Modern humans have always loved water and most people take great pleasure from bathing and swimming. We are entranced by the sea. Worldwide, wherever they are economically caught or gathered, fish and shellfish are especially desired by humans in their daily diet. Random examples at Tiwi Beach or Kosi Bay on the eastern African shore illustrated this. Studies on children in the USA and elsewhere have led to the suggestion that modern people of the Far East, who have been the most persistent eaters of seafoods, are on average intrinsically more intelligent than European or African populations. Was it seafoods that had a particular quality? Could not the flowering of classical civilisations in the Mediterranean basin, and the laggardliness of central Europeans be laid at the door of a seafood diet over millennia?

Afloat on the Indian Ocean or wandering its shores, whether in eastern Africa for much of my life or, for a short while, in India, watching people gathering shellfish and going to extraordinary dangerous and life-threatening lengths to catch fish, and enjoying the results of these harvests, I *knew* that there had to be a solution inextricably entwined with that ocean shore.

No modern apes or their ancestors ate seafoods. If bipedalism first showed itself in forest apes who lived beside swamps and lakes in central Africa, their putative descendants became extinct. They may have occasionally eaten freshwater fish, but it was not part of their regular diet. The beneficent effect of long-chain fatty acids in all fish was not experienced. Chimps have always lived alongside African lakes and rivers and have not developed brains like mankind,

100

presumably because they stuck to their normal forest-habitat diet. Gorillas who have been observed wading chest-deep and on two legs in water have remained stubbornly vegetarian.

Other large land-mammal species such as bears and cats catch freshwater fish when the opportunity offers, and have not developed large brains. Cats and dogs are carnivorous and their diet is meat from the top of the food-chain. If all the known early hominins diverged from forest apes because of a greater intake of animal protein, including occasional freshwater fish and shellfish, they all eventually become extinct. Lacustrine and riverine central African habitats were apparently not the solution to the enigma of the big brain.

The core-population, the missing link, evolved somewhere else. That 'somewhere else' had to be on the Indian Ocean shore and the special component that it could provide was seafood. *Australopithecus* species who did not evolve further from a bipedal hominid in three million years all eventually became extinct and they had the opportunity in all that immense time to adapt to a consistent diet of freshwater fish in the chain of lakes and rivers of the Great Rift Valley. Clearly, they did not change their eating habits. There is little doubt that the gracile *Australopithecines* developed an omnivorous diet and probably occasionally ate other mammals, as do modern chimps, and maybe they were occasional opportune scavengers of cat's kills.

An *Australopithecine*, like its cousin the ancestor of the chimpanzees, would have had to invent efficient methods of catching freshwater lake and river fish. They are difficult to catch without nets, baskets, hooks or harpoons. Even with these aids, which *Australopithecines* did not have, patience and time is required and there is that universal problem of predators lurking beside freshwater. Freshwater fish are not natural food for apes. Bipedalism may have been originally developed for freshwater wading in search of succulent plants and even crabs or other shellfish, but it did not help with catching quantities of lake fish.

Baboons and other monkeys have been recorded as occasional seafood eaters but that is not their natural or sustained diet. Irregular and occasional consumption of freshwater fish and shellfish or seafoods were not the panacea. We are considering genetic mutations and physical adaptions requiring thousands of generations. It had to be sustained high consumption of seafoods, maybe for unbroken periods of hundreds of thousands of years. There was no lack of time in our ancestral story.

Australopithecines who migrated down the river roads to the ocean, pursued by deteriorating habitat during cold, dry climate cycles after population explosions in warm, wet cycles within the expanded forests and their fringes, had to adapt to a littoral food environment or expire. Many must have failed to adapt.

Anybody who has spent much time beach combing tropical seashores knows that the most abundant and obvious food is that found and harvested along the shore. There are fruits and roots within the coastal forest and insects and small mammals, as there are in inland forests, but the cornucopia of the reefs is something that no lake or river can begin to approximate. Even where there are no reefs, huge quantities of sand-mussels, crabs and other burrowing shellfish can be found at low tide in estuaries, and turtle's eggs are lavishly provided when they come ashore to lay.

For those hominins that were able to adapt their diet to include regular exploitation of the masses of tidal zone shellfish, and to learn to harpoon octopus and fish left behind in pools with a simple sharp stick, there was an extraordinary and unique opportunity denied any other ape. I came to believe that our direct ancestral line evolved on the shores of the Indian Ocean. If they were confined to that environmental niche in order to survive when their cousins expired, littering the Great Rift Valley and elsewhere in the interior with the fossil evidence of their extinctions, they were probably on the seashore for a very long time.

Or maybe the question of the time necessary will be subject to review as research into epigenetic effects proceeds. The proposal that nutritional and environmental stresses can profoundly affect the genes that are transferred to offspring because certain genes can be 'switched off' in response to the behaviour or environment of recent ancestors is fascinating. It could mean that important anatomical change can be relatively rapid. Perhaps the greatest enigma confronting the whole matter of human, and all mammal evolution, is the apparent shortage of fossils of transitional forms. If epigenetic effects in response to environmental catastrophe provide relatively rapid evolutionary change, then this enigma is more easily understood.

Dr Rolf Reik and associates of the Babraham Institute in Cambridge had this to say on their website.

Epigenetic gene regulation: control by the centre.

Imprinted genes are only expressed from either the maternal or the paternal allele. Most imprinted genes occur in clusters, and their expression and silencing is often regulated by imprinting centres located within the cluster. Our recent work shows that there are at least two different types of imprinting centre. The first controls higher order chromatin structure, and partitions genes into expressed or repressed domains. The second controls repressive chromatin modifications through a non-coding RNA.

There are about 80 imprinted genes in the mouse genome, and most of them are conserved in humans. They have important roles in mammalian development, including the regulation of fetal growth, postnatal adaptations and metabolism, and adult behaviour. Most imprinted genes are clustered in the genome, and within a cluster share regulatory elements such as enhancers or chromatin boundary elements (also called insulators). The clusters can be up to 1Mb or so in size and contain several imprinted genes. An important discovery was that of 'imprinting centres' (IC), that is regulatory elements in the cluster that control expression and imprinting of the majority or all genes in a cluster. How imprinting centres work is not known.

We are interested in a cluster of imprinted genes approximately 1 Mb in size which is located on distal chromosome 7 in the mouse, and on 11p15.5 in the human where genetic or epigenetic defects in the cluster are associated with the fetal overgrowth and cancer condition - Beckwith-Wiedemann syndrome. The cluster contains approximately 14 imprinted genes, and can be further subdivided into two domains. ...

... observations [previously described in detail] lead to a model in which expression of the non-coding RNA in early embryos results in targeting of repressive histone marks to the region, which serve to stably silence adjacent genes. It will now be important to elucidate the molecular mechanism of this epigenetic marking process which involves non-coding RNA. This regulation of regional silencing by an imprinting centre bears striking similarities to the mechanism of X chromosome inactivation. This raises an interesting hypothesis by which the evolution of X inactivation and imprinting may be intricately linked.

Comparative genomic and functional work is required to explore this hypothesis further.

This abbreviated dissertation is technical but it indicates where future work may take us.

No doubt, these studies into genetics should be coordinated with work on probable mutational effects of cosmic radiation bursts. It is a complex matrix of evolutionary processes which are considered together. No thread of the canvas can be sensibly isolated and examined on its own.

But, no matter how anatomical genetic changes were triggered, there had to be a coincidental powerful agent which facilitated the jump from *Australopithecus* to *Homo,* and thereafter along the chain of evolution to ourselves. Was seafood that vital and unique facilitating agent; seafoods for a greater or lesser length of time?

*   *

I cannot forget that we are still 'semi-aquatic apes' in many obvious ways today. Water-therapy has long been prescribed for a number of human ailments, including arthritis and mental disease, where it has been standard procedure for many years. Roman and every other classical civilisation practised it. Greeks revered swimming with dolphins. In the Bible there is frequent reference to washing and anointing. Research at the Thrombosis Research Institute in London, reported in *The Daily Telegraph* (22 April 1993), showed that regular cold baths boost the production of sex hormones, help sufferers from severe stress and chronic depression, improve poor circulation and raise the number of white blood cells which fight virus infections.

An experience which is either a luxurious indulgence or a therapeutic treatment today is to have our naked skin massaged using a variety of unguents. Induced sweating in saunas or steam rooms and by mud packs of various kinds are considered useful to promote well-being and combat skin ailments and ageing. These activities by modern people cannot always be irrelevant and coincidental.

104

SIX : *THE DRIVING FORCE*
Prolonged seafood diet forces development of the brain and neural system.

"The biochemistry regarding the big human brain did not fit with the savannahs which everyone saw as the site of origin of *Homo sapiens*. How could one challenge this view which was held with such strength, simply on some biochemical calculations which suggested a role for seafoods? When Stephen pointed out that the physiology fitted with a marine origin, then Homo aquaticus was born."

Michael Crawford & David Marsh in *The Driving Force* (1989)

"The conventional view of a hunter and gatherer, killing wild animals and developing a big brain through the competitive effort, is not sustained by the nutritional evidence in relation to the big brain. The land food chain in terms of providing for the special nutrients such as docosahexaenoic acid (DHA) known to be needed by the brain, is very poor and all land based animals lost relative brain capacity as their bodies evolved into bigger and bigger dimensions. The rhinoceros at the age of four years weighs a ton but its brain is no more than 350g. A human child at four years of age is about 20kg but already has over 1.3kg of brain. Even the gorilla has a smaller brain than the chimpanzee although it is in a much bigger body.

"The ecological niche which supplies the DHA, trace elements and other crucial nutrients is the land water interface. The oysters, mussels, scallops, winkles, salmon, cod, herring and the like are the richest sources."

Prof. M.A.Crawford :
Editorial comment, *Nutrition and Health* v9 No 3 (1993)

In 1989, Michael Crawford was Head of the Department of Nutritional Biochemistry at the Nuffield Institute in London and a professor at Nottingham University. David Marsh was a professional researcher specialising in evolutionary theory. In their book, *The Driving Force* (1989), they proposed a new look at all biological evolution on Earth, suggesting an added dimension to the Darwinian theory of evolution. They took a close look at the problem of the evolutionary jumps from bipedal hominin to modern human.

The new dimension they proposed was the particular role of nutrition and the physical environment with which it is interlocked. They suggested that random genetic mutation is just one of several factors causing evolution. The environment, which influences nutrition and behaviour in all plants and animals up the food chain, is the dominant factor. All is cause and effect, all is integrated. The environmental habitat governs behaviour which is enormously important to evolution but the *DRIVING FORCE* is the food that all creatures consume, and food is a vital facet of the environment.

Michael Crawford reminded me in a personal letter in 2003:

Darwin stated there were two forces in evolution, "Natural selection and conditions of existence, of the two the latter is the most powerful." ... The conditions of existence were the most powerful. Darwin was right.

Environmental change, whether induced by climate or because a species migrates, means change to diet and behaviour. Food is the fuel and chemical agent for every minute and obscure activity within living organisms from the ancient simple bacteria to modern mammals. From the moment an ovum is fertilised by a sperm in a mammalian womb, nutrients enter the new living system and eventually a hugely complex, mature animal walks the earth. In the case of higher primates, like the hominins, this complexity is at its greatest and the maturing process takes years. Two distinct essentials contribute to this miracle: the DNA recipes within the two seminal cells and the nutrition that is fed to the growing and developing animal.

Molecular changes in the genetic controls are caused by nutritional changes and random mutations add to them. Evolution proceeds by jumps when nutrition and environment are favourable and the engine of positive feedback is running. If a change in nutrition is sustained, affecting hundreds and then thousands of succeeding generations, chemical changes to genes in the DNA recipe occur causing permanent changes to the species. The magnitude of the nutritional change determines the potential for biochemical activity and the number of generations experiencing the new diet determine how much genetic change there can be. If there is sufficient time, all genetic changes possible can take place.

But nothing is static, the environment changes as climate changes, species migrate, behavioural and cultural adaptations amend diets, natural selection is at work: evolution is continuous.

Without some braking and refining process, there would be a disastrous proliferation of strange forms and aberrations within a family of species. It is here that natural selection and 'survival of the fittest' play their essential roles, culling off unfit developments and aiming for stability. It was an exciting addition to a simplistic 'ladder-like' Darwinian theory which struck me like a blinding light.

Evolution, Crawford and Marsh repeatedly pointed out as long ago as 1989 with many examples, progresses often in extraordinary jumps. These take place with the development of organisms which are able to exploit nutritional surpluses, occurring because prey species expand, or when competition has been reduced by widespread extinctions. Amazing jumps are usually followed by periods of relative stability with refinement interspersed by minor jumps and extinctions.

The acquisition of more geological and astronomical data recently has improved understanding of recurrent mass extinctions. Whenever they occurred there were opportunities for species that were waiting to expand but unable to do so because the environment had been fully exploited until then by already established species. A vacuum is filled by a spectrum of rapidly expanding and evolving species which complement and interact with each other, aiding both processes of nutritional driving forces and natural selection.

The biochemical exposition is complicated but rests, most simply, on the proposition that as life itself becomes more complicated and plants and animals expand in complexity and feed on each other, feeding on other species lower in the chain, they ingest organic matter already developed for specific uses by their prey, whether animal or vegetable. Metabolic effort is not required to build these foods chemically for diverse purposes: organisms can use energies, advanced organic chemicals and DNA resources already in the foods they eat to increase their own complexity. The upward spiral of positive feedback runs ever faster until environmental limits are reached and natural selection operates the brake. The principle of survival of the fittest does not stimulate evolution; contrarily, it operates when mutation from external radiation and nutrient-driven and environment-adapted evolution in a stimulating environment is too successful. A quotation from *The Driving Force* is appropriate:

> We could sum up our approach by saying that we see all life forms and their evolution as examples of physics and chemistry in action. The process can be considered as a series of chemical reactions in which genetics, organisms and their environments interact. Variability occurs in both genetics and chemistry but the evidence indicates that, of the two, chemistry is the more coercive.

Further on in the book, while describing biochemical complexities that favour genetic evolution rather than random mutation from external sources, the authors write:

> .... a very simple mechanism can now be proposed which would lead to permanent genetic change. If the introduction of a new nutrient suppresses its synthesis by the cell, it would have the effect of a suppressor sitting on the DNA: just as in cell specialisation. If the new chemical input becomes permanent, then total deletion of the DNA segment would not be noticed. .... if that covered section is rewritten, then new ideas could be expressed in a heritable manner.

Here is one of several examples given:

> The conventional view is that the horse achieved its present shape and form through competition to run fast, the slower members being filtered out. We suggest it happened the other way around. Nutrition induced change in form, and genetic change, if and when it occurred, would have operated within the confines already set by nutrition.

But nutritional driving forces affect different parts of the organism in different ways. Michael Crawford, in a letter to me, wrote:

"The mistake current evolution theory makes is to consider food as food. ... The evidence we have accumulated in our laboratory clearly shows that there are different nutritional principles (and hence foods) involved in body growth on the one hand and brain growth on the other."

Crawford's thesis of a seashore location for hominin evolution began with the particular study of the biochemical effects of a prolonged seafood diet producing a nutrition-based evolutionary driving force on the brains of land mammals. Conclusions drawn from an examination of dolphins, seals and the other aquatic mammals were at the core of their theory. What fascinated him and his colleagues was that as they developed their argument it increasingly coincided with Sir Alister Hardy's physiological and behavioural proposals for a seashore phase in human evolution. They came to the specific seashore hypothesis from other, more general studies. An aquatic hominin hypothesis was not an objective of their research.

If changes of food and behaviour become reasonably permanent, DNA recipes are altered and evolution surges ahead. Particular seafood nutrients are the most powerful ingredients in expanding the neuro systems and brains of mammals and a hominin who exploited the food of seashores and experimented with a new lifestyle under stress of climate-induced environmental change could enter an exploding phase of positive feedback. The biochemical detail of this argument, that seafoods are the most powerful neural building blocks for higher orders of mammals with large brains, such as whales, dolphins or apes, is complex. But it has been subject to extensive research. Its application to evolution during a possible seashore phase in the development of *Australopithecus* and the near-certainty of prolonged periods during later evolutionary jumps of the *Homo* line is the novelty provided by Crawford and his colleagues.

Any mammal which has had a sustained seafood diet during a prolonged period of time undergoes profound physical and behavioural change. The examples are numerous, besides the obvious ones of the ocean-going mammals such as whales and dolphins. Different species of the seal, sealion and otter families are aquatic or semi-aquatic forms of land mammals which have adapted to the oceans. Crawford proposes that the relatively great changes these species made were stimulated by nutritional driving forces.

Research into the effects of high seafood diet continued in the years since Crawford and Marsh published *The Driving Force*. Michael Crawford at the Institute of Brain Chemistry and Human Nutrition at the London Metropolitan University, had published a number of papers by 2003. Research supported the original thesis and expanded the concepts.

With the growing general acceptance of nutrition and evidence of migrations of *Homo erectus* and *Homo sapiens* along seashores of the Indian Ocean rim having an effect on the evolution of *Homo* species, after millions of years of stagnation in the *Australopithecus* and *Paranthropus* groups, Crawford and colleagues were able to be more definite.

Crawford and colleagues produced a paper, *Evidence for the Unique Function of DHA during the Evolution of the Modern Hominid Brain.* I quote from it:

> The accepted dogma regarding the evolution of *Homo sapiens* is that he was originally a hunter and gatherer on the African savanna. A study of savanna and other African species show that as they evolved larger and larger brains, the relative size of the brain diminished logarithmically with increase in body weight. A cebus monkey of 0.9 kg body weight has 2.3% of its body weight as brain, a 60 kg chimpanzee 0.5%. The larger gorilla at 110 kg has only 0.25% brain which is physically smaller than the chimpanzee's brain.

The chimpanzee, our closest cousin, is omnivorous like a baboon and does not eat fish and the gorilla is almost entirely vegetarian. The authors go on to state:

> We might hypothesize that *Australopithecus spp* could not mount this heroic metabolic effort [the evolution of a large and complex modern brain] either which explains why their brain capacity was constrained by their land based diet at 400-500 cc for 3 Myr and explains why coastal foods fits the rapid recent expansion to 1.3 kg after 3Myr of static brain size.

I am reminded, once again at this point, of Professor Philip Tobias discussing the evolutionary needs of developing a unique nervous system to enable bipedalism in hominids. Crawford and his

110

colleagues have shown the vital importance of specific nutrition for the development and maintenance of an advanced brain and nervous system. Tobias wrote (in 2005):

> If proprioception plays an important part in the control of the upright posture and poise of the head, does it differ between humans and the apes? If there are differences, what is their nature? ... Are they differently, perhaps uniquely developed in humans as compared with quadrupedal animals? Are these nerve tracts denser from some areas of the body than others? Are they more intricate, with more cross-connections, in humans than in apes?

Perhaps seafood for long periods was the ingredient that aided this specific essential and unique development?

George Monbiot, commentator in the British *Guardian* newspaper, reported in 2006:

> During the Palaeolithic era, humans ate roughly the same amount of Omega 3 fatty acids as Omega 6s. Today we eat 17 times as much Omega 6 as Omega 3. Omega 6s are found in vegetable oils, while most of the Omega 3s we eat come from fish. John Stein, a professor of physiology at Oxford who specialises in dyslexia, believes that fish oils permitted humans to make their great cognitive leap forwards. The concentration of Omega 3s in the brain, he says, could provide more evidence that human beings were, for a while, semi-aquatic.
>
> Stein believes that when the cells that are partly responsible for visual perception - the magnocellular neurones - are deficient in Omega 3s, they don't form as many connections with other cells, and don't pass on information as efficiently. Their impaired development explains, for example, why many dyslexic children find that letters appear to jump around on the page.

Those scientists most concerned with the connection between seafoods and brains and the nervous system inch towards this view.

Letten F. Saugstad, a respected scientist and investigator in several fields, published this in 2006 (*Nutrition & Health*, 18. 3):

> We migrated *out of Africa*, the cradle of human evolution where optimal conditions prevailed, to all over the world

where various different epigenetic factors have contributed to our differences. Notably, there is now good mitochondrial DNA evidence that the migration out of Africa was around the coastlines, testifying to a long prior acquaintance with a marine coastal habitat. Recognising our marine heritage, the necessity of abundant seafood availability as crucial in the evolvement of our great brain, we have to admit that a superior brain function has been replaced by brain dysfunction with our high protein diet of last century, neglecting food for the brain.

The additional point being made clearly in this passage, supported by those scientists working in this discipline, is that not only are seafoods essential to the evolution and good health of our brains, but that a lack of them and a high intake of other protein foods, such as lean meat from wild herbivores, reduces brain function and with epigenetic effects over just a few generations there could be a reduction of some brain functions.

Mankind could not have evolved a large brain on the dry savannahs of Africa and it may be that prolonged absence of N-3 (DHA) fatty acids in diets in different parts of the world has resulted in behavioural and cultural change in their native populations. A return to a high seafood diet, of course, restores those functions. This raises possible answers to the question as to why certain people, living in certain regions in recent time, seem to have greater intellectual dynamism, and others do not.

Behavioural and cultural 'jumps' occur for several reasons: mutation from external forces such as bursts of excessive cosmic radiation, environmental change which provokes different practical responses and, perhaps most important of all, nutrition. Nutrients are of principal importance because they fuel the brain which has to deal with all the other factors. Those particular fatty acids, obtainable primarily from seafoods, and it must be remembered, from freshwater fish in smaller concentrations, is the necessary nutrition for a special combination of feedback mechanisms.

*   *

In the important BBC TV documentary series, *Ape Man* (2000), Dr Leslie C Aiello described differences between the two early hominin groups. Both 'gracile' *Australopithecus* and 'robust' *Paranthropus* were

112

co-existing on the African savannah fringes about 2,500,000 years ago, as proven by their fossils. *Paranthropus* had heavy skulls to support strong jaw muscles to enable chewing of tough roots in a dry savannah environment. And they had large bellies similar to gorillas for digesting large quantities of a rough vegetarian diet, as demonstrated by Donald Johanson's Lucy skeleton from the Hadar.

The gracile *Australopithecus* were smaller and had slighter skulls than *Paranthropus* and have been shown to have been occasional carnivores. Careful examination of rough stone fragments found alongside gracile fossils revealed that they may have been used to crudely butcher meat and break open bones which proved two facts, that gracile *Australopithecines* were simple tool-users and meat eaters. Aiello stated that it was the gracile *Australopithecus* that evolved a larger brain to body weight ratio than *Paranthropus* over time, and there had to be a reason. Both were upright walkers. Why was there divergence, and why did meat eating begin, requiring simple stone tools?

Dr Aiello proposed a theory which might explain a larger relative brain size in *Australopithecus africanus*. Recognising that the *Paranthropus* group were vegetarians, she stated tellingly that: "vegetarians don't have big brains." She explained that the consumption of meat, especially brains and the rich marrow from broken skulls and bones, would start a feedback mechanism connecting tool-making and brain expansion through the principle of survival of the fittest. The best tool-makers were the best meat extractors who developed the bigger brains, and so on. Aiello and her colleagues were therefore proposing that land-animal protein consumption (particularly brains and marrow) was the driving force. (Dr Aiello had previously proposed this idea in 1995 in a paper co-authored by P.Wheeler.)

This idea was a whisker away from acknowledging a seafood concept as proposed by Michael Crawford more than ten years before the TV documentary series. Having come so close to a nutrient-driven answer to evolution eventually proceeding to the *Homo* range, why did she not examine seafoods? The detailed scientific research of the biochemistry was readily available. The Aquatic Ape Hypothesis had been around for forty years. An ideal opportunity to float a seashore concept, however lightly, had been missed again. Aiello and others were persisting in the confrontational stance of excluding the seashore; and the hypothesis that tool-using by early hunter-gatherers, which facilitates meat-eating, was learned during sojourns at the seashore where shell fish had been a critical factor. As years passed, I could not understand the maintenance of this dogged, excluding viewpoint. What was it about the Seashore Hypothesis that these scientists specialising in palaeanthropology considered it to be anathema?

Even on the matter of scavenging from the kills of big cats and wild dogs on the savannah, which is almost always proposed as the forerunner of hunting, there is essential practical contradiction.

The problem of nakedness is considered first. The Savannah Hypothesis proposes that nakedness was selected because it enabled hominins to easily copiously sweat and therefore keep cool during the 'marathon running' activity necessary for hunting plains antelopes with the simple weapons available to *Homo erectus*. Earlier hominins who did not make tools, and therefore throwing spears or bows-and-arrows, could not hunt plains antelopes. Natural selection of those with less fur being the best hunters, and so on, is a circular argument. If a hominin had fur, did not sweat from eccrine glands and had not developed a stature and gait capable of sustained and speedy tracking of antelopes it could not begin to hunt antelopes.

A belief that *Australopithecines* became naked, grew in stature with greater brain to body ratios in order to hunt, and then evolved to the early *Homos* has to be discarded. The lean meat of antelopes is not a driving force for brain enlargement in excess of the needs of a larger body mass. There can be no doubt that hyenas regularly consume more bone marrow and brains than hominins ever could have. Hyenas did not develop big brains relative to body mass.

Lyall Watson, in *Lightning Bird* (1982), pointed out that early hominins would not have actively or aggressively scavenged, any more than modern primates do in the wild. Hunting small animals preceded scavenging (if indeed hominins ever regularly scavenged), because it is always easier to kill insects, reptiles, birds and small mammals than to chase predators off their kills. palaeoanthropologists conventionally see hominins learning to hunt as a result of becoming carnivorous on the savannah plains from chasing cats and dogs off kills by group action. Watson, citing Adrian Boshier, a naturalist who spent many years living in the wilderness without firearms, shows that it requires far greater effort, both physical and psychic, to chase predators away from kills than to catch and eat the variety of small animals which modern baboons also catch and eat. Baboons are

114

intelligent primates and quickly learn to scavenge from modern humans' rubbish tips and dustbins because they are faster than humans. Baboons are the scourge of human camping sites in wilderness, learn how to open the zips of tents, and race away with ease when confronted. But they don't chase cats or dogs off their kills, because they are not faster than them. They steal fruits, vegetable foods and sweetmeats from humans. But, they do eat small animals they have caught and have not developed large brains.

There is another simple argument which has been universally ignored by palaeoanthropologists who routinely propose scavenging as a precursor to hunting. It is the undeniable fact that people absolutely abhor the smell of dead meat. We cannot abide the aroma of carrion and are instinctively repelled. This is quite clearly a genetic imprint. We watch with feelings of disgust as pet dogs or cats eat 'bad' food. More importantly, it goes beyond a psychic reaction. Our digestive systems cannot handle the bacteria especially associated with rotting meat and we die from some of them. Any bacteria which work at breaking down both meat and vegetable matter causes us distress. We cook our food to kill bacteria and the economy of the Indian Ocean in the last two thousand years has been boosted by trade in spices. The cuisines of all tropical countries employ cooking with pungent herbs and spices. All of this is hardly coincidental or the result of rapid mutations in modern mankind's genes over the last few millennia. My conclusion is that far back, before *Homo erectus* learned how to defend themselves from the major predators, they learned the painful lessons of the savannah: don't mess with the scavenging cats and dogs and keep away from their kills. The aroma of carcasses was not an invitation to scavenge, as it is for hyenas and jackals, it was a signal to get away fast. Lions eat carrion and will guard a decaying elephant corpse for days as they gradually consume it.

Maybe when *Homo erectus* and their *Homo sapiens* descendants, had learned how to hunt large mammals with coordinated group action armed with spears they also learned that meat, however fresh, was more easily digested if cooked first. Hominids are not habitual red meat eaters. Modern hunter-gatherers, such as the San-Bushmen of the southern African savannah, butchered their prey after the kill, often after carrying it back to their camp. To do this, either at the kill or at the camp, they had to have already perfected their ability to combat cats and dogs and keep them away.

Maybe the universal enjoyment of the social occasion of a barbecue by people today, like a seaside holiday, has its origin that far back. The caricature of overweight suburban men quaffing beer, telling jokes and guffawing around a barbecue while the womenfolk sit together gossiping and tending the rampaging children is a mirror of ancient society as poignant as the picture of a modern family group exploring rock pools at the seashore.

A conventional hypothesis suggesting that an opportunistic meat-eating driving force was learned on the savannah plains and big brains evolved there with positive feedback and survival of the fittest must fail. Apart from the biochemical evidence which is conclusive enough, logic suggests that during the millions of years of opportunity for the wholly-carnivorous cats and dogs, they should have become the dominant species with enormous brains and huge intellects. It must be reiterated that the only wholly-carnivorous warm-blooded mammals with large brains, relative to body size, and exceptional intelligence are those that live within the oceans. It is dolphins, killer whales and seals with whom we disport harmoniously in aquaria and 'sea-worlds'. And every time we make a face when we have forgotten to clean out the kitchen refuse bin, we are aware of our ancient genetic inheritance rejecting scavenging as a dangerous pursuit.

It may not seem relevant, but it should be noted that modern hunter-gatherers such as the San-Bushman, and modern iron-age peoples of Africa, sustained themselves mostly on vegetable foods. The San's principal food was gathered by women and iron-age people's provision was cultivated. Meat, whether hunted by the San or herded by those with iron-age culture, was an occasional luxury often associated with ritual or ceremony. Hunted or herded meat was provided by men and required considerable energy and organisation to acquire. Animals, whether hunted or herded had mystical and religious significance. Animals were related to them in their cosmos and vegetable foods were common to all higher forms of animal life.

*   *

By 2016, archaeological discoveries at the southern Cape region of Africa showed that modern humans, *Homo sapiens*, of the African Middle Stone Age developed the particular insights and abilities to conceive and execute abstract decoration. It was considered to be the

116

dawn of all artistic expression, and the dates were 70-100,000 years ago. This is described and discussed more fully in a later chapter.

The cave sites which provided the definitive evidence also had contemporary middens with abundant evidence of a seafood diet. Middens (garbage tips) with quantities of seafood shells and other discards proliferate along southern African coasts, proving consumption by seashore-living people, but these archaeological sites with coincidental, newly-discovered artistic relics and shell middens, with dates going back to before the out-of-Africa migrations of *Homo sapiens* were electrifying. Archaeologists and anthropologists who were aware of the scientific nutritional evidence of a prolonged seafood diet, assumed, with good reason, that the 'jump' to artistic expression may have been linked to seafood eating.

Professor John Parkington of the University of Cape Town published an important popular book, *Shorelines, Strandlopers and Shell Middens,* in 2006 which is devoted to this particular subject. He describes the importance of seafood in the development of brains and neural systems.

It became an established theme that the enlargement and complexity of the modern human psyche to include decoration, jewellery-making, sculpting and, later, rock-art painting and engraving was probably first experienced at the far end of Africa. From there, it has been proposed by John Compton and others, it spread to eastern Africa during climate change stimuli and thence to the rest of the world with the out-of-Africa diaspora of about 75,000 years ago. The Cape, it was proposed, was the seat of the last great step in cultural evolution leading to civilisation. It was suggested that this was possible because of the unique character of the Cape coast and its shellfish nutriments, proven by the middens.

This is controversial, but the evidence of seafood and a cultural 'jump' was clear. I was delighted and awaited the extension of the theme to include a merging with the Seashore Hypothesis to explain the whole of our unique and extraordinary evolutionary trail. However, the exclusion of the seashore from a general theory has been maintained. John Compton of the University of Cape Town in his encyclopaedic *Human Origins* (2016):

> In much the same way that our bigger-brained genus *Homo* evolved from the australopiths who made the behavioural shift to eating carrion, our species [*Homo sapiens*] evolved from those among our predecessor species who ate seafood.

117

The shift to eating carrion was greatly facilitated by the use of stone tools (Oldowan) to break open bone-encased fatty marrow and brain not accessible to lions. But eating seafood did not require any new tools or skills or nearly as much daring as the scavenging or stealing of carrion. ... Unlike the scavenging or hunting of large game, the collection of seafood was far less dangerous and did not require learning complex skills. Adopting and sustaining a seafood diet was a no-brainer for those living within reach of the seashore.

Sadly in my view, Compton pursues the carrion-eating proposition for the 'jump' in brain size and intelligence from *Australopithecus* to *Homo erectus* and onwards. I have discussed this in some detail earlier and will only remark here that it is not only lions who would prevent the hominins from getting at marrow and brain of a kill. It was the ubiquitous hyenas with especially adapted jaws who are the African marrow and brain eaters. To get at carrion marrow and brain, hominins would have to chase away both lions and hyenas; and then have the undisturbed leisure time to crack open large bones and skulls with stone tools which they had fortuitously kept ready. I cannot begin to imagine a widespread practice of this activity, let alone it being so regularly extensive over such long time that it resulted in the dramatic evolution of brains and anatomy of early hominin species.

Much later, *Homo erectus* would devise group tactics for combatting hyenas with spears if it was an imperative. They probably had the mental ability to plan ahead and carry marrow-bone-cracking stone tools. But their predecessors, who are the ones assumed to be the first to benefit from the marrow and brains, would not.

Having made those comments, I say that Compton could hardly have been more successfully succinct in preposing a general Seashore Hypothesis.

*

For those who seek a more scientific explanation for the nutritional 'driving force', I quote the whole of the abstract of this paper: *Brain-specific lipids from marine, lacustrine, or terrestrial food resources: potential impact on early African Homo sapiens*, by C. Leigh Broadhurst, Yiqun Wang, Michael A. Crawford , Stephen C. Cunnane, John E.

Parkington and Walter F. Schmidt, published in *Comparative Biochemistry & Physiology*, Part B 131 (2002).

The polyunsaturated fatty acid (PUFA) composition of the mammalian central nervous system is almost wholly composed of two long-chain polyunsaturated fatty acids (LC-PUFA), docosahexaenoic acid (DHA) and arachidonic acid(AA). PUFA are dietarily essential, thus normal infantyneonatal brain, intellectual growth and development cannot be accomplished if they are deficient during pregnancy and lactation. Uniquely in the human species, the fetal brain consumes 70% of the energy delivered to it by mother. DHA and AA are needed to construct placental and fetal tissues for cell membrane growth, structure and function. Contemporary evidence shows that the maternal circulation is depleted of AA and DHA during fetal growth. Sustaining normal adult human brain function also requires LC-PUFA. *Homo sapiens* is unlikely to have evolved a large, complex, metabolically expensive brain in an environment which did not provide abundant dietary LC-PUFA.

Conversion of 18-carbon PUFA from vegetation to AA and DHA is considered quantitatively insufficient due to a combination of high rates of PUFA oxidation for energy, inefficient and rate limited enzymatic conversion and substrate recycling.

The littoral marine and lacustrine food chains provide consistently greater amounts of pre-formed LC-PUFA than the terrestrial food chain. Dietary levels of DHA are 2.5–100 fold higher for equivalent weights of marine fish or shellfish vs. lean or fat terrestrial meats. Mammalian brain tissue and bird egg yolks, especially from marine birds, are the richest terrestrial sources of LC-PUFA. However, land animal adipose fats have been linked to vascular disease and mental ill-health, whereas marine lipids have been demonstrated to be protective. At South African Cape sites, large shell middens and fish remains are associated with evidence for some of the earliest modern humans. Cape sites dating from 100 to 18 kya cluster within 200 km of the present coast. Evidence of early *H. sapiens* is also found around the Rift Valley lakes and up the Nile Corridor into the Middle East; in some cases there is an association with the use of littoral resources.

Exploitation of river, estuarine, stranded and spawning fish, shellfish and sea bird nestlings and eggs by

Homo could have provided essential dietary LC-PUFA for men, women, and children without requiring organized hunting by fishing, or sophisticated social behaviour. It is however, predictable from the present evidence that exploitation of this food resource would have provided the advantage in multigenerational brain development which would have made possible the advent of *H. sapiens*. Restriction to land based foods as postulated by the savannah and other hypotheses would have led to degeneration of the brain and vascular system as happened without exception in all other land based apes and mammals as they evolved larger bodies.

If the gracile *Australopithecine* forms were omnivorous and occasional meat-eaters, like modern chimps, who migrated back from the seashore up the eastern African rivers, having learned their tool-using skills beside the sea, it must be asked why the 'robust' species were still surviving and vegetarian less than two million years ago. Perhaps the *Paranthropus* group is evidence of those branches of our tree which never spent time at the seashore.

The *Paranthropus* group has been divided into two main branches. The *robustus* species is associated with South Africa and *boisei* with East Africa. They had large 'nutcracker' jaws suitable for crunching roots and tough vegetable fibres. Maybe they could be considered to be more like a chimp in lifestyle than their *Australopithecine* cousins, a sort of 'super-chimp', but they had a problem which eventually doomed them. They survived longer than their gracile, omnivorous *Australopithecus* cousins who jumped the evolutionary hurdle to the *Homo* range, but their inheritance had bequeathed them a body which irrevocably stood and walked upright, and this was their downfall.

Their diet was unable to develop their brains further and the greater range of climate changes in the Pleistocene era caught up with them. In drier conditions, the forest fringes about the lakes declined and could not adequately sustain them. Having become bipedal they could not function efficiently in the arboreal environment of the deep rainforest and they could not compete with the other primates whose home it was. Each cold, dry glacial period brought them close to extinction and eventually predators probably killed them off. They could not run fast enough.

The 'gracile' *Australopithecines* apparently disappeared several hundreds of thousands of years earlier than *Paranthropus*. Many groups in the interior no doubt suffered the same fate as *Paranthropus*, but the main cause of their disappearance from the fossil record must be that they evolved through the jump to the first *Homos* on the seashore. Seafood gave them bigger brains and 'survival of the fittest' in the seashore life honed their anatomy.

*

While the last of the *Australopithecus* and *Paranthropus* species wandered the margins of the African rivers and lakes, some surviving for a while and others expiring, evolution of the missing core-population along the Indian Ocean littoral continued, driven by a sustained and regular seafood diet.

Frequent immersion in seawater and the problem of dried salt, sand, shells and seaweeds in residual fur completed the trend to nakedness. Ducking and diving in the sea consolidated changes in their breathing equipment and allowed them to produce an ever-increasing range of sounds. Continued practice in swimming strengthened the hip joints and the straightness of their stance enabling easier walking and safer running: 'marathon running' abilities of hip and joint facility. Increased lung and thoracic capacity from the diving and swimming experience gave them more stamina for trekking long nomadic distances. They grew stronger, taller and slimmer.

Their relative brain capacity kept pace with body growth and intelligence increased as varied experience stimulated cultural evolution. The carrying of simple tools and the results of fishing and shellfish gathering in surging seawater on coral reefs was the obvious path to inventing carry-bags. Simple tool-making was learned to increase the efficiency of fishing, reef-gathering and food preparation, and eventually for hunting. The learning process for the invention of hunting spears is easily imagined when considering the use of sharpened sticks to snag octopus and other soft seafoods, and then to spear fish.

Careful rearing of slow-maturing children was a survival imperative exacted by natural selection, and socialising by females became more complex. This seashore trail along our direct *Homo* ancestral line seems to be the most obvious progression. It was a long and rugged road, hundreds of thousands of years long, braving cyclical ice-ages, cosmic events and many environmental shocks. Parasitical and invasive diseases were hurdles that were leaped by being beside the sea when they ravaged the general primate populations of savannah and forest.

All possible interacting genetic, behavioural and environmental factors had to play their powerful roles for our extraordinary modern species to diverge from their primate family ancestral bases. Positive feedback was the engine, seafoods were the fuel, the littoral environment was the anvil and natural selection was the refining process. The missing link in logic that had bothered me was in place.

Seafoods were the facilitator!

Here is a final quotation:

> When [the Aquatic Ape Theory was] originally presented (Hardy, 1961) and more recently reviewed and expanded (Morgan, 1972; 1982; 1991), this theory has not addressed the question of how human brain development could have occurred.
>
> Optimal mammalian brain development dependant on lipid nutrition and brain complexity is, in considerable part, a function of the complexity of structural lipids. Normal development of the neonatal human brain relies heavily on two long chain polyunsaturated fatty acids ... Both are available in abundance in shore-based seaweed, molluscs, invertebrates and in fish. On land, these fatty acids can only be obtained by carnivores consuming meat, and then only in low concentrations. ... A marine-based phase of human evolution would provide both the nutrient and energy requirements a larger brain would require.

Stephen C.Cunnane, Lawrence S.Harbige & Michael A.Crawford: *Nutrition and Health* v9 No.3 (1993).

SEVEN : *HOMO ERECTUS*
The appearance of the first *Homos*.
The Pleistocene ice-ages began.

When discussing the evolution of the *Homos*, that genus of species quite distinct from the earlier range of more primitive hominins, two different tracks may be followed. They are closely inter-related and can confuse. There is the path of anatomical or genetic evolution and there is the path of cultural evolution, and different people at different times and places are described with either and both criteria. The genetic definition sticks to Latin-based taxonomic names, *Homo erectus* etc., and cultural evolution is usually defined by the tools in general use, Early Stone Age, palaeolithic, neolithic, Late Stone Age and so forth. This is compounded by differences in stone tool culture identities and periods applied in Europe and Africa. In this book, African terms are used. Lay-people are sometimes muddled by this, with good reason.

~~~~~~~~~~~~~~~

The fossil evidence shows that there were two coexisting families of hominin species in Africa for a time. Both families were buffeted by climatic and environmental stresses, and both adapted to meet them or became extinct. They were the *Australopithecus* and *Paranthropus* groups and the early true *Homos*. The anatomical differences between the two lines are substantial apart from skull size and shape. *Australopithecus* and *Paranthropus*, though bipedal, were smaller and did not have a pelvis suited to long marches across the land, which later *Homos* developed. They used tools of wood, bone and suitable stones but they did not make them, and their brains, though progressively larger than their ape cousins, were still small.

The critical difference between the two families of species is that all the *Australopithecus* and *Paranthropus* types became extinct and the surviving descendants of the early *Homos* are ourselves. It has to be presumed that at least one branch of *Australopithecines* evolved into the *Homos*.

123

Raymond Dart, the pioneering South African palaeontologist, proposed that bones and antelope horns were used as tools long before stones. He was passionate in this belief which was supported by bones found with *Australopithecus* remains at Makapansgat and elsewhere. Bones, whether found on the veld or discarded in a midden, present a great variety of possible uses without much alteration, if any, whereas a stone tool has to be imagined within the natural lump of rock. Making a stone tool, therefore, is an advanced mental facility, requiring abstract or creative imagination, which it is assumed that *Australopithecus* did not have. It was one that early *Homo* developed.

In 1964 when it was still believed that *Australopithecus* proceeded in a simple unbroken 'ladder' line to ourselves, Louis Leakey, Tobias and Napier gave the name *Homo habilis* to the first species they reckoned had the mental ability to make stone tools. It was assumed that *Homo habilis* might have represented a phase when there was still some genetic interaction with *Australopithecus africanus* whom they resembled, but they had a rather larger brain and skeletal differences.

Homo habilis is often known as *Homo ergastor*. Some authorities suggest that *H.habilis* was the first manifestation of a hominin with a larger brain and this subsequently evolved as *H.ergastor* and then *H.erectus*. That assumes a 'ladder', or lineal progression of evolution. There is academic controversy about the need for this separate species designation since it is seemingly the earliest manifestation of *Homo erectus*. In other words, the *Homo* line might as well be described as commencing with *Homo erectus* which over more than a million years had several regional variants. Maybe, the same process was occurring with earliest *Homo* as there was with the *Australopithecines*; that the variations of *Homos,* were extinct branches from a common core-people. It is that core which I see as the possible 'missing link' whose discovery awaits us on lost ancient Indian Ocean shores and it is from the successful 'core' that *Homo erectus* descended.

The proliferations of early *Homo* species suggested by differences in skull shapes has been challenged. Discussion about whether *Homo habilis* or *Homo ergastor* were the defining 'first' *Homo* species, differentiated from the *Australopithecines*, are probably irrelevant. Fossils with attributes which scientists have defined as *Homo habilis* parallel the period when *Homo erectus* existed and therefore discussion continues as to whether the two are separate species living in parallel for several hundred thousand years or variants of one early *Homo* species.

Presently, there are at least ten subspecies of *Homo erectus* which have been described and five related species, such as *H. ergastor* and *H.habilis*. It has been argued that many of these subspecies and related species are unnecessary since they likely represent regional variations in skull shapes and sizes of the same order as modern humans scattered around the world today. I follow that argument and would prefer to consider all the Homo people as *Homo erectus*. What principally distinguishes them, in my opinion, is their culture which developed and evolved as required during the enormously long period of about two million years since the appearance of the first distinct *Homo habilis* fossil.

Adaptation to regional geography and the climate cycles undoubtedly caused regional variations from the main line, but were these variations different species? Latest genetic evidence proves that *Homo* species did indeed interbreed (Neanderthals and modern humans for example) and therefore should they be described as separate species? Presumably not, but this requires a re-constitution of taxonomy. Genetics today is causing much re-thinking.

Recently, Professor Lee Berger of the University of the Witwatersrand in Johannesburg announced the discovery of fossils in September 2013 of possibly fifteen individuals in a cave near the famous Sterkfontein complex. Careful analysis suggested to him and his team that these hominins were sufficiently advanced in brain size and skeletal structure to be classified as a separate species within the *Homo* genus. He named them *Homo naledi* and the official description was announced in September 2015. At the time of writing (2017) dating has not been possible, but it has been estimated that these hominins probably lived at about 2M years ago, coincident to *Homo habilis*. In the defining paper, *Homo naledi, a new species of the genus Homo from the Dinaledi Chamber, South Africa* (eLife 2015;4:e09560 of 10 September 2015) Berger wrote in the Abstract:

> Homo naledi is a previously-unknown species of extinct hominin discovered within the Dinaledi Chamber of the Rising Star cave system, Cradle of Humankind, South Africa. This species is characterized by body mass and stature similar to small-bodied human populations but a small endocranial volume similar to australopiths. Cranial morphology of H. naledi is unique, but most similar to early

Homo species including Homo erectus, Homo habilis or Homo rudolfensis. While primitive, the dentition is generally small and simple in occlusal morphology. H. naledi has humanlike manipulatory adaptations of the hand and wrist. It also exhibits a humanlike foot and lower limb. These humanlike aspects are contrasted in the postcrania with a more primitive or australopith-like trunk, shoulder, pelvis and proximal femur. Representing at least 15 individuals with most skeletal elements repeated multiple times, this is the largest assemblage of a single species of hominins yet discovered in Africa.

Several authorities commented on Berger's announcement which gained wide publicity. It seems acceptable that the hominins were somewhere in transition from *Australopithecus* to *Homo erectus*, but whether they were on a straightforward 'ladder' or were a lost pocket which expired on the South African Highveld is not known, and maybe this will never be determined. Acceptable dating may be impossible. There has been criticism of Berger's methods and over-hasty publication, and exploitation of the media. From the viewpoint of the Seashore Hypothesis, *Homo naledi* easily joins the ranks of those many groups of hominins who migrated inland from the seashore core-people and eventually became extinct due to their inability to survive the rigours of climate, lack of a sustaining diet and the pressures of predators.

Until *Homo erectus* was fully developed, with tool-making capabilities, control of fire and advancing cognitive and social abilities, I believe all intermediate populations were unsustainable over time outside the seashores of eastern Africa. If there was a 'ladder' of human evolution it began with *Homo erectus*, and that 'ladder' had its foot planted on the seashore.

Here is a list of some of the generally-accepted African hominin species. There are others which may be lesser variants such as the newly described *Homo naledi*. Eurasian variants, such as *Homo heidelbergensis* are also well established and described. Brain capacities are approximate and there is notable variation. There are other variants which are not included.

Genus/Species	Aprox. date	Brain capacity
Australopithecus/		
Paranthropus	4M - 1.5Mya	450-500 cc
Homo habilis	2.5Mya	750 cc
Homo ergaster	2.1Mya	900 cc
Homo erectus	1.9Mya - 200Kya	1,000 cc
Homo sapiens	200Kya	1,400 cc
(*Homo*		
neanderthalensis	400Kya (?) - 30Kya	1,500 cc)

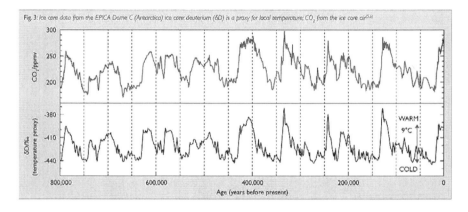

Data from the EPICA ice cores - British Antarctic Survey

Glacial-interglacial cycles during the later Pleistocene Era.
These cycles are relaxant to the most active period of variation.

Tim Bromage and Friedman Schrenk found a hominin jawbone and other fossils in the Great Rift Valley near the shore of Lake Malawi in 1991-92. These bones were dated to about 2.3M years before present, at the beginning of the Pleistocene and at a time of high humidity and lake levels. Philip Tobias described the jawbone as probably that of *Homo habilis*, the earliest of its line found at that time. Other examples of early *Homos*, whether *habilis*, *ergastor* or *erectus*, have been found at Olduvai (1.8 - 1.7M years ago), Koobi Fora (1.9M years ago) and Dmanisi in the Caucasus (1.8 -1.6M years ago).

When it was discovered that the robust *Paranthropus* and *Homos* must have co-existed for some hundreds of thousands of years, the evolution of the true *Homo* line was thought to have developed in parallel after an event of species deviation. This usually occurs because of geographical separation over sufficient time for random or environment-driven mutation to make cross-breeding no longer possible. How this happened has not been explained in conventional hypotheses.

Following the reasoning suggested in the previous chapter, that *Australopithecine* types began dispersing away from the seashore during climate fluctuations between three and four and a half million years ago, I suggest that the reason for the divergence is simple. Migrations during succeeding stages of evolution occurred from time to time when stimulated by population pressures (caused by glacials) or environmental shocks. The core populations continued to evolve on the ocean littoral. For a long period, maybe hundreds of thousands of years, intermingling and hybridisation between the two was possible, but eventually a particularly long geographical separation occurred, probably as a result of desertification in the immediate interior, and genetic gaps between the two groups might have been too great for cross-breeding to continue.

The Pleistocene series of cyclical severe ice-ages extended by long cool-dry periods, and interspersed by warm-wet interglacials, started about 2.3 million years ago and minor extinctions and stimulations of all land-animals followed each of them. Succeeding *Australopithecine* and *Paranthropus* species who had been able to survive in the interior until then could not weather the severe shocks of this Pleistocene epoch. Those in the interior disappeared forever from the fossil record. *Paranthropus*, the vegetarians, survived longer than the gracile and omnivorous *Australopithecus*, probably because they inhabited more restricted and protected forested environments. They were specialists and eventually succumbed to severe changes in their environment provided by ice-ages. The *Paranthropus* branch of the hominin line might almost be nicknamed 'super-chimps'.

The *Australopithecine* species disappeared from the fossil record several hundred thousand years before *Paranthropus*. I suggest that they did become extinct on the savannahs but survived on seashores where they evolved into what we have described as *Homo*. *Homo habilis* and later *H. erectus* variations, armed with tool-making and other more advanced culture because of greater cognitive ability began to populate the whole planet where practical.

There is a tantalising possibility for the emergence of the *Homo* range of our direct ancestors. Looking for recent reports of supernova activity I found interest in the discovery of oceanic layers of iron isotopes which show evidence of there being a close supernova sometime within the last 5M years, perhaps at the beginning of the Pleistocene, 2M years ago. Further on in my search, the Wikipedia online encyclopaedia provided this quote:

> In 2002, astronomers discovered that roughly 2 million years ago, around the end of the Pliocene epoch, a group of bright O and B stars called the Scorpius-Centaurus OB association passed within 150 light-years of Earth and that one or more supernovae may have occurred in this group at that time. Such a close explosion could have damaged the Earth's ozone layer and caused the extinction of some ocean life (consider that at its peak, a supernova of this size could produce that same amount of absolute magnitude as an entire galaxy of 200 billion stars).

> Reference : Comins, Niel F.; William J. Kaufmann III (2005). *Discovering the Universe*, 7th edition, New York, NY.

The lack of time definition is typical of the problems scientists still encounter in pinpointing past events of this kind. Estimates place the supernova which caused the iron isotope deposits to have been only 100 light-years away which would have undoubtedly resulted in severe radiation and caused extinctions and mutations.

If it occurred at about 2M years ago, it may have triggered the evolution of *Australopithecus* to *Homo habilis* A supernova closer than about 200 light-years is believed to have two principal effects: ultra-violet radiation sufficient to blow away the ozone layer and therefore endanger life not naturally protected sufficiently by dark-skinned pigmentation, and the bombardment by cosmic radiation which causes accelerated mutation and interferes with the genetic structures of life forms.

Whatever the trigger, I believe the particular *Australopithecines* of the coastal core-population responded to the opportunities of those times. Their bodies continued to be trained by the specialist athletic demands of the seashore lifestyle. Their brains and nervous systems grew in complexity and power under the stimuli of the seafood nutritional Driving Force. Coastal *Australopithecines* were affected like all animals during adverse climate cycles, but they had their special advantage. Seafood-driven brain development in their particular circumstances enabled a jump in cultural evolution.

It was not only brain development that surged ahead during the shocks at the beginning of the Pleistocene. The emerging *Homos* at the seashore, being dependent on seafoods at this time, practised wading, swimming and diving daily, and this would have stimulated the further straightening and strengthening of their legs and pelvic structures. In turn, this improved walking and running ability. Persistent changes in their air passages and larynx, with simultaneous perfecting of breath control in the brain to make deeper diving possible, increased the range of sounds they could make and an articulated language beyond simple shrieks and barks became possible.

Regular swimming and diving strengthened lungs and enlarged their chests giving them greater stamina for long marches and sustained running, which enhanced hunting ability on land when it was needed. All larger land mammals can run much faster in bursts with their four legs; it is the marathon running capability of humans which is another of the enhancements that a seashore lifestyle would have promoted.

Their height increased from an average of less than 1.4 metres to 1.8 metres. They stood straight and tall. The function of eccrine sweating to dispose of excess salt increased and nakedness became complete.

There was dynamic cultural feedback for the enlarging brain from success with meeting varied seashore opportunities. There were any number of challenges more easily encountered every day than in a savannah or lacustrine environment. Tools were devised to make shellfish easier to collect and prepare. Simple spears made it easier to catch fish and octopus. The use of driftwood as floats is a reasonable speculation. The magic of being confronted daily by the chaos of an ever-changing ocean, with overriding tidal cycles governing reef gathering, had a rare effect on minds growing in awareness. Some concept of time, however dim, had to result. Larger catches presented the opportunity for more sophisticated socialising. Bolder swimming and diving both increased fishing success and developed an adventurous psyche. The idea grew of purposefully migrating up and down the coast to explore, as well as for immediate survival.

I was particularly struck by a description I came across in an authoritative travel book, describing men swimming and fishing far at sea off Pacific islands, sometimes supported by floats. This seems particularly important to me and I quote from *Mystic Isles of the South Seas* by Frederick O'Brien (1921):

> " ... He would be three miles out, swimming, with a small log under arm for support, and often he might be in company of thirty or forty of his tribe, who, with only the same slight aids to keeping afloat, would be fishing leisurely. They carried their tackle and their catch upon their shoulders, and appeared quite at ease, with no concern for their long swim to shore or for the sharks, which were plentiful. They might even nap a little during the middle afternoon."
>
> "When our people wanted to sleep at sea," said McBirney, "if there were two of them, though we never bothered to take along logs, one rested on the other's shoulder."
>
> One listened and marvelled, and smiled to think that, had one stayed at home, one might never know these things.

O'Brien was an astute observer and a serious travel writer. His little gem of a book, written in the early 20th century has many interesting insights on the people of the Society Islands at that time, before their culture was too badly corrupted by Western Civilisation. Knowledge of the oceans and their use of the sea in everyday life, handed down over thousands of generations, provides useful sources for a study of the seashore lifestyle in modern humans. There are other older sources than O'Brien's, of course, but his book is very readable.

There is another passage in O'Brien's book which delights me and I quote it here. O'Brien had been questioning Polynesian elders and chiefs in rural Tahiti about the origins of their people. In addition to clear and definite descriptions about migrations from the south-east Asian mainland and the vicissitudes of their movements through the already-populated islands of Indonesia and Melanesia, one respected source made this remarkable statement:

The chief had said that in former times men retained their *pareus* except when they went fishing, at which time they wore a little red cap. He did not know whether this was a ceremonial to propitiate the god of fishes or to ward off evil spirits in scales. **Man originated on the seashore, and many of the most primitive habits of humans, as well as their bodily differences from the apes, came from their early life there. Man pushed back from the salt water slowly.** (My emphasis)

*

Systematic tool-making, especially the sculpting of hand-axes, commenced. Communication became more sophisticated and reasoning ability to solve abstract problems commenced. The production of hand-axes made possible the construction of crude boats as improvements to driftwood floats, and our earliest seafaring tradition was born. Island-hopping was tried with success. I have on more than one occasion watched fishermen at sea, once off Cape Cormorin of southern India, on crude but efficient sailing rafts made from two or three carefully selected and roughly-shaped logs lashed together. This image was off Cape Cormorin in 2004.

As numbers increased during favourable warm-wet periods, the *Homos* also explored up those rivers which their *Australopithecine* ancestors had followed. They learned to control fire and use skins and suitable vegetable materials to make clothing. Regular hunting was pursued as a survival imperative to provide clothing in cooler highland and sub-tropical zones and efficient carry-bags for their slow-maturing babies and tool-kits on the march. The invention of spears, either hardened by fire or tipped with stone points, enabled them to combat large predators. The means for making clothes and bags from skins and the ability to control the magic of fire made them masters of the environment beyond the widest capability of *Australopithecus*.

Perhaps the need for skins as protective clothing promoted organised hunting of large mammals and not the other way round? This has not been proposed by anthropologists as far as I know and meat-eating always seems to be the primary explanation for hunting.

*   *

I have often flown over the great lakes of the African Great Rift Valley. I have visited them on the ground and marvelled at this extraordinary terrestrial aberration. Africa has no great tectonic mountain ranges like the Alps, the Andes or the Himalayas. But it has its Great Rift Valley running from the Red Sea to the Zambezi delta. The region of the lakes and the rivers that run along the Rift or close to it have provided much evidence of human evolution from 4,500,000 years ago when the first *Australopithecines* appeared in the present record. Where *Australopithecus* or its ancestors have been found some distance from the Rift in the South African highveld or near Lake Chad, there are riverine routes to those places. I have always been awed by the area; as if emotion, intellectual excitement and bubbling knowledge are pure products of those environments. Insights have often came to me unbidden and suddenly.

Lake Turkana is the scene of definitive discoveries of early hominid fossils. From an airliner at 35,000 feet, almost the whole of the area can be seen. The sun reflects with blinking brilliance from the centre of the long slim lake, running 175 miles from north to south. From that height the opal glare seems to strike from a burnished surface of finely ground milky crystal. On either side, the land is at first glance a uniform chocolate, streaked daintily with faint markings. On the eastern horizon, there are the distant teeth of mountains at the far side of the Chabli Desert. Craning one's neck and looking northward, the dusty distance shows where the Rift continues into the mysteries of Ethiopia. It is not only the awesome vista that thrills, it is its time dimension of four million years of human history that gives it uniqueness. There is nowhere else on this planet that can compete with the vast extent of the four dimensional view from the tiny window of a speeding airliner.

Our planet Earth, with its totally integrated dynamic systems which James Lovelock called Gaia, seems to present a slow-changing picture of the past when the only way we contemplate it is through the medium of physical geology. The solidity and rigidity of stone lulls us into a concept of excruciatingly slow change. This is far from the reality of the Pleistocene which we now know was normally cool with frequent warm, interglacial periods with sharp climatic shocks caused by random events.

Prof. Roland Oliver, could still suggest in his excellent book, *The African Experience* (1991), that early hominin populations were minute and grew achingly slowly:

> ....the total hominid population of eastern and southern Africa at any period up to the emergence of *Homo erectus* is likely to have been of the order of some tens of thousands.

There are hundreds of thousands of baboons and smaller savannah monkeys, maybe millions, living in Africa today during the present warm interglacial despite enormous pressures from humanity. Even after relentless slaughter by modern humans over 3,000 years, and the decline in vegetation cover in the Sahara and southern semi-deserts during the same period, there were still about 1.25 million modern African elephants surviving in 1980 in small artificially-constricted zones. During the warm interglacials, different species of savannah baboons and elephants evolved and multiplied before expiring again during climatic shocks, filling niches and then becoming extinct. Hominins were affected in the same way. There can be no doubt that populations swung dramatically with climate change, but I wonder if they fell to such low levels suggested by some authorities. The best place to be was always along the Indian Ocean littoral.

I am satisfied that all creatures move rapidly to fill the whole of an available suitable environment. Niches are quickly filled when environmental factors are favourable and a nutritional driving force is at work. Genetic evolution proceeds in jumps to plateaux imposed by natural selection and survival of the fittest until a new opportunity appears within the chaos of the general system to promote another jump. Climatic fluctuations continually generate change in the environment which affect different living species in different ways. Extinctions occur when favourable conditions disappear over such a wide area and for long enough that species cannot keep up, leaving room for other species.

In the same way, populations expand exponentially to fill congenial environments, stabilise when natural selection prohibits further increase and contract when conditions are adverse. The actual structures of societies, their manners, laws and style follow the same rule. Genetic evolution, population growth or decline and the composition of societies have the same mechanisms, the same kind of laws apply. It is one of the harmonies of a Universal Law.

At the end of the Pliocene and during the first climatic cycles of the Pleistocene in which *Homo habilis* fossils were dated, the evolution of this new line proceeded at the seashore and the occupation of the most suitable parts of the interior of Africa were accomplished. Some expeditions failed while nutritional stimulation and the learning process continued beside the ocean. Others followed until a refined species capable of sustained success had evolved. A date of about 1.7M years ago may be assumed to be reasonable. Following the natural law, the brake on proliferation was applied and there was stability. Aberrant types which had been exploring possible niches were now superfluous and withered outside the mass of societies. Illustrating this special time, there was one of those lucky fossil discoveries which has become a marker.

Homo erectus living along the Great Rift Valley and the river systems crossing the nearby savannahs were physically well-developed, tall and slim. This was demonstrated by a remarkable fossil skeleton which Kamoya Kimeu discovered and excavated with Richard Leakey and Alan Walker in the Nariokotome dry river bed near the shore of Lake Turkana in 1984. It was the complete remains of a boy who lived and died on the shore 1.4 to 1.6 million years ago. Richard Leakey and Alan Walker wrote:

> .... because it is a youth's skeleton and so complete, it offers us a unique glimpse of growth and development in early humans. At five feet four inches tall, the boy from Turkana was surprisingly large compared with modern boys his age: he could have grown to six feet. Suitably clothed and with a cap to obscure his low forehead and beetle brows, he would probably go unnoticed in a crowd today.

This example of very early mankind is particularly important. The skeleton shows how close people of the *Homo* family are 1.4 million years apart. It also illustrates the importance of nutrition. The boy who lived on the ancient lake shore probably had a rich diet of freshwater fish, different roots and tubers, grass seeds, fruits, locusts, honey and occasional feasts of meat. He was as tall and robust as a modern African living in similar surroundings. He was much taller than 20th century African hunter-gatherers such as the San-Bushmen confined to the harsh environment of the Kalahari Desert, or Pygmies living in the Congo rainforest, both with restricted diets.

The illustrations which follow are instructive. The reconstruction of the *Homo erectus* teenage boy from the Great Rift Valley was built up from the skeleton. There have been other reconstructions, particularly of the head. Like the image of a naked modern woman swimming with dolphins which was included earlier, it is images like these which tell me more than a thousand words in academic papers.

HOMO ERECTUS

The 'Nariokotome Boy', *Homo erectus.*

Probably 1.4 million years ago from the Great Rift Valley in Africa.

This reconstruction from an almost complete skeleton is in the Musee Nacional Prehistoire in Les Eyzies, France.

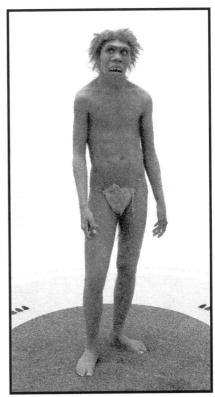

HOMO SAPIENS

A young man,
typical *Homo sapiens* of present-day Europe, 2007.

(Photographed by the author.)

HOMO ERECTUS

An evocative reconstruction of a *Homo erectus* female by John Gurche, in the Smithsonian Institute.

It is based on a fossil from Koobi Fora in the Kenyan Great Rift Valley, probably 1.75 million years ago.

HOMO SAPIENS

A guide in the Kahuzi-Biega National Park in the Congo (DRC) in 1985.

He was descended from Pygmies, and he was typical of his people.

(Photographed by the author.)

The great variation in appearance exhibited by modern people must be similar to variation amongst *Homo erectus* people.

But the boy who fell into the mud and died of septicaemia beside Lake Turkana still had a small brain compared to modern humans despite his physical similarity to us. Richard Leakey's associate on the Nariokotome Boy fossils, Alan Walker, talking on a TV documentary in 2001, stated that there was evidence that the communication node in the boy's brain was developing, but it appeared that he was not yet capable of an extended vocabulary. Walker's conclusion was based on the fact that the opening in the boy's vertebrae was too small to carry sufficient nerves to operate a talking function.

I found this fascinating. Here was possible evidence of a brain having been promoted by the nutritional seafood driving force and the complex of the nervous system being held back because of more slowly evolving changes in the bony skeleton. No doubt the boy was a member of the early range of *Homo erectus* who could communicate well with a large vocabulary of different barks and calls and used complicated gestures and grimaces, but was unable to articulate clearly yet. Probably breath control was already fully functional, because of the diving and swimming, but advanced intricacies of movement in tongue and lips was not possible. 1.4M years ago was still very early in *Homo's* development. Walker emphasised that although he had a relatively small brain, below the neck he was similar to a modern human.

Walker also disclosed that the boy's spine had been damaged and had twisted probably from some accident or contact with a large animal as a child. Maybe that childhood damage had interfered with the proper development of the nervous system and the spine itself? Was the boy crippled? In any case, more evolution beside the ocean was necessary. What we do know for certain is that between the time the Nariokotome boy lived and the emergence of modern mankind, speech was fully developed. Until a series of nearly complete *Homo erectus* skeletons are discovered and analysed, a time line cannot be drawn.

There is no doubt that *Australopithecus* and *Paranthropus* walked upright and could swim, but *Homo erectus* was much better at both. They could outwalk the shifting environment during the changes of the Pleistocene Ice-ages. *Homo erectus* moved out of eastern, northern and southern Africa. They became the first hominin colonials or refugees, ranging across the Earth wherever the environment was suitable for them. Roland Oliver in *The African Experience* (1991) wrote:

> Men equipped mostly with Acheulian tools [hand-axes like those found prolifically at most Early Stone Age sites] penetrated to every part of Africa saving only the fully forested regions of the Congo basin and the Guinea coastlands. In climatic terms, they learned to inhabit on the one hand areas much hotter than the highlands of eastern and southern Africa, and on the other hand areas that were somewhat moister and covered with denser vegetation.

It is noteworthy that Acheulian hand-axes are the well-prepared and aesthetically created stone tools that have been discovered from this period all over the Old World where these very early people penetrated. Having spent many millennia colonising Africa, they had learned to survive and thrive in the habitats that Africa provided during successive climate changes. In Central Africa if you travel a mere few hundred miles here and there, you can find canopy rainforest, *mopane* deciduous woodland forests, dry savannah thornbush, grassland, high plateaux, scrub and desert. *Homo erectus* met all these habitats and understood them, learning which to avoid and which were good. Their levels of technology and bushcraft were sufficient to cope with exploring the tropical and semi-tropical zones of Eurasia. Using spears in a disciplined group, they had learned how to defend themselves from cats and dogs in open country. Their strength was their general competence and physical stamina; their limitations were their need to be close to water and their inability to cope with the coldest weather. They were especially practised at combing the beach, their native habitat. Provided they did not try to go too far north in Eurasia, they were safe.

We must not lose sight of *Homo erectus'* particular seashore origins or the special role that the seashore life and seafood nutrition continued to play. The conventional speculation suggests that *H. erectus* spread gradually over the continents of the old world, following paths that suited and settling in favourable habitats. That is reasonable, but neglects the Seashore Hypothesis.

With advancing culture and greater adaptability, *Homo erectus* ranged Africa more successfully than their ancestors and cousins. As they continued to evolve along the seashore with its nutritional driving force, groups moved off. Similarly to their *Australopithecus* cousins in past ages, they followed paths of least resistence and moved up and down the coast before trying river routes into the interior. Why trek inland when there were many miles of familiar and safe empty beaches ahead? They would only have tried the internal pathways of the rivers when confronted with a geographical barrier, and it is significant that the only barriers on the eastern African coast are those provided by the swampy, mangrove filled deltas of the rivers whose sources are at the highlands on the edges of the Great Rift Valley.

I was dispirited by a remark made by a scientist in a TV documentary film. She said that *Homo erectus* was remarkable for struggling through jungles, deserts and over harsh mountain ranges to spread through Asia. This indicated, once again, the extended blinkered vision of those who hold to the Savannah Hypothesis. Following seashores and river valleys is easier, safer and more natural than struggling with inhospitable inland terrain. What she had not considered was the obvious probability that *Homo erectus* was a seashore traveller and had explored and settled the familiar Indian Ocean littoral of the Asian continent before attempting colonisation up rivers. They did not cross mountain barriers and raging deserts to reach hospitable river valleys. They walked around them along the seashore. Eventually they reached the islands of Indonesia and during ice-ages many of those islands were linked by dry land.

Stephen Oppenheimer reckoned in *Out of Eden* (2003) that until about 2M years ago Africa was still joined to Arabia at the southern end of the Red Sea, at least periodically, and therefore there was a natural dry pathway out of Africa along the northern shores of the Indian Ocean as well as the route up the Nile and then into the Levantine region of the Mediterranean. Oppenheimer sees this as the period when *Homo erectus* found it easiest to begin their diaspora.

Tim Redfield has made a special study of the Red Sea and the Strait of Bab el Mandeb. He responded to my specific question about the assumption of a relatively late time for the opening of the Red Sea and the closing of the Bab el-Mandeb land-bridge by kindly sending me a pre-publication paper in September 2003 prepared by himself, W.H. Wheeler and M. Often. They had carried out exhaustive work on the data available at that time from several disciplines and had done field work in the Afar triangle. Their conclusion was that by 2M years ago the Red Sea was open. They wrote :

Tectonic reconstruction (supported by paleontologic and isotopic data) suggests that a "land bridge" connected Africa and Arabia, via Danakil, up to the Early to Middle Pliocene.

And again :

By middle Pliocene time this seaway (the straits of Bab el Mandeb) had fully formed, and the Afar Depression was isolated from Arabia. Short periods of renewed land connection may have resulted from sea level fall during glacial maxima.

Oppenheimer's assumption of a continuously free path on a land bridge at this place for *Homo erectus* until ± 2M years ago is not definitely supported, but that does not mean that they could not migrate into Arabia and eastwards along the sea shores. During a severe ice-age, the sea could have been low enough for the strait to dry at about 2M years ago, since it was continuing to deepen at that time, or they crossed on crude rafts. This is not the picture of a major stream of migration from 2M years ago, especially during a favourably wet and warm interglacial when the sea was high. However, I do not see that as a problem. *Homo erectus* passing around the northern end of the Red Sea, along the southern shore of the Suez land-bridge, would not have been following a map with a compass. If they were migrating along the coast, it made no difference to them whether they moved from African to Arabian shores at Bab el Mandeb or Suez.

The main purpose of Oppenheimer's discussion of the land bridge at the southern entrance to the Red Sea is in finding support for his thesis that *Homo erectus* during succeeding migrations until the peopling of the world by modern mankind were primarily 'beachcombers' following sea shores in their wanderings.

I agree with his thesis absolutely for different reasons. Oppenheimer was explaining why it seems from fossil evidence that hominins penetrated Asia and the Far East before they colonised Europe. Beach combing from the northeast African Rift Valley directly to southern Arabia is an obvious answer. My enthusiasm for the idea began many years ago and follows very simply from my thesis that *Homo erectus* was still very much a child of the seashore. One to two million years ago, *Homo erectus* would have followed seashores wherever possible during an expansionist period because that was the familiar and happy path.

*   *

A fossil-hunting pioneer, Eugene du Bois, found part of a hominid skull in 1891 beside the Solo River, near Trinil in East Java, and this fossil was dated by stratification at various times to up to more than a million years ago. Until more fossils were discovered and advanced dating techniques were devised, this was the earliest sure evidence of the spread of *Homo erectus* around the world to far practical limits of that time.

By the 1990s many palaeontological sites providing early *Homo* fossils had been explored as far apart as Swartkrans in South Africa (25ºS. latitude), along the Great Rift Valley, Ternifine in Morocco, Soleilhac in France (about 44ºN latitude), Torralba in Spain, Narmada in India, Luc Yen in Vietnam, Sangiran and Perning in Indonesia and, in China, Yuanmou, Yungxian, Nanzhou and Beijing, famous for 'Peking Man' (about 40ºN latitude). Obviously, the spread of *Homo erectus* was universal in Africa and Eurasia within tolerable climatic limits: an area below about 45ºN latitude. As the climate varied, which also controls vegetation and deserts, so their numbers and mobility varied. At times they were absent from large zones where it had became too cold, desertification had spread or other shocks such as vulcanism or flooding prompted moves. Survival depended on an ability to 'pulse' with the 'pulsing' of the climate, vaguely akin to the annual migration of birds with time extended to periods of thousands of years.

Athena Review (Volume 4, Number 1) in 2004 produced a special feature on the latest general information available on *Homo erectus* sites. Latest published information was reviewed and notable sites were listed with indications of different periods of migration or residence. Probably the oldest examples of *Homo erectus* in Eurasia are the fossils recovered at Dmanisi in Georgia, dating from 1.8 Mya with skull sizes similar to *Homo habilis* in Africa. Fossils from Sangiran in Java have been almost certainly dated to 1.8 Mya which is coincident to earliest estimates of the first hominin 'out-of-Africa' migrations. There seems no doubt that soon after the jump to the *Homo* line, this new species had the ability to migrate relatively enormous distances and exhibited the desire to do so.

143

Not only were these early migrants anatomically of the African *Homo erectus* species, but they carried with them the intellectual and cultural abilities of the Early Stone Age. Confirmation of tools made by *Homo erectus* in Indonesia was revealed at the Indo-Pacific Prehistory Association Congress in March 2006. Richard Stone in *Science* magazine reported on photographs of small chalcedony tools exhibited by Harry Widianto. The sedimentary layer in which they had been found at Sangiram in the Solo river basin had been dated to 1.2 - 1.6M years ago. Russell Ciochin of Iowa State University stated that argon technique had refined these dates to 1.58 -1.51M years ago. These dates are similar to tools found at Majuangon in China with a date of 1.66M years ago.

The peopling of all the habitable zones of Africa-Eurasia, following the great highway of the tropical seashores, by early *Homo erectus* is a clear foreshadowing of later migrations. The migrations of *Homo erectus*, with their anatomically maturing bodies is a milestone around 2M years ago which is surely of equal significance to the appearance of the first erect bipedal hominins. It is their intellectual ability to visualise tools within lumps of rock and then make them which is so special. There is no doubt they made tools of various kinds from other materials which have not survived. Many animals have used objects as tools, but only mankind can visualise sculpture however crude. It shows extraordinary changes within the brain and the mind, unique to our ancestral line.

Much has been made of the ability of chimps to use a small stick or grass stem to pick grubs out of knot holes in branches of trees, and similar feats of tool-using. There are birds which exhibit precisely the same facility. Otters crack open shells to get at the molluscs within. Birds pick up shells and fly up to drop them on rocks to break them open. There are any number of examples of tool-using or genetically-implanted behaviours employed by the whole range of animals. It is an ever-expanding marvel that even the most insignificant creature has the ability to learn how to adapt to its environment and to use common everyday materials or competence to enhance their ability to get at food. But this is a quantum leap away from visualising and making a general-purpose tool in a material which has no apparent relationship to the final product.

All over the world, Early Stone Age *Homo erectus* visualised the classical general-purpose Acheulian hand-axe in chunks of various types of suitable rocks, and sculpted them. Chimps never made hand-axes, neither did the *Australopithecines*; they could not visualise a tool within a lump of rock. Creativity, in its earliest dawning, began with *Homo erectus.*

In *Athena Review*, Roy Larick, Russell Ciochon and Yahdi Zaim detailed the complex and painstaking research that has gone into producing dates for the *Homo erectus* fossils which have been discovered in Java. Their measured conclusion from the geological evidence associated with the hominin fossils gave them confidence to state :

> Our results give the first radiometrically calibrated scheme for the emergence of this part [of] Sunda [the name given to the SE Asiatic region encompassing Java and Sumatra], as well as for the arrival, entrenchment, and disappearance of *Homo erectus.* This human ancestor occupied south Sunda for at least half a million years beginning more than 1.6 mya. With an occupation of this duration, we may now speak of an evolutionary sequence for Sunda *Homo erectus.* With our sedimentary framework and argon-argon chronology, nearly 35 Sangiran dome *Homo erectus* fossils can be seen in evolutionary sequence. Sunda *Homo erectus* followed a parallel evolutionary trajectory to that known for fossils in East Africa and the Caucasus. Cranial capacity increased and sexual dimorphism became more nuanced.

An interesting speculation was proposed by the same authors that the spread of earliest *Homo erectus* from Africa into the corridor from Spain to China and Java was related to an unstable geotectonic 'highway' which they name the Tethys Corridor. Their concept was that the migrants: "took advantage of open linear landscapes to migrate north from the Rift [in the East African highlands] to the Caucasus, and then both ways across the Tethys corridor - west towards Gibraltar, east to the Himalayan foreslope and then east to current Java." The assumption is that they were following familiar geography to that of their actively volcanic homeland of the African Great Rift Valley. I have a number of objections to that theory which I have discussed elsewhere regarding *Homo* migrations. The most natural and obvious pathways at any time are the tropical seashores and then up rivers, and not across varied geography and mountain barriers.

I can understand the idea that early *Homo* migrations occurred along the tectonic fault which produced the Caucasus and Himalayas.

It could be visualised that the migrations proceeded north until the mountain barriers were reached and then spread west and east. This assumes that the migrants were long time residents of the African Rift Valley and felt compelled to follow an inland route across those enormous distances, somehow propelled through deserts and marginal lands where active vulcanism and tectonic drift were creating new mountain chains. Rather than follow a route which exhibited these barriers to easy travel, I suggest that they were intentionally migrating away from the erupting volcanoes and earthquakes of the Great Rift Valley.

I see a simpler and more understandable scenario: that *Homo erectus*, whether directly along the Great Rift Valley from the interior or along the familiar coastal strip, arrived at the Red Sea confluence of the Rift and the Indian Ocean during favourable periods of population explosion. Following the Indian Ocean shores and making use of the Mesopotamian and Indian rivers, they would have penetrated easily to the Caucasus region, taken a short-cut across the Indian sub-continent, as well as wandered around it, and naturally ended up at the extremity of land at that time which was Java. Using the great river-roads of Indo-China and China, migrants settled in any number of suitable places, some of which have provided significant fossil finds. The migration and settlement zone called the Tethys Corridor and the 'Tethys Realm' proposed by Larick, Ciochon and Zaim encompasses a general area within easy reach of Indian Ocean and Mediterranean Sea seashores and the rivers debouching onto them. There is no difficulty in understanding why *Homo erectus* settled where their fossils have been found. If there is a problem, it is determining how and why they migrated to those sites.

During the severe cold periods of an ice-age, populations of all Early Stone Age people declined and perhaps they disappeared from much of the ice-bound Eurasian continent, leaving pockets along the tropical and sub-tropical belt. Malaysia and Indonesia are known examples where pockets survived. In Europe there is the obvious example of the Neanderthals. Nevertheless, during the warm interglacials the only parts of Earth *Homo erectus* did not penetrate, taking their advancing Acheulian Early Stone Age technology with them, were the higher northern latitudes of Eurasia, Antarctica, the Americas, Australia and oceanic islands. Colonisation of those parts had to wait for further evolutionary progress to specialised

146

technology, further growth in reasoning ability and later surges of population from Africa.

There was no incentive or imperative for them to trek through mountain ranges or wander unknown harsh terrains. There was plenty of room along the familiar seashore and riverine highways.

The disastrous tsunami in the Indian Ocean on 26 December 2004 reminded me that here is another reason for the difficulty of finding fossils of ancient seashore-living hominids and early *Homos*. Tsunamis are catastrophes, but do not eliminate seashore life. In December 2004, maybe 20% of people on the highly vulnerable Andaman and Nicobar islands were killed or injured. It is particularly notable that in the Nicobar Islands it was recent immigrants from India who perished and the indigenous islanders survived almost intact by noting the early signs and running inland. But seashores are changed, beaches and sandbanks dramatically shift, bodies and other detritus are buried.

Tsunamis and giant tropical cyclonic storms have an effect on the shape of seashores which are dramatic and short-term, not to be compared with the slow long-term changes resulting from continental tectonic movements and the expansion and contraction of ice-sheets. But they are an additional factor in considering where ancient seashore fossils might be found, and they are an incentive to move along.

EIGHT : *THE PARTICULAR INTERGLACIAL PERIODS OF 650-550,000 YEARS AGO*
The dawn of modern mankind.

In the last twenty years or so, stimulated by concern about artificial global warming, work on deep ice-cores obtained by drilling in the Antarctic and Greenland ice has revealed much-refined dating and measurement for world temperatures. Greater precision can be applied to dating the warm and cold periods which have affected mankind's evolution and migrations. When it is warm, populations explode and migrations occur; when it is cold and there are ice-sheets over the northern hemisphere land masses, populations shrink and adaptations through survival of the fittest occur.

Very roughly, there have been cyclical swings between warm and cold periods with ice ages approximately every 100,000 years during the Pleistocene Epoch which began about two million years ago, coinciding with the emergence of *Homo erectus*. Arbitrary boundaries are applied according to which criteria are used, geological or environmental, and either 1.8M or 1.6M years ago are usually quoted. The conclusion to the Pleistocene is decided by the end of the last ice age at 12-10,000 years ago when the Holocene Epoch containing the present warm period begins. It is during the Holocene that agriculture is the dominant trait of northern hemisphere people.

Although variations in climate have always produced ice ages when large parts of the planet were covered with glaciers and ice sheets, it is during the Pleistocene that a clear cyclical pattern is observed. About every hundred thousand years there is a long period of cold climate with glaciation, extensive northern hemisphere ice sheets, a reduction of rainfall with desertification and a lowered ocean level with the drying out of shallow seas and straits. Between the periods of ice and cold there are shorter warm 'interglacials' with extended land area in the northen hemisphere habitable by mankind and other mammals with great increase in populations, more rain and the flooding of land bridges. We are presently experiencing a warm interglacial. The cycles are caused by the Earth's wobbles and eccentric orbit, but there are several other factors which distort the process so that the cycles are prolonged or shortened. There are sudden spikes and unexpected anomalies in the record. The chaos within our fluid atmosphere and oceans, changes in the Sun's radiation, the dragging effect of increased reflection from large ice sheets which increases cooling and sudden unexpected events such as massive volcanic explosions or meteor strikes all have their influence. The evolution of mankind and other mammals is obviously much affected by this constant stirring of the environment with its occasional unexpected violence within the longer term cycles.

There have been two significant points for evolution in the Pleistocene where the cyclical temperature ranges of cold and warm changed. At about 800,000 years ago the cold periods became more severe and from about 650,000 years ago the warm periods had higher temperature spikes. Some authorities propose that this is because of longer term cosmic cycles influencing the sun's radiation. (See the graphs shown earlier.)

Whether our global temperatures are presently affected by artificial production of carbon dioxide or not we are at a mild thousand year cyclical high temperature spike within the Holocene epoch, and we should be devoting more political and scientific energy towards understanding it rather than being concerned with the very short-term of a few decades into the future. If we are at the cusp of a warm spike we could be heading into a cool period with great possibilities of disaster for our civilisation with its huge burden of expanding urban populations. Some scientists see this as a possibility.

*

In November 2006 there was much attention in the press and TV news to the announcement that geneticists, led by Dr Pääbo, at the Max Planck Institute for Evolutionary Anthropology in Germany had determined that *Homo neanderthalis* had broken away from the main *Homo* line at about 500,000 years ago, suggesting 516,000 as the mean. They also proposed that the original group had been of the order of 3,000 individuals. This new genetic evidence of Neanderthal divergence was a substantial advance in our knowledge and the date of 500,000 BP added excitement.

I had always been particularly interested in this period. Climate change was occurring. There was a warm peak at about 650,000 BP, separated by a shorter than usual cold period from the next warm period centred around 575.000 BP. After 500,000 BP there was a shift the pattern. At about 430,000 BP there was a lower than usual temperature dip followed by a higher than previous warming. Thereafter, the warmings have been warmer and the coolings have been colder, leading to the present. There is archeological evidence that since about 650,000 years ago there was acceleration in the cultural evolution of *Homo erectus* and their variants.

There was a general shift in the pattern. The warm peaks are massively higher, leading to the present. It was as if the Earth's climatic cycles were intensifying, becoming more abrupt, and mankind's evolution and pace of life was forced to accelerate with it.

I had also come across reports of a possible close supernova at about then. The evidence was scarce and provides speculation only, based on anomalies in ocean floor sediments. Severe bursts of cosmic radiation, such as that resulting from a nearby supernova, cause chemical changes in the atmosphere which show in sediments in ice sheets or ocean floors. The ice-sheets of Greenland and Antarctica are very useful for detecting strange chemicals in the atmosphere and dating them, but earlier than two hundred thousand years the evidence is limited. Ocean floors are the clue to earlier events, but it is difficult to be scientifically precise. However, if there had been a nearby supernova at about 500,000 years ago, as has been suggested, it would explain a number of divergences in genes and behaviour which were occurring at that time.

In 2008, A.M.Soderberg and forty-two other scientists published an article in *Nature* describing their "serendipitous discovery" of the "extremely luminous X-ray outbursts at the birth of a supernova". This particular aspect of a supernova explosion had not been known before the extraordinary good luck in catching this evidence of particular cosmic radiation. It shows, once again, how massive energy outbursts occur during common galactic events, some of which can be very close to Earth according to the random chance of our chaotic universe.

*   *

150

Lake Naivasha, Kenya, in 1965 - how the environment of Olorgasailie might have looked 600,000 years ago.

The Olorgasailie archaeological site is in the Great Rift Valley about sixty kilometres directly southwest of Nairobi. At the height of the dry season the Great Rift Valley there is burnt by the tropical sun until the leafless acacia scrub and the land itself merges into shades of dusty grey. It can be hot and very dry. I visited the site in 1987 when the temperature in the shade of the picnic shelters was a searing 41.5ºC (107ºF).

During the rainy seasons there is a fine view from the Ngong Hills. At the escarpment rim in the crystal air you see into the vast depths of the Rift, a thousand metres below you. Between rain showers on clear days, instead of looking through dust haze at a parched land coloured in pale pastels, you stare over rich green, extending maybe ninety kilometres to the blue volcanoes on the southwestern horizon. Beyond Olorgasailie volcano there is the faint shadow of 2,500 metres high Meto on the Tanzanian border and Gelai looms beyond, towering over Lake Natron. Out of sight, the Ngorongoro volcanic massif cradles the famous crater game reserve. To the west, above the Rift, the Serengeti Plains sail away to Lake Victoria and, to the southeast, clouds often hide the lurking giant of Kilimanjaro.

Experiencing the Great Rift Valley at Olorgasailie during the greatly differing dry and wet seasons emphasizes the contrast between the seasons in all of eastern-southern Africa. Northern Europeans living in their green lands most aware of warmth or cold, or any modern urban dwellers cocooned in their cities, may not understand the truly vital importance of the rains in much of Africa, the Mediterranean basin and southern Asia. The transformation of savannah from bare trees, dry rivers and baking dust to green vegetation, foaming torrents and mud is not just an interesting geographical phenomenon, inconveniencing tourists. It is the annual renewal of life itself. When rains are delayed or fail, as they often do, animals and humans suffer a misery that people in northern Europe cannot begin to feel no matter how many TV documentaries they view or newspaper stories they read. And presently we are in a benign climatic cycle.

Living through the capricious march of the seasons in rural Africa makes one aware of how fragile life was for ancient mankind and their large mammal companions. The evidence of many extinct species including *Australopithecines* is there. It also shows how important it was to be able to move, to be a nomad, and colonise wherever there was a suitable niche. And if there was pressure from behind or because of climate changes, then the nomads moved on fast to survive, generation by generation.

Around six hundred thousand years ago Earth was experiencing the beneficence of a prolonged warm interglacial period. Across the whole spectrum of life, species were making jumps in evolution, variations were proliferating and were replacing established plants and animals. Those that had survived the previous ice-age but were slow to adapt and fill new niches were pushed aside and many expired. This was a recurrent theme of the cycles of the Pleistocene.

Half a million years ago is a time-span that our minds are incapable of comprehending, yet that was the approximate age that I was contemplating at Olorgasailie. The environment then would have been something like it is at Lake Naivasha to-day. Below the foot of the Olorgasailie volcano is the location of the archaeological site (1º34'S. 36º26'E.) where an Early Stone Age complex was excavated by Louis and Mary Leakey from 1942 and Glynn Isaacs gave much time to it in the 1970s when he carried out the definitive excavation.

The earliest evidence of *Homo erectus'* occupation of the site gives a time scale of between 900,000 and 700,000 years ago. Richard Potts, Anna K. Behrensmeyer, Alan Deino, Peter Ditchfield and Jennifer Clark reported in *Science* on 2 July 2004:

> Hominin fossils from the African mid-Pleistocene are rare despite abundant Acheulean tools in Africa and apparently African-derived hominins in Eurasia between 1.0 and 0.5 million years ago (Ma). Here we describe an African fossil cranium constrained by $^{40}Ar/^{39}Ar$ analyses, magneto-stratigraphy, and sedimentary features to 0.97 to 0.90 Ma, and stratigraphically associated with Acheulean handaxes. Although the cranium represents possibly the smallest adult or near-adult known between 1.7 and 0.5 Ma, it retains features observed in larger *Homo erectus* individuals, yet shows a distinct suite of traits indicative of wide population variation in the hominins of this period.

This evidence shows that Early Stone Age *Homo erectus* people occupied this pleasant site for many hundreds of thousands of years, off and on, but around 600,000 is the period that interests me.

Six hundred thousand years ago, during that warm interglacial, when Early Stone Age *Homo erectus* worked a stone tool industry there, they had established a series of settlements, or camps, on the shores of the now-vanished lake. Fossils from the ancient settlements had been set in preserving silt over millennia as the lake rose and fell and layers of dust and ash from nearby volcanic eruptions defined the time strata.

Most of the stone tools found at Olorgasailie were Acheulian hand-axes, the standard Early Stone Age, or palaeolithic, manufacture from South Africa to central Europe and Asia. They were universal tools, shaped to fit comfortably in a hand's grip and probably used mostly for working wood or bone, butchering and skinning carcasses and preparing skin clothing. There was no stone on that ancient lake shore, but plenty of lumps of stone and water-rounded pebbles were carried there for craftsmen to work on. Ancient men or women carried stones in leather bags over their shoulders from the nearest rocky gorge a few miles away to the pleasant camp by the lake. The earliest principles of trade and craft specialists were established and this is an important portal in human development which had been entered by that time. For there to be trade and a semi-permanent craftsmen's settlement, there had to be enough of a suitable language for communication and minds capable of quite complex reasoning.

It was flat country half a million years ago when palaeolithic *Homo erectus* lived there in rough camps making stone tools, the women gathering vegetable food in the lush lacustrine forest and savannah scrub surrounds, the men catching fish in the lake and occasionally butchering kill from the hunt; living the good life. Other clans came there for recreation by the water and to exchange particular foods and skins for the hand-axes produced in the workshops of Olorgasailie. Probably, they brought the raw rock for conversion to tools as part of the exchange.

Standing at the site, I visualised the silver sparkle on blue waters stretching away to the eastward and the grassy parkland under giant yellow-boled fever trees. Strange, extinct antelopes and short-necked giraffes would be grazing and browsing at a distance and giant hippos snorting in the water. A distant trumpeting might have stirred the community of people sitting about a smoking fire. Huge extinct elephants (*elephas recki*), much taller than to-day's giants, would be moving down to drink a hundred gallons or so of water and bathe together with happy snorting and squealing.

I have seen a fossil elephant leg bone from the excavations placed alongside a similar modern one in the site museum. They were identical but for the fact that the extinct one was twice as big. Maybe it is the animal fossil bones that have been exposed and dug up at Olorgasailie that are most important. Apart from extinct giant elephants, the area has yielded bones of extinct species of hippos, zebras, various antelopes and, of particular interest, a large savannah baboon (*Theropithecus oswaldi*). According to anthropologist Glyn Isaac's description:

> More than eighty adult and juvenile baboons were eaten at this camp, and the bones were mostly smashed to extract the marrow.

Glyn Isaac described an interesting parallel in modern times, citing the modern click-speaking Hadza people of northern Tanzania, related culturally to the southern African San-Bushmen:

> ... [they] occasionally band together and go out at night to surround a clump of trees or a rocky knoll where a baboon troop is sleeping. They dislodge the animals by shooting

arrows and then club as many as possible to death as they break out of the circle.

Early Stone Age bands would have thrown stones rather than shoot arrows, but the technique was exactly the same. Throwing missiles is a very ancient method of attack and is still universally practised successfully today as any TV news clip of street rioting will show.

In recent years there has been much palaeontological and archaeological exploration in Europe. Many universities with expanded faculties and local authorities have devoted resources to the task and several fascinating sites have been investigated and analysed. Whereas *Homo erectus* and their descendants originated in Africa, moving outwards into Eurasia during favourable climate cycles, evidence of these movements and knowledge about the Early Stone Age people involved has been extended by study mostly at their destinations rather than at their origins.

The Orce region in southeast Spain was brought into great prominence by Dr. Josep Gibert in 1989 when he proposed that he had evidence of *Homo erectus* possibly as old as 2M years ago. Later, he and his colleagues published a paper detailing their arguments. The journal *Antiquity* published *Two 'Olduvan' assemblages in the Plio-Pleistocene deposits of the region, southeast Spain* by Gibert and his associates in 1998. The argument for a *Homo* presence at about 2M years ago was based on dating of stone tools by faunal association and palaeomagnetic study of contiguous strata. Gibert proposed that early *Homo erectus*, contemporary with those of East Africa, crossed the Strait of Gibraltar when sea levels were low, and supported this with evidence that other large African mammals have moved north into Europe at various times. Gibert's thesis was subject to much controversy and the matter was exacerbated by the discovery of a tiny finger bone in the Cueva Victoria of that region. Discussion, in which Prof. Phillip Tobias of the University of the Witwatersrand took part, proceeded on whether the bone was hominid or equine with chemical analysis eventually coming down on the side of hominid.

I see no reason to doubt that *Homo erectus* crossed into southern Spain two million years ago. The logic of them following prey animals north across the Strait of Gibraltar is perfectly reasonable. They were certainly in Iberia a million or more years later. The ability of early *homos* to beachcomb their way around the Indian Ocean, or the Mediterranean Sea, is a central theme of this book, and

155

so is the assumption that evolution beside the seashore provides natural facility in crossing stretches of water. No navigational or intellectual skills were necessary for elephants, hippos, rhinos, apes or *homos* to head off from Africa for Spain, because they could clearly see the other side. It would have looked to them as if they were crossing a large lake or the mouth of a deep bay.

Josep Clols and Lluis Beotas revealed further definitive information from the Orce region (37ºN. Latitude) and Cueva Victoria, resulting from continuing excavation and research, in their article in *Current World Archaeology* (No 20, 2006). They wrote:

> We found evidence of human presence ... The minimum estimated age for the sites is 1.3 million years for Venta Micena, 1.25 million years for Barranco León-5, and 1.2 million years for Fuentenueva-3. Evidence of our ancestors comprised fragmentary human fossil bones - a piece of an infant's skull that included two parietal and the occipital bones, two humeral fragments and part of a molar. We also found hundreds of Olduwan-type tools made of flint or quartzite.

In 2004, Clols and Beotas continued with extensive work in the Cueva Victoria which lies near Cartagena (± 38ºN. latitude). Human remains in this large cave complex were found with those of over sixty species of vertebrates. The authors point out that one of the most important facts to emerge from this complex is the positive identification of African mammals, specifically *Theropithicus oswaldi*, a primate, and *Hippopotamus antiquus*. They crossed the Strait of Gibraltar from Africa and there can be no doubt that *Homo erectus* did too.

In 1992, an assemblage of bones was found in a deep cave at Atapuerca (42º35'N. 3º07'W.) in Spain. It was reported that they made up 30 youthful individuals who died about 300,000 years ago. At that time it was decided from their skulls that they were within the range of *Homo erectus* and may have been directly ancestral to the Neanderthal people of Europe. Now, it is known that Neanderthals diverged 500,000 years ago.

The Atapuerca mountains in northern Spain have provided several cave sites with early human remains. In March 2008, Eudald Carbonald and several colleagues published a paper, *The First Hominin in Europe* in *Nature* vol. 452, which aroused much excitement.

Their findings from the cave-site, Sima del Elefante in the Atapuerca, were supported by good dating of a human jawbone with some teeth and a collection of stone tools and flakes. The date was established from the layer TF9 at $1.22 \pm 0.16M$ years ago. Their paper stated: "Peopling of Europe occurred much faster and in a more continuous manner than previously thought." They preferred to consider the people there to be of the *Homo heidelbergenses* or *Homo antecessor* species, but these differentiations to *Homo erectus* have still to be clearly established.

I continue to believe that *Homo erectus,* and closely related offshoots, moved rapidly all over the world when climate and environment were suitable from about 2M years ago, and retreated or expired when it was not. It is heartening that firm evidence of this spread is continually revealed.

In 1994, there was the exciting revelation that part of a *Homo* skeleton excavated at Boxgrove in Sussex (50ºN latitude) had revealed a date about 480,000 years ago and that this man had stood taller than the Neanderthals of 35,000 years ago. As in Spain, there is discussion about the precise species of the hominins living in north-west Europe at that time, as revealed by Boxgrove. *Homo heidelbergensis* is favoured by many. The date of about 500,000 years ago, a date coinciding with the existence of 'modern' behaviour at the Olorgasailie site in Kenya, became widespread when Early Stone Age sites across Europe were analysed.

An extensive flint industry was described at Boxgrove. More than 20,000 chips were studied and reassembled painstakingly to show that large stones had been worked to produce hand-axes. A permanent camp had existed in that place where specialist craftsmen had sculpted quantities of the ubiquitous tool of the Early Stone Age. It was an uncanny mirror of Olorgasailie far away in the Great Rift Valley of tropical Africa and within the same time-scale. Similarly to Olorgasailie, animal bones showed that they had been broken open and had been butchered and scraped. Microscopic analysis proved that some of the bones at least belonged to animals which had been butchered before being gnawed later by carnivores. Although it was commonly assumed that early people were hunting larger mammals by that time, this evidence proved it. Cats or dogs were scavenging carrion discarded by men, not the other way around.

In 2005, there was the discovery of stone tools at Pakefield (52º28'N.) on the English Suffolk coast. Tools and flakes at

Happisburgh in Norfolk (52º49'N.) enhanced the Pakefield finds. Simon Parfitt and colleagues revealed that *Homo erectus*, or a closely related species, was living along the present East Anglian shores during an earlier warm period, about 700,000 years ago. Chris Stringer, commenting specifically on this, stated that 700,000 years ago represented the oldest evidence of *Homo* north of the Alps. It is apparent that the climate of northern Europe was mild at that time and the environment was satisfactory for people with Early Stone Age culture to follow river roads to the western ends of the Eurasian continent as far north as 50º latitude. Excavations at Happisburgh and Pakefield created a sensation when published. Although much earlier examples of early humans have been found in Spain, some considerable distance southwards and obviously in a warmer zone whatever climate cycle was being experienced, it can now be safely assumed that whenever the climate provided an environment with food suitable for Early Stone Age mankind, they migrated there.

At Bilzinsleben in Thuringia (51ºN latitude) there was evidence of three round shelters or structures and a variety of stone artifacts ranging from anvils for breaking bones, through hand-axes to more finely-worked stone points and scrapers. Here was another camp dated to about 500,000 years ago when the Earth was basking in a warm interglacial.

Near Torralba in Spain where an ancient shallow lake and marsh had existed about 500,000 years ago there were hand-axes and a variety of butchered bones in what seemed to be artificial assemblages. It could be concluded that animals had been herded to boggy places where it was easy for a group of hunters to converge and kill them. Probably meat from carcasses was taken from there to camps after butchering.

The Schöningen site (52ºN latitude) near Brunswick in Lower Saxony produced the lucky find of perfectly preserved and finely made spruce-wood spears or javelins. There could be no doubt that they had been used for hunting.

What kind of advanced early people lived in these varied places across Europe and further north than any previously discovered examples of the *Homo* range? Dr. Leslie Aiello in the BBC series, *Ape Man*, described the remarkable find of a complete skeleton in a tunnel at Altamura in Italy (40ºN latitude), again dated to that magic Interglacial of 500,000 years ago. Although the skeleton was fixed to a rock wall by limestone accretions, a careful analysis was made. This was not *Homo erectus* of a million or more years ago. It had a larger skull and a clearly different occipital ridge compared to the older species.

There seems no doubt that these early people roaming western Europe, going as far as the climate cycles allowed, were the ancestors of the Neanderthals. They were the divergent European group, themselves evolving from a common *Homo erectus* of the African core-people, who were to inhabit the lands from the Mediterranean to Britain and Germany. Divergence proceeded to speciation which eventually reached a peak when they were snuffed out at about 30,000 BP. This line of descent lived through the harsh and protein-deprived environments of several cyclical glacial periods, roughly centred at about 750Kya, 650Kya, 550Kya, 450Kya, 350Kya, 275Kya, 150Kya and the most recent ice-age. No doubt their genes were periodically refreshed by new infusions from Africa until speciation made this difficult and then impossible, but they never passed through the gate to *Homo sapiens*.

As long ago as 1960 a subspecies of Early Stone Age mankind which was discovered near Heidelberg in Germany had been defined as *Homo erectus heidelbergensis* (Heidelberg Man). This definition has been amended and broadened to describe the species which populated Europe during that warm period about 500,000 years ago. It was *Homo heidelbergensis* who lived in camps, worked specialist industries to make a variety of stone tools and used bone and wood to make other tools and weapons for hunting. Some tools seem to have been made for their decorative value rather than for their utility. Decoration had previously been thought a refinement confined to a much later cultural phase. *Homo heidelbergensis* had lived and worked in communal homesteads and without doubt had sufficient reasoning and communicating abilities to have developed simple society and technology. As at Olorgasailie in Kenya they traded with other clans.

Dr Lesley Aiello described how the skull of *Homo heidelbergensis* from Greece revealed a capacity of 1200-1300 cc. She demonstrated that a typical earlier *Homo erectus* skull supported a brain of about 900-1000 cc and *Homo sapiens* about 1400 cc. *Homo heidelbergensis* was at the dawn of modern humankind.

*   *

159

I am wary of ladder-like evolution narratives and the naming of *Homo erectus* variants as different species, but here is the conventional view. In Europe, it is described that *Homo erectus* evolved to *Homo heidelbergensis* and then *Homo Neanderthalis.* It was a continuing progress with the names principally defining increasing brain size and skull shape. Culture was progressing too, quite markedly. Stone tools became more refined and specialised. In parallel with Olorgasailie, Boxgrove shows how communication and social structures, all tied to increased reasoning and planning abilities, were becoming more complex. What of the other massive branch of the migrations out-of-Africa during the Pleistocene?

*　　　*

Homo erectus in southeast Asia proceeded on their own path of evolution in response to their particular environments.

Genetic evidence shows that modern indigenous people of that region possess the African Eve mitochondrial DNA inheritance. And the rest of humanity has a betaglobyn marker which appeared first in southeast Asia, also at about 200,000 years ago. This shows that not only did the African Eve migration reach to the furthest extent of habitable Asia, but that genes from those regions filtered back to Europe and Africa. Long-distance nomadism, most probably by beach combing, and the pulsing of human migrants back and forth during climate cycles seems proven beyond doubt. It was not always one-way. Genetics confirms what was intuitive reasoning as little as fifteen or twenty years ago.

Alan Templeton in *Nature* in 2002 suggested that there was "ubiquity of genetic interchange between human populations", and that there was some integration between different geographical populations of *Homo erectus.* It is a common-sense assumption which I have always accepted.

Apart from the universally recognised Australian Aborigines, similar aboriginal people have been described in southeast Asia; notably Malaysia (the Semang), Thailand and the Andaman and Nicobar Islands, and southern India. These people were referred to as the Negritos. It is interesting that George McCall Theal in his exhaustive *History of South Africa* (vol 1 : 1910) describes the Semang aboriginal Negrito people of Malaysia with as much accuracy as modern anthropologists. The difference is that in Theal's day there

160

were many more living in their ancient culture and Theal makes a direct comparison with the Khoisan of southern Africa. Theal (1910):

> In South-Eastern Asia there are people living today, such as some of the inhabitants of the Philippine Islands, the Andamanese, and the Semang in the Malay Peninsular, who are so like the Bushman that it is almost certain they are of the same stock. The type must have been fixed in their common primeval home in some far remote time, and the changes in each that have since taken place have been so small that the close relationship may still be seen. ...
> The points of resemblance between the Bushmen and the Semang are so numerous that they cannot be accidental. ...

Theal details them and uses the work of Skeat and Blagden in *The Pagan Races of the Malaya Peninsular* (1906) as his reference. Because scientists and historiographers of that time wrote in a style that offends political correctness today does not mean that we should ignore their research or opinion. After all, they were observing at first hand people who have since been much changed by absorption into modern societies. The least affected aboriginal Negrito people of south-east Asia are those still living on the southern Andaman Islands where one of their languages, or dialects, spoken by maybe 250 survivors has not been recorded.

Modern research synthesized in a website maintained by the Andaman and Nicobar Associations shows that opinion held at the beginning of the 20th century by historians like Theal in South Africa about the close relationship between the Khoisan genetic group in southern Africa and the Negritos of south-eastern Asia is consistent with today's voluminous research. One is led to an understanding that the remnants of the Khoisan and the Negritos are examples of descendants of those people who were living in the tropical zone of Africa before the 'out-of-Africa' migration of about 80,000 years ago. Here is a brief extract from the Andaman Association website maintained by George Weber:

> Another trait that needs a brief mention in a treatment of the Negrito is characteristic of a majority but not all Andamanese towards short stature. Indeed, the Andamanese are often called "pygmies" although not all are short enough to deserve the label. Nonetheless, on average they are quite short in relation to other human groups. They

share the trait of shortness with populations who have lived for a genetically significant number of generations in thick forest: the African pygmies, the Veddas of Sri Lanka, the Barrineans of Australia and the other Negritos, Negritoids and Veddoids. Short stature may be an adaptation independently acquired by each population or a genetic trait going back to the original founding population - we do not know yet.

The trait of steatopygia links the Andamanese to the South African Khoisan (Bushmen and Hottentots) in a fascinating way: the two populations are very remote from each other but they are the only living groups with steatopygia. This is especially relevant since steatopygia is genetically controlled and is thought to be very ancient indeed.

Modern Melanesians, distinct from the Negritos, who inhabit Indonesian and Pacific Ocean islands physically resemble sub-Saharan Africans and are culturally distinct from their Polynesian neighbours. Whereas Polynesians are aware of their recent trans-oceanic origins, the Melanesians have no origin-legend other than that they came from out of the Earth, suggesting very ancient roots. Many Africans who do not have a history of recent migrations have the same kind of origin-legend. Respected travel-writer Paul Theroux commented largely on this in *The Happy Isles of Oceania* (1992) describing an extensive journey through much of the western Pacific.

Melanesians have special somatic similarities with Negroid Africans, particularly their dark skin and rich head of tightly curly hair. I have always been fascinated by the possibility that they are evidence of a migration directly from Africa into tropical Asia perhaps in a later period than the original modern people 'out-of-Africa'. Perhaps they migrated around the Indian Ocean rim at about 60,000 years ago when there may have been a surge in energy by population increases as a result of a warm period. It was then that Cro-Magnon people (a common term for the European branches of the out-of-Africa migrations) were moving purposefully into Europe. Whereas the Semang and similar peoples originated in Africa maybe during an outsurge of migration 500,000 years ago, reflected in their genetic similarity to the Khoisan, Melanesian origins were 'modern'.

At some time during the last ice-age, Melanesians could have been pushed south-east into a pocket of islands where they became isolated and retained their racial integrity. If Australian Aborigines

162

survived as a distinct genetic group from earlier than the last Ice-age with the 'African Eve' DNA marker which proves their descent, then it would not surprise me if Melanesians, directly from Africa, also discretely survived, isolated on their densely rainforested islands and keeping later migrants at bay. They have a reputation for fierceness and insularity and did not integrate happily into 20th century Western culture. Although the great mix of ancestry in the south-east of Asia and Oceania makes following DNA trails complicated, some research suggests that the people of Papua-New Guinea highlands are from a migration as old as that of the Australian Aborigines, but may not have been from the precisely similar root. In other words, both peoples had ancestors who came out of Africa at an early stage, about 74,000 years ago, and mixed with existing late *Homo erectus* populations, but in their passage around the ocean shores there was some genetic divergence.

*

The technology of boat building to aid fishing probably led to tropical sea voyaging earlier than is presently acknowledged. I believe people were commonly paddling and sailing on rivers and lakes, along coastlines and island-hopping in the calm season of monsoon systems in the tropics by 600,000 years ago. European *Homo heidelbergensis* people and those who lived around the ancient lake at Olorgasailie would have had the expertise. Rafts of shaped logs lashed together and dug-out canoes were in use before recorded history all over the tropical world. They are as ubiquitous as axes, scrapers, knives, arrow-heads, clothes or carry bags. The technology is not complicated and I cannot ignore mankind's powerful aquatic trait.

The discovery of the tiny *Homo Floresiensis* people, a seemingly aberrant remnant of the last direct descendants of the true *Homo erectus* line in Asia, on the island of Flores, which was not joined to the mainland during the Pleistocene, makes it certain that people had the capability of crossing short stretches of sea of the order of 10-20 kilometres for maybe hundreds of thousands of years.

The presently-defined species *Homo erectus* colonised most of habitable Africa by at least 1.8 million years ago and had begun crossing into Eurasia. It seems that they must have crossed the Strait of Gibraltar by 1.3 million years ago. There is no absolute date for the first movements into Arabia, but we may be certain that they colonised most parts of Eurasia which were habitable by 1M years ago.

Latest evidence from excavations on Java show that *Homo erectus* reached the ancient Sunda lands, which comprised the western islands of Indonesia which have been joined to Indo-China during the height of ice-ages when ocean levels were lower. *Homo erectus* reached Java between 1.8 and 1.6 million years ago. The find by Eugene du Bois in 1891 on the Solo River was the signpost to this most important proof that the first 'out-of-Africa' movements by *Homo* is of this order of time. On the island of Flores, which is one of the string of lesser volcanic islands lying to the east of Java, and which was not joined to Sunda during ice-ages, stone tools have been found. Theodoor Verhoeven reported stone tools of about 700,000 BP on Flores in 1968. Other scientists, led by Paul Sondaar, dated volcanic layers with stone tools at about 800,000 BP in 1994. Mike Morwood and others (1998) confirmed the dates of volcanic layers with tools and proposed that Early Stone Age people had crossed the sea to Flores about 840,000 years ago.

At that time, *Homo erectus* had learned to cross short stretches of open sea and this is a clear punctuation point in mankind's maritime history. Not only did they have the technical expertise to build canoes and rafts, they had the social organisation and capability to plan voyages across the sea. The fact that land can be seen across the divide between Sumbawa, part of the Sunda lands, and the Komodo Islands and Flores makes it easier to understand the capability of these early people. They were not yet venturing across the sea over the horizon; that had to wait for further evolution to modern humans.

Since the strait between Sumbawa and Flores has strong tidal streams, I have always imagined that simple canoes made labouriously from forest trees were used for exploration rather than clumsy rafts. *Homo erectus* did not have time schedules governing his canoe building and his stone tools were capable of cutting wood; and many hands make light work. When exploration was complete, movements of family groups could always follow on rafts, husbanded by men in canoes.

As the climate swung, bursts of migrants moved fast or drifted in trickles; and expired or retreated when adverse conditions were experienced. These migrants met parallel or earlier migrant groups and undoubtedly mixed to some degree. This maintained the continuity of *Homo* evolution and the healthy mixing of genes and culture.

Whatever earlier movements occurred in sublime times along easy seashore and river routes, Early Stone Age people had surged across all the accessible warmer parts of Eurasia by at least a half million years ago. I believe that this activity happened in a series of relatively rapid jumps when climatic pulses suited and not in some immensely slow linear migration. Unfortunately, the warm interglacials and ice-ages not only created the stimulations and brakes on mankind and other large mammals, they also destroyed palaeontological evidence. Sites which have recently revealed *Homo heidelbergensis* in Europe are actually quite rare.

Homo erectus had learned to tame fire before one million years ago and this must have been central to their ability to move about in temperate southern Africa and Eurasia and survive normal winters. Mankind today, during the present warm period, cannot survive more than a few days of a northern European winter without fire, clothes and shelter. Fire and the ability to hunt large mammals for clothing extended their geographical and environmental range, extended the variety of foods in their diets, diversified their social structure and enabled them to respond to greater challenges.

It has been claimed that the earliest proven use of fire outside Africa has been shown in hearths excavated at Gesher Benet Ya'aqov in northern Israel by a team led by Naama Goren-Ibar of Hebrew University. The date of the hearths is about 790,000 BP. Obviously, fire was in use outside Africa long before this date, but no absolute evidence has yet been discovered. Earliest definite control of fire is proven from a hearth at Chesowanja in Kenya at about 1.4M years ago.

Homo erectus and its *heidelbergensis* variant or successor were both curbed by the Ice-ages which pushed glaciers and ice sheets over much of Eurasia. Without the ice-ages, who knows what manner of people we might have been today with an unbroken line of evolution in the higher temperate zones. Would there have been massive and grievous species divergence between a speculative *Homo europeanensis* and a *Homo africanus*?

The northern limits of survival for Early Stone Age people in Eurasia moved back and forth to the pulsing of the Ice-ages. Further interrelated physical, technical and social evolution was necessary for innovation in shelter, communal cooperation and specialist

165

tool-making and -using. Fishing and hunting methods had to be modified in the face of a variety of harsh terrains and scarce prey. Without the next stages of innovation, they could not have survived the long-term cooling of an Ice-age after a warm interglacial. Perhaps more significantly, they could not have survived the more severe shocks of temporary climatic aberrations bringing on short-lived cold periods often lasting as little as a hundred years. In Europe there have been several of these in historical time which have caused famine, plagues, refugee migrations, population decimation and cultural trauma. We only have to look at the 'Barbarian' invasions of Europe and the plagues of the 14th century of our present era to see what can happen.

The earliest migrants of *Homo erectus* into cool temperate parts of Eurasia during warm interglacials did not survive the next Ice-age, because of lack of technologies. *H. heidelbergenses*, though better equipped, had similar difficulties. Some nomads probably retreated back to Africa and exchanged new knowledge with those who had stayed at home. New expertise steeled by ice-age experiences in the melting pot of the northern temperate zone was allied to people of Africa who had made their own progressive advances. It was an explosive mixture and projected humankind forward. The magic of this progress was that refreshing sojourns all around the African and Asian Indian Ocean shores with long periods of seafood diet provided sufficient brainpower growth to use the shocks of alternating cycles to make extraordinary cultural jumps.

During the cold times, many who were settled at the far end of South Africa could not ride out the extremes of climate and refugees trekked back to the tropics along the river and seashore highways. These refugees from the far south may have provided a greater stimulus to cultural advancement in certain directions than exhausted remnants from Eurasia. Genetic mixing amongst these native Africans added to the beneficent effects of restorative millennia-long periods of exposure to the seafood driving force on the Indian Ocean beaches.

In passing, it is necessary to remark on speculation that *Homo erectus* penetrated the Americas long before the accepted period of modern mankind's migrations from Siberia during the last sixty thousand years. There are proposals that Toca de Esperança in Brazil reveals evidence of tools claimed to be from 300,000 years ago, and Sandia Cave in New Mexico from before 100,000 years ago. This is speculative and there is academic argument about the veracity of dating, but I see no reason why *Homo erectus,* or an east Asiatic sub-species or diverging race, should not have been in the Americas at that early time. There were four ice-ages between 500,000 and 100,000 years ago with warm interglacials between them. During an ice-age, sea levels were low and the Bering Strait was a land bridge and during a warm time there was a more equable climate along the northen Pacific rim when the Bering Strait was flooded. Both extremes suggest that *Homo erectus* probably did not have the technology to manage either the icy climate or the sea passages. But there were hundreds or thousands of years of climatic transition and I have no doubt that relatively small parties of Early Stone Age people could have managed it. That they did not survive into more recent time because their numbers were inadequate for sustained population growth does not surprise me either.

*

Alan Templeton in the journal, *Nature,* in March 2002, proposes three major waves of emigration 'out-of-Africa' There was the first major colonisation at around 1.7M years ago. Recent analyses by Larick, Ciochon and Zaim show that this colonisation reached Java in that order of time. The second that is detected from fossil evidence is in the time range from about 840,000 to 420,000 years ago. During that range, there were several warm interglacials promoting population growth. The third is the spread of modern people during the last 100,000 years.

Christopher Stringer and Robin McKie in *African Exodus* (1996) describe a number of sites in Asia which also fall into this particular out surge of Early Stone Age people from Africa. This book is essential reading for those who wish to have an understanding of the details of *Homo* migrations available at that date. Unfortunately, Stringer, at the time he was writing, missed the essential ingredient which would answer many of the questions he was still pondering: the seashore dimension and the vital addition of long-term seashore living. Amongst other sites, Stringer notes 350,000 year old skulls at Yungxian in China, with larger skulls than earlier *Homo erectus,* and those who lived at Olorgasailie about 600,000 years ago.

The period from the emergence of *Homo habilis,* about 2.3M years ago, until the time of Olorgasailie and the other comparable sites around the world shows remarkable brain growth. It is hardly surprising that the culture of Olorgasailie had become complex, including those quite modern concepts of specialist craft groups and inter-clan trading.

Stephen Oppenheimer in *Out of Eden, The Peopling of the World,* (2003):

> ... new human species with larger brains and more skills appeared in Africa. As the climate briefly warmed after each glacial maximum, the Sahara would become green for a few thousand years and the new human species would venture out to try their luck in Eurasia. By 1 million years, brain volumes of various human species living both within and outside Africa had increased from 400 to 1,000 cm³, and even into the modern size range [± 1,400 cm³]. In other words, human brains had grown to three quarters of their modern range before we [*Homo sapiens*] came on the scene.

Oppenheimer is unable to account satisfactorily for this extraordinary growth, which continued to the level of the Early Stone Age people at Olorgasailie and then the emergence of modern humans. Even in 2003 he does not examine the effect of seafood nutrition and the stimulation of seashore living.

Lyall Watson in *Elephantoms* (2002) is taken with the proposal that the seashores of South Africa were important for the development of larger-brained Early Stone Age people, the kind of people who lived at Olorgasailie. He refers specially to 500,000 year-old 'Saldanha Man', found at Hopefield in 1953 near the Atlantic Coast, and recent discoveries at Langebaan beside the seashore within Saldanha Bay.

*   *

In codifying the general development of mankind during the long time scale since the emergence of the first distinctive *Homos*, by 2004 a new taxonomic nomenclature was emerging, in the same way that the family and species names of the pre-*Homo* ranges of hominids had been proliferating. This is a problem which will augment as more fossils are discovered presenting an ever-increasing complexity of subtle and not-so-subtle skeletal changes, illustrating evolution's advance over hundreds of thousands of years in sudden jumps. Jumps are followed by periods of divergence and stabilisation, but during those stable periods, enhanced or delayed by local climate change, migrations occurred suggesting regional speciation within time periods, all with their own names. Some species failed and became extinct, like the Neanderthals. As knowledge increases and complexity grows when viewing hundreds of thousands of years, it is increasingly difficult to describe human evolution accurately in simple and pithy narrative.

Sarah Milliken of Oxford University described in *Athena Review* the two approaches to the human ancestral tree after the advent of the *Homo* line:

> ... palaeoanthropologists can be polarised as being either "lumpers" or "splitters". "Lumpers" believe that the number of species of early Homo has been overestimated ... "Splitters", on the other hand, believe that the number of species of early *Homo* has been underestimated, and an extreme advocate of this view might recognise the coexistence of at least half a dozen of them in the lower Pleistocene.

The 'splitters' have enjoyed a period of discussion and speculation about the emergence of the *Homo* genus, as distinct from the *Australopithecines*. Some academics have suggested, for example, that *Homo habilis* is not of the *Homo* group at all and that the first species to be so described has to be *Homo ergastor*.

The period of 800-600,000 years ago, during which there were two glacial periods and three warm interglacials was particularly productive of genetic splitting. Latest research shows that Neanderthals split from *Homo erectus* during this time. Other divergencies in Eurasia are discerned. The ancestry of the Neanderthals as distinct from the main line of the *Homos* continues to be subject to some debate. It could be asked : which of the two was the main line? *Homo neanderthalensis* in Eurasia, or *Homo sapiens* in Africa? A report in the London *Daily Telegraph* in May 2008 illustrates this.

Links between humans' ancestors redrawn
By Roger Highfield, Science Editor
06/05/2008
The family tree of mankind has been redrawn by a new computer analysis that attempts to sum up what it means to be human. Many attempts to compile evolutionary trees that

169

link humans with their apemen relatives are hampered by how they try to divide fossil skulls into categories such as 'flat-faced' or 'protruding-faced', when in reality these traits vary over a spectrum.

Instead, Dr Rolando González-José of the Centro Nacional Patagónico-CONICET, Puerto Madryn, Argentina and colleagues used geometric measurements from many human and ape fossil skulls, and condensed them into four parameters, reflecting variables such as skull roundness and facial retraction.

They classified 20 skulls pertaining to our species, our living nearest relatives: gorilla and chimpanzees, and the most important and complete cranial remains from relatives such as the gracile australopithecines (*Australopithecus afarensis* and *A. africanus*), robust australopithecines (*Paranthropus boisei, P. robustus, P.aethiopicus*), *Homo habilis, Homo erectus, Homo ergaster, Homo heidelbergenses,* and *Homo neanderthalensis*.

The biggest surprise to arise from the analysis published in *Nature* concerns *Homo habilis*, which lived between 2.3 and 1.6 million years ago. An analysis published in 1999 concluded that this ancestor should no longer even be considered human (that is, assigned the genus, or group of species, called *Homo*) and some have suggested that the honour of being at the base of the human family tree should go to *Homo rudolfensis*.

But the new analysis disagrees. "Simply put, *H. rudolfensis* presents a more retracted face than *H. habilis*, and a more globular and rounded cranial vault," says the team. "These particular and subtle differences confer a more derived aspect to the *H. rudolfensis* skull and place it in a derived position with respect to *H. habilis*", says Dr González-José.

They conclude that species currently assigned to the genus *Homo* are indeed a single family, with the two-million-year-old *Homo habilis* at its root, and that, much more recently, *H. sapiens* and *H. neanderthalensis* were evolutionary cousins, rather than offshoots of the same species. They also find one ancestor, *H. heidelbergensis* should not be viewed as the last common ancestor among Neanderthals and modern humans. Instead, it sits on a branch that leads to the Neanderthals. Earlier on, that branch joins the one that led to our ancestors.

In other words, what this team concluded is that the 'splitters' indulge in unnecessary and ultimately unproductive exercises in speciation based on small and inconclusive variations in fossil skulls. Any modern observer, travelling about the world for a few days, and observing the faces and skull sizes and shapes of the myriad of travellers in international airports has to have doubts about deciding on ancient species and evolutionary theories based on subtle differences in skulls. Genetic research has shown that Neanderthals and modern humans in Europe, 'Cro-Magnons', interbred and all Europeans today carry traces of Neanderthal genes.

The broad sketches I have drawn in this book of how I see the evolutionary trail seem to me to be unaffected by these pedantic arguments.

Speculative divergence of *Homo erectus* about 500,000 years ago.

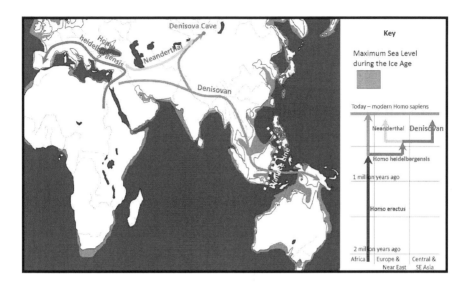

Image from Wikipedia, 2017

Late genetic research at the Max Planck Institute has identified a new variant of *Homo erectus*. It is the Denisovians and there is insufficient evidence presently to describe them as a new species. Maybe, there is a reluctance to proliferate *Homo* species descriptions since genetics also proves interbreeding between these variants. The Denisovian gene is detected in modern people across eastern Eurasia.

This diagram from Wikipedia illustrates one example of speculation on the movement of three main *Homo erectus* variants during the period 800-400,000 years ago. It also shows the extent of land uncovered during a glacial period.

The Denisovians are identified from DNA extracted at the Max Planck Institute from a finger bone discovered in the Denisova Cave in Siberia.

The progress of technology in determining genetic trails from minute portions of recoverable DNA is bound to have a great impact on the narrative of human evolution. Now, is an exciting time.

NINE : *AFRICAN EVE*
Remarkable genetic research and events a quarter of a million years ago.

Much recent literature or comment about the later phases of evolution of mankind features specific genetic studies made at Berkeley, California. In a large sample of women with diverse ethnic origins, researchers traced a particular DNA marker which is carried by the human female. The male counterpart is lost in the process of union between the sperm and the ovum. This research has become famous because the result suggested that there was a common worldwide Mitochondrial Eve in the African population group appearing sometime about an abrupt warm peak at about 250,000 years ago. This concept has become popularly known as that of the African Eve. Christopher Stringer and Robin McKie in their book, *African Exodus* (1996), wrote:

> The study [the original Mitochondrial Eve research of 1987 by Wilson, Cann and Stoneking at Berkeley] produced three conclusions. First, it revealed that very few mutational differences exist between the mitochondrial DNA of human beings, be they Vietnamese, New Guineans, Scandinavians or Tongans. Second, when the researchers put their data in a computer and asked it to produce the most likely set of linkages between the different people, graded according to the similarity of their mitochondrial DNA, it created a tree with two main branches. One consisted solely of Africans. The other contained the remaining people of African origin, and everyone else in the world. The limb that connected these two main branches must therefore have been rooted in Africa, the researchers concluded. Lastly, the study showed that African people had slightly more mitochondrial DNA mutations compared to non-Africans, implying their roots are a little older.

The date this experiment suggested for a common ancestor was somewhere between 142,500 and 285,000 years ago. A quarter of a million years ago becomes the popular date in general use. It is noticeable that there was a particular high warm temperature spike at about 250,000 BP with cold periods either side followed by a lesser warm from about 220,000-200,000 BP.

More recent studies (2013) suggest dates for this theoretical genetic diversion at about 160,000 BP, between about 200-140,000 BP. This time scale fits into a cold glacial period, which reinforces the reminder that this experiment is a guide to evolutionary diversion at about these times. Natural selection will operate with greatest impact at either limit of a climate cycle with its corresponding environmental stresses. To determine the most accurate Eve, the genes of all people on Earth would have to be included in the model, and even then there would be argument.

After publication of the first genetic experiments at Berkeley in 1987 suggesting an 'African Eve', a storm of controversy raged. It lay between those who believed in a steady and worldwide evolution through the whole of the *Homo erectus* and *Homo sapiens* period towards the present racial divisions seen in mankind, and those supporting an African Eve with modern diversions occurring during the Neolithic period of *Homo sapiens*.

More recent certainty that *Homo neanderthalensis* evolved from *Homo erectus* in Europe and western Asia along a separate evolutionary path to mainstream *Homo sapiens* in Africa, has put paid to the concept of a worldwide evolution of one genetic family. If Neanderthals split from the main *Homo* line at about 500,000 years ago in Europe, and this seems now to be generally accepted, where else did this occur in the vastness of the Eurasian landmass?

The apparently unique aberration of the recently discovered *Homo floresiensis* fossils in Indonesia may yet lead us to other extinct Asian equivalents of the Neanderthals, but it would seem that this particular example is evidence only of how a severely isolated pocket of *Homos* can diverge quite easily in a period of less than a few hundred thousand years. In 2010 the Max Planck Institute established the DNA of another variant which was named Denisovian, after the cave where a small bone was discovered in Siberia. There is insufficient other evidence to describe this mutation fully, but fragments of the DNA appears in modern people in east Asia.

More experiments and research have increasingly supported the original genetic evidence from Berkeley. Other techniques using other protein markers have been used. They exploited new advances in biochemistry and the ever-increasing knowledge and volume of research into DNA. The genes of our cousins, the chimps and gorillas, have been brought into the studies and, coincidentally, clarity in our relationship with them and our divergence from them to the hominin line and *Australopithecus* has been enhanced. More sophisticated computer modelling has confirmed how the modern races of mankind diverged only in the last 80,000 years.

Stringer and McKie in *African Exodus* (1996) cited one particular work as being most important, among several others. It is the compilation of enormous research over two decades by Professor Luca Cavalli-Sforza of Stanford University published in his *The History and Geography of Human Genes* (1994), co-authored by Menozzi and Piazza.

Stringer and McKie wrote:

> More than 70,000 frequencies of various gene types in nearly 7,000 human population types are included, combined with anatomical, linguistic and anthropological studies. It is an august body of work that comes down fairly and squarely on the side of the Out of Africa theory. We conclude a definite preference for the rapid replacement model [of Eurasian peoples by Africans], states Cavalli-Sforza.

Comparing genetic distances between modern people and the archaeological and fossil evidence of their separations, Joanna Mountain and Cavalli-Sforza prove a good correlation which is quoted by Stringer and McKie. It shows that Negroid Africans separated from non-Africans about 100,000 years ago, southeast Asians from Australians and New Guineans at about 55,000 years ago, Caucasoids from northeast Asians about 42,000 years ago and northeast Asians from Amerindians about 25,000 years ago. Later researches quoted by Stephen Oppenheimer refine these conclusions enormously and 80,000 years ago is reckoned to be the time when African Negroid genes became distinct from all other races, indicating a major migration out of Africa.

In 1997, another two separate experiments with the male line of descent supporting the African Eve hypothesis were reported. In these cases research into the mutations of the Y chromosome, passed on through the male line, showed that the Khoisan (Bushman) people in southern Africa is the only race to have so many ancient genetic remnants of archaic *Homo sapiens*. Dr Michael Hammer, of the University of Arizona, analysed the Y chromosome of 1,500 men of diverse ethnic groups from around the world. He stated in an interview:

> One way of looking at this is that the Y chromosome traces back to people who lived in Africa. We have evidence that the Y chromosome in all men today trace back to one African male at some time in the past. It is possible that this male was not anatomically modern. He may have been more like Homo erectus, one of our hominid ancestors, but the Y chromosome survived the change in the way we look. ....
> The oldest branch of the [human family] tree that traces all the way back to Adam is represented today by the Khoisan people [of southern Africa]. Something like 20% of the Khoisan men have this old, old Y chromosome. We don't find it at all in European populations and it is present in very low levels, 2% or 3%, in other African groups.

Dr Peter Oefner of Stanford University reported similar findings from his genetic investigations. He stated that research showed:

> .... a unique mutation occurred, resulting in one [symbolic] son who defined the new line and whose descendants eventually reached a majority in Africa. Some offspring of this lineage left Africa to populate the entire globe.

Further refined study in genetic divergence amongst modern races show that African people were the oldest modern human stock. The ratio of genetic variations was African 199: European 98: Asian 73. The numbers from this experiment are dramatic.

Dr Max Ingman, who researched at Uppsala University, in 2001 published an article in *BioScience Productions* in which he wrote:

> For the last fifteen years or so, molecular anthropologists have been comparing the DNA of living humans of diverse origins to build evolutionary trees.

He summarised the arguments about the two approaches to divergence and concluded:

> The most important date, in relation to the competing evolutionary theories, is the time when all the sequences coalesce into one - the 'mitochondrial Eve'. .....
> From this study [the 'Population Genome'], a date of 171,500 years ago was obtained which fits remarkably well with that proposed in the recent African origin hypothesis.

It is interesting that Prof. Philip Tobias in South Africa published papers based on simpler research into genetic differences between the Khoisan and the general African Negro population of Africa as long ago as 1971. In an address to the Royal Society of South Africa, he stated:

> ... in general, Bushmen and Hottentots [the Khoisans] share a common sub-Saharan pool of genetic alleles: Khoisans have more in common genetically with Negroes than either group has with any non-African peoples. [But] .... Many facts have accumulated to confirm what the somatic evidence formerly indicated, namely that in numerous characteristics Bushmen differ appreciably from southern African Negroes. ...

In April 2008, Professor Himla Soodyall of the University of the Witwatersrand was reported in an interview with Shaun Smillie in *The Mercury* of Durban. He described how a man in the Colesberg District of the Northern Cape had demonstrated the oldest DNA described in living people. Soodyall stated:

> This man carries the most ancient DNA signature, going back to a period between 90,000 and 150,000 years ago. ...
> What we had were that branches of the mitochondrial tree in Africa were not fully resolved. Now we are able to look at those branch patterns more accurately.

The *New Scientist* reported on 8 October 2014 a remarkable archaeological discovery by Andrew Smith of the University of Cape Town in 1910. A fossil skeleton, buried in a seashell midden about 2,300 years ago at St.Helena Bay, on the south west coast of South Africa, yielded DNA. Analysis showed that his ancestry diverged about 150,000 years ago; the oldest recorded from actual genetic evidence, but comparable to the man from Colesberg, above. The St. Helena man had changes to his inner ear proving that he was a 'marine forager' who spent much time in the cold sea of that west coast. He was a Seashore Man!

Out of this welter of information derived from research experiments and actual DNA, it seems to me that the general structure of human movements and evolution in the last half million years has been reasonably well established. What was principally established? It is that around 200,000 years ago a major genetic diversion occurred within the main *Homo* thread. It is when *Homo sapiens*, modern mankind, is identified.

In western Eurasia the Neanderthals diverged probably 400-500,000 years ago and became habituated to the cooler, more rigorous regime of the temperate zones which moved north and south to the rhythm of the ice-ages. In the rest of Eurasia, mostly confined to the south of the tectonic barriers of the Caucasus and Himalaya ranges, *Homo erectus* proceeded with evolution in less-demanding tropical and sub-tropical cycles. There is the strange Denisovian variant to consider; where did this deviation occur and why? The genetic experiments show that modern *Homo sapiens* evolved quite separately in Africa, away from Eurasian population groups at about 200,000 years ago.

All humanity at this time was descended from the same root, but at about 200,000 years ago we had become four main branches: Neanderthal, Denisovian, advanced *Homo erectus* and emerging *Homo sapiens* in Africa.

Why was modern man, *Homo sapiens*, evolving separately in Africa? It can only have been the effect of the continuing access of the core-people to seafood on the eastern African shores.

*

Homo Neanderthalensis are the presumed descendants of *Homo erectus* in Europe, via *Homo heidelbergensis*, and parts of western Asia where their fossils have been found. The region best known for Neanderthals is south western France although the original site after which they are named is in Germany. The speciation of the Neanderthals away from the main *Homo* line is now reckoned to have been at about 500,000 years. As learned cultural behaviour prompted greater tolerance of colder conditions, their anatomies adapted. The Neanderthals developed heavy, more powerful and shorter bodies than the main African *Homo* line to combat repeating ice-ages. Their brains were on average larger than their African contemporaries, possibly in response to their larger physical bodies.

It is interesting that fossil material of larger than average skulls was also found in southern Africa where it would have been cold during Ice-ages. Evidence from sites such as Hopefield in the Western Cape of South Africa (Saldanha Man), The central high plateau of South Africa (Florisbad Man) and Broken Hill in Zambia (Rhodesian Man) suggests that a parallel evolution towards a Neanderthal-type was happening in the more temperate zones at the end of Africa during Ice-ages. But it is noted that these African skulls were not Neanderthals; they lacked the heavy brow ridges which are definitive for the European variant. These African variants have sometimes been named *Homo helmei*.

Debate about Neanderthals' abilities in creative or symbolic activity raged for many years. The archaeological site in the Grotte du Rennes at Arcy-sur-Cure in France and others in eastern Europe have been important, but there are any number of sites attributable to Neanderthals. Discoveries of animal teeth probably used in necklaces, the use of other material for jewellery, the employment of ochre and manganese ore for decoration, the invention of specialist small tools and symbolic burial all show that Neanderthals were not only masters of their temperate and cyclically icy environment but they were also parallelling *Homo sapiens* in cultural evolution. Their culture and social organisation was maybe simpler and less diverse, reflecting their constricting environment, but it was not necessarily intellectually inferior. Dates for these Neanderthal sites range from their extinction about 30,000 BP back to more than 60,000 years ago.

An editorial article in *Current World Archaeology* (No. 20, 2006) describes latest findings of Neanderthal-origin artefacts in the Grotte des Fées at Chatelperron. It is stated that :

> Neanderthals were much more like modern humans than had been previously thought. Bristol University's Professor Zilhao and colleagues from France have concluded that sophisticated artefacts - such as decorated bone points ... Were the work of Neanderthals around 44,000 years ago.

There is no doubt that *Homo sapiens* in Africa were more complex and diversified in their culture, but the Neanderthals were not stereotypical brutish cave-men of myth. The explanation for the more 'advanced' culture of the African core-people at the time of their first meetings with Neanderthals in the main body of eastern Europe, maybe 60-50,000 years ago, is because they had the advantage of two or three hundreds of thousands of years of a warmer climate and superior seashore nutrition. They were tropical people and in their long trek from eastern Africa around the shores of the Arabian Sea and then up the great river valleys to the Black Sea, the Mediterranean and onwards they had learned to master the new environments fast, always sustained by sojourns on seashores with abundant seafoods. The Seashore Hypothesis maintains its presence.

Homo sapiens were from the core-population of Indian Ocean people, the Neanderthals were the deviants whose genetic and cultural development had been influenced by the harshness of their temperate European environment, subject to the severe stress of several ice-ages, and isolated from the driving force of seafoods. Nevertheless, as Professor Zilhao has been quoted as saying:

> ... The fact that both anatomically modern humans and Neanderthals had the capacity for human cognition and symbolic thinking suggests the origins of such mental activities may date way back to before the two species split from their common ancestor.

We have circled around to my fascination with the Olorgasailie example of Early Stone Age people and their 'modern' cultural behaviour.

*

While much academic, professional and public attention was focussed on Neanderthal exploration in Europe, some work in the East produced similar evidence. Thought was given to the concept of the survival of an Asian parallel equivalent of the Neanderthals in pockets of south-east Asia and the islands of Indonesia.

Found in Java, Solo Man was long considered to be a candidate and Dr Alan Thorn, who excavated at Lake Mungo in Australia, believed that there was fossil continuity between Java and Lake Mungo at least until 30,000 years ago when the lake dried. At

180

Ngandong a *Homo erectus* skull was dated in 2000 to between 53 - 25,000 BP. Pockets of descendants of this ancient species were able to survive until comparatively modern time, surviving the several ice-ages of the Pleistocene within the warm tropical embrace of southeast Asia and the Sunda Islands.

And then there was the extraordinary and astonishing discovery of fossils of small 'pygmy' people in September 2003. They continued to live in the forests of the island of Flores. This showed that there were definite pockets of descendants of Asiatic *Homo erectus* surviving until relatively recent time. They were nicknamed the 'Hobbit' and their skulls were about "the size of a grapefruit"; their height was about one metre. This shock revelation was made by Professors Mike Morwood and R.P.Soejeno during a news conference at the Australian Museum in Sydney on 28 October 2004. These strange aberrations, cut off from the mainstream of human evolution for maybe 700,000 years, were named *Homo Floresiensis*. The upper limit was suggested by Morwood's previous dating of stone tools on Flores of that order of time.

Controversial argument immediately occurred with opinions that the 'Hobbit' was merely a modern Pygmy-type offshoot of modern humans with a small brain caused by pathology. There are modern Pygmy-type people living in the dense rainforests of Indonesian islands, similar to the Ituri in the Congo. However, this was countered by evidence that although there was a small brain, it had a structure, especially of the frontal lobes, which coincides with advanced intelligence and the brain capacity relative to body mass was not too dissimilar to a scaled-down *Homo erectus*. Bones of six or nine other individuals have been found which show that the 'Hobbit' was not some isolated individual aberration. Unfortunately, there has only been one skull found.

In the *Scientific American* magazine of February 2005, Kate Wong wrote an extended review of the 'Hobbit' people. She quoted several authorities who have speculated or discussed the possible reason for the evolution of these small people. The consensus seems to be that they were descendants of later *Homo erectus* who became isolated on the island of Flores and this constriction to a limited environment resulted, over millennia, in their small size. Comparison with modern Pygmies or Bonobo chimps, constricted within the Congo rainforest, is obvious. Arguments that the condition of the 'Hobbit' people was caused by similar afflictions of pathological

181

microcephalic dwarfism as experienced in modern human dwarfs have been dismissed by experts. Dwarfs in our modern society are an occasional aberration, have small bodies and large heads and seldom survive a shorter than usual lifespan; the Hobbit people of Flores have a 'normal' structure though small.

In May 2006 *Science* magazine included an article on recent investigations of the skeleton of *Homo Floresiensis*. Fossils indicated that its shoulder and upper arm structures were almost exactly similar in relative dimensions to the only nearly-complete skeleton discovered so far of ancient African *Homo erectus*: the Nariokotome Boy from 1.6M years ago near Lake Turkana. This is flimsy evidence perhaps, but is the only available fossil link, and it tends to prove the proposition that *Homo Floresiensis* is a direct descendent of *Homo erectus* who got lost and degraded on their isolated island.

In *Science* of 30 March 2016, Thomas Sutikwa, Matt Tucheri and others announced more accurate dating of the Flores fossils. It was established that their dates were in the range of 100,000 to 60,000 years ago and it was assumed that *Homo floresiensis* became extinct at about 50,000 years ago, which coincides nicely with the arrival of *Homo sapiens*.

In a TV documentary examining the discovery of early human occupation of Flores, a re-enactment of the crossing of the straits between Sumbawa and Flores was attempted to illustrate the probabilities. This was achieved with some difficulty because of the tidal streams that run in the channels. Here is the general description of the streams in the Selat Sape [Strait of Sape] which divides the islands of Sumbawa and Komodo and is typical of the other channels between Komodo and Flores. From the British Admiralty *Indonesia Pilot vol. II* (1983) :

> Tidal streams in Selat Sape have a semi-diurnal character and are only slightly affected by the monsoon in the Flores Sea. The tidal streams are weakest about 5 days after the moon's quarters, the maximum rate then averages 3 knots for both N-going and S-going streams. Very strong tidal streams with a maximum rate of 4 to 6 knots occur from 2 to 5 days after full moon and new moon. When the moon's greatest declination occurs during this period a rate of 8 to 10 knots may be expected ...

Observation of the streams, and practical experience over time probably resulting in the loss of some explorers, would show when it was best to attempt crossings of the various straits and channels separating the Indonesian Islands. However, when there was prolonged glaciation during an Ice-age the sea levels are considerably lower. Examination of maritime charts shows that these straits would have been either dry or much narrower. The Selat Sape between Sumbawa and Komodo may have shrunk to no more than 4-5 kilometres, and maybe less, and the straits between Komodo and Flores could have been dry.

If *Homo erectus* was able to make the crossing from Sumbawa to Flores, did they progress to the end of the chain of islands as far as Alor? I am sure that they did, and maybe fossil evidence will one day prove it.

Homo sapiens migrated as far as the Sunda Islands and across to Australia at about 70,000 years ago and remnants of these 'aboriginal' people are scattered in pockets throughout south-east Asia. They were pushed into mountainous regions by migrating farmers during the last 2-3,000 years. Legends about them are told today. No doubt the 'Hobbit people' were similarly pushed aside and isolated by early *Homo sapiens*, in the same way as the Cro-Magnons behaved towards the Neanderthals in a similar but different scenario in Europe. Australian Aboriginals were moving towards extinction under pressure from people of the Industrial Age and their diseases just a century ago, until rescued by Victorian enlightenment. The Khoisan of South Africa were severely affected by measles and smallpox in the 18th century. The San-Bushmen of southern Africa faced extinction from cultural and political pressures at the hands of modern post-colonial African governments. It is an old story.

Who knows what other strange offshoots of the *Homo* line may await discovery in remote parts of Indonesia, Malaysia or Indo-China? I had long believed that remnants of people descended from the several 'out-of-Africa' migrations survived for long periods in isolated tropical eastern Asiatic pockets. The Flores discovery did not take me by surprise.

Stephen Oppenheimer, reviewing the larger skulls of Africa from the period of 250-150,000 years ago and their similarity to skulls found in Java (Solo), China (Maba and Dali) and at Narmada in India, suggests that they represent the last discernable movement of late *Homo erectus*, or *Homo helmei*, people from Africa into Asia sometime

183

before 150,000 years ago. Genetically, they were children of Africa, sisters of the large-skulled people of southern Africa. They did not deviate into a separate species like the Neanderthals because they did not have to react to the climatic challenges of several European ice-ages, and possibly because their African ancestry was from a more recent time than ancestors of the Neanderthals.

As Christopher Stringer has put it, in Asia there was much shuffling of the 'genetic pack of cards'. Old genetic strains were mixing with new migrants from Africa while genetic distances were not too great for speciation to have taken place. Interbreeding was possible and occurred until recent time. Geographic distance did, however, have effects and the differing somatic racial appearance of Asiatics and Australasians show how this is manifested amongst today's people. Because of the shuffling of the genetic cards along the tropical shorelines of eastern Africa and southern Asia, a discrete and widespread genetic type like the Neanderthals did not generally emerge. There were gaps in time between waves out of Africa into Asia, stimulated by the climatic cycles, but not great enough.

It has been established by recent genetic research that all the people outside Africa deriving from *Homo erectus*, with the obvious presumed exception of *Homo floresiensis*, did interbreed and hence they are not technically different species.

Middle Stone Age people, also described as 'archaic *Homo sapiens*', who had evolved in Africa during the period of 250,000 to 150,000 years ago were genetically distinct from the Neanderthals and Denisovans of Eurasia. Divergence had occurred and it was irrevocable, but this divergence had not proceeded to the boundary of speciation. This supposes an interaction along the seashores from eastern Africa to Indonesia and further into Australia, and would be more confirmation of the basic 'beachcombing' trait in all people. As Springer eloquently described it: there was a shuffling of gene cards back and forth.

*   *

Fossil evidence was sharpened with the publication of information in 2003 about three skulls discovered in the Afar region of Ethiopia, where the Great Rift Valley debouches into the Red Sea. (It is remarkable how many transition species are found at this critical junction beside the warm sea, rich with seafoods.) The skulls had been discovered in 1997 but their significance was only realised later. Dr Tim White of the University of California, Berkeley, who has worked often in this region, was one of the leaders of those who identified the fossils. He told Associated Press in 2003: "They're not quite completely modern, but they're well on their way. They're close enough to be called *Homo sapiens*." White and his colleagues placed the fossils in a subspecies which they named *Homo sapiens idaltu*. They were dated to between 160,000 and 154,000 years ago. Their report was published in *Nature* on 12 June 2003: *Pleistocene Homo sapiens from Middle Awash, Ethiopia*.

More recently, fossils have provided earlier dates than these. 200,000 years ago becomes an established threshold of modern mankind in Africa. From an editorial article in *Athena Review* v.4 (2), (2005) :

> Now, two early *Homo sapiens* skulls called Omo I and II, discovered in 1967 in the Kibish Formation on the Ethiopian Omo River and originally thought to be 130,000 years old, have been significantly redated to about 195,000 years ago. Using both geo-chemical dating methods (40AR/39AR) and soil analysis, a team of American and Australian scientists including Ian McDougall, Francis Brown and John Fleagle (2005) have thus recast the Omo remains as nearly contemporary with the oldest genetic projections for our species.

For many years previously, controversy had existed over the two logical but different routes to the development of modern mankind's proliferation into the spectrum of races which we know today. Based on somatic evidence, the evidence of anatomy and general appearance, it had long been thought that the different races evolved through random mutation and reaction to the environments in different geographical locales over long time from ancient stock, presumably *Homo erectus*. The alternative was the 'out of Africa' process which proposed evolution of *Homo erectus* proceeding towards geographical speciation which was overtaken by the explosion of modern *Homo sapiens* people migrating relatively late into Eurasia. The extinction of the Neanderthals about 30,000 years ago becomes a pillar of this theory because it is undeniable and the same thing could have happened everywhere.

Superficially, I found both routes attractive at different times. Undoubtedly, many Europeans tend to look like the common view of a Neanderthal; short and stocky with big bones and heavy skulls; more hairy than other races with some individuals very hairy indeed, rugged faces which could often be described as rather ugly. There are the persistent legends of troglodytes and goblins living in the forests. The somatic difference between Europeans and Africans and the Middle Easterners and Far Easterners of Asia are dramatic. These physical differences in appearance are what I have always considered to be one of the most attractive attributes of our modern species of mankind. It is a joy to belong to such a diverse species. Chimpanzees are so boring in their apparent conformity!

Luckily, the debate has been resolved though modern science. My adherence to the Seashore Hypothesis has continued to be vindicated. Stephen Oppenheimer in *Out of Eden, the Peopling of the World*, (2003) quotes genetic data suggesting a date for African Eve at 190,000 years ago, coinciding nicely with other genetically-based estimates and the onset of a glacial ice-age lasting for sixty thousand years. It also coincides nicely with the fossil evidence from Ethiopia.

Adding to what I have described above, he provides greater understanding of the mechanism of the research itself and how this has been used to trace the movements of people out of Africa, into Asia and thence through Europe and Australia. There can be no doubt that all people on our planet today have an origin in Africa about a quarter of a million years ago. Where there remained some obscurity and lack of knowledge, this was in the matter of the degree of interbreeding between people out-of-Africa and existing populations who had migrated earlier and evolved separately over the previous million years or so.

Oppenheimer shows that there was a break in our direct ancestry between those who remained in Africa and those who migrated out of the continent at a date about 80,000 years ago. Some evidence of Neanderthal genes in modern Africans can be attributed to the more recent movement of people back into northern and eastern Africa.

This break seen in the genetic record is reflected in fossils. In Palestine, fossils have been found of both Neanderthal types and *Homo sapiens* at about 120,000 - 90,000 years ago. The two species were apparently not intermingling; there is no way of knowing. But it shows that modern people had moved out of Africa through the Suez land-bridge at that time. There is no trace of them further north of the Levant, and it must be assumed that they were not able to adapt to desert conditions prevailing there at the time. However, there is evidence in genetic trails that some of this earlier out-of-Africa movement traversed the seashores as far as Indo-China . It is notable that there was a high temperature cycle spike around 125,000 years ago.

At about 80,000 years ago the principal exodus of *Homo sapiens* with Middle Stone Age culture was begun successfully. Stimulated by whatever local environmental circumstances prevailed, they migrated along the tropical Asiatic seashores and up the great rivers of south Asia rather than around the Mediterranean, and that saved them from a similar failure to the earlier attempt and gave them more time to adapt along the Indian Ocean rim. From that date onwards, the fossils of modern people and their Middle Stone Age artifacts are found across Asia, into the Indonesian islands and down into Australia.

Stephen Oppenheimer in *Out of Eden* comes closest to considering a particular detail of the Seashore Hypothesis of any palaeanthropologist I have read. He discusses the motives for modern humans, *Homo sapiens,* pursuing a 'beachcombing' trail when migrating into Asia from the Horn of Africa during the later Pleistocene epoch. His suggested practical reasons for this will resonate with anybody who has studied the seafood nutritional contribution to *Homo* evolution. Earlier, I quoted Oppenheimer's remark: "Beach tucker has the added advantage of remaining available when the savannah dries up during an ice-age."

Christopher Stringer, appearing in a TV documentary series, when suggesting that modern Stone Age hunter-gatherers who were proven shellfish eaters had migrated along seashores stated tellingly: "The world was one long beach and generation by generation they moved along it."

I was struck by that evocative description and wished that I had devised it myself !

*   *

The southern coast of South Africa continued to provide excitement and controversy about the evolution of modern people. John Compton in *Human Origins* (2016) describes at length the importance of Pinnacle Point, an archaeological site near the modern town of

Mossel Bay in the Western Cape Province of South Africa. Follow8injg the great success of excavation at Blombos Cave which provided decorated ochre pieces in what was hailed as the first time mankind had left evidence described as artwork, Pinnacle Point is both confirmation and an extension of the theme that this coast was something of a pivot in late human cultural evolution. John Compton weaves a narrative story which proposes this coastline was a principal originating source of *Homo sapiens'* wholly modern cognitive abilities.

Curtis W. Marean of the Institute of Human Origins, School of Human Evolution and Social Change, Arizona State University, led the excavations and this is the abstract from his paper, *Pinnacle Point Cave 13B (Western Cape Province, South Africa) in context: The Cape Floral kingdom, shellfish, and modern human origins*. Journal of Human Evolution, 19 March 2010.

Genetic and anatomical evidence suggests that Homo sapiens arose in Africa between 200 and 100 ka, and recent evidence suggests that complex cognition may have appeared between ~164 and 75 ka. This evidence directs our focus to Marine Isotope Stage (MIS) 6, when from 195-123 ka the world was in a fluctuating but predominantly glacial stage, when much of Africa was cooler and drier, and when dated archaeological sites are rare. Previously we have shown that humans had expanded their diet to include marine resources by ~164 ka (±12 ka) at Pinnacle Point Cave 13B (PP13B) on the south coast of South Africa, perhaps as a response to these harsh environmental conditions. The associated material culture documents an early use and modification of pigment, likely for symbolic behavior, as well as the production of bladelet stone tool technology, and there is now intriguing evidence for heat treatment of lithics. PP13B also includes a later sequence of MIS 5 occupations that document an adaptation that increasingly focuses on coastal resources. A model is developed that suggests that the combined richness of the Cape Floral Region on the south coast of Africa, with its high diversity and density of geophyte plants and the rich coastal ecosystems of the associated Agulhas Current, combined to provide a stableset of carbohydrate and protein resources for early modern humans along the southern coast of South Africa during this crucial but environmentally harsh phase in the evolution of modern humans. Humans structured their mobility around the use of coastal resources and geophyte abundance and focussed their occupation at the intersection of the geophyte rich Cape flora and coastline. The evidence for human occupation relative to the distance to the coastline over time at PP13B is consistent with this model.

Marean states in the conclusion to this detailed and defining paper:

> Modern humans are the sole terrestrial mammal that, in some cases, has a persistent use of marine resources that develops into a coastal adaptation characterized by technological and cultural peculiarities that are rather rare for hunter-gatherer economies. In some situations this coastal adaptation ultimately cultivates dense populations, richly complex material culture and social institutions, and "sea-centric" cultural proclivities well expressed among ethnographically and archaeologically documented hunter-gatherers in coastal California, Chile, Australia, and other areas of the world. Pinnacle Point provides us with a glimpse of the origins of the coastal adaptation.

What is being suggested is that Pinnacle Point helps to define the origin of wholly modern humanity and that it was this environment which provided the stimulus or breeding ground for the cultural 'jump'. Marean and colleagues, and other scientists at Cape Town like John Compton, seem satisfied that it is the southern African Cape coastlands which provided the unique environment for this momentous advance in the development of the human psyche. John Compton in his book devotes particular space to describing the particular role of seafood in this leap forward at the Cape. The re-wiring of *Homo sapiens'* brain and mind to extend existing abilities of talking, using abstract language, trading, planning and visualising, to include the creation of decorated objects and personal jewellery, which may be defined as art with no intrinsic or practical value, is indeed one of the most exciting watersheds of pre-history.

Dating proves that all along this coast hunter-gatherers with a high proportion of seafood in their diets had jumped over the line to complete modernity before the out-of-Africa migrations into Eurasia of about 80-75,000 years ago. To be able show where it happened from fossil and related hard evidence at more than one site is a truly extraordinary coup for palaeanthropologists and archeologists.

189

Langebaan Lagoon, Cape west coast - site of 'Eve's footprints' dated to about 120,000 years ago.

Storm's River mouth, Cape south coast, in the vicinity of Blombos Cave.

Haing studied the Seashore Hypothesis for about forty years, I had to be delighted with the conclusions reached by the scientists involved in the Cape investigations. However, I was dismayed by their assertion that it was probably the particular circumstances on that coast at that time which had stimulated seafood consumption and brought about the massive evolutionary jump in culture. The idea, pursued at length by John Compton on the basis of the archeologists' conclusions, that this was then carried the length of Africa and diffused thence into the rest of the world by migration of a discreet group from the Cape makes no sense to me.

Curtis Marean describes the climate at the Cape when this cultural jump was occurring to be harsh of a cold climate period. This could understandably be a stimulus to evolution through natural selection and is reasonable as an explanation. But, there is also emphasis on the rich biodiversity of flora providing good nutrition. A sudden switch to seafoods, thus enabling increased brain complexity, is not explained by this scenario. These people were not apparently starving and being forced to eat seafoods for survival. Pinnacle Point, and Blombos, might prove seafood eating at particular points in time, but do not prove that it started then. My broad Seashore Hypothesis is quite unaffected by these Cape archaeological sites, exciting and momentous as they certainly are.

Apart from anything else, the revelations do not change the generally accepted time or place of *Homo sapiens* evolution from *Homo erectus* or another late variation. *Homo sapiens* first appears in the fossil record in the Great Rift Valley of Ethiopia at the other end of Africa. I have referred to the Omo River fossils above, and here is a defining announcement on their dating.

Stratigraphic placement and age of modern humans from Kibish, Ethiopia
Ian McDougall, Francis H. Brown & John G. Fleagle

In 1967 the Kibish Formation in southern Ethiopia yielded hominid cranial remains identified as early anatomically modern humans, assigned to Homo sapiens. However, the provenance and age of the fossils have been much debated. Here we confirm that the Omo I and Omo II hominid fossils are from similar stratigraphic levels in Member I of the Kibish Formation, despite the view that Omo I is more modern in appearance than Omo II. 40Ar/39Ar ages on feldspar crystals from pumice clasts within a tuff in Member

191

I below the hominid levels place an older limit of 198 ± 14 kyr on the hominids. A younger age limit of 104 ± 7 kyr is provided by feldspars from pumice clasts in a Member III tuff. Geological evidence indicates rapid deposition of each member of the Kibish Formation. Isotopic ages on the Kibish Formation correspond to ages of Mediterranean sapropels, which reflect increased flow of the Nile River, and necessarily increased flow of the Omo River. Thus the 40Ar/39Ar age measurements, together with the sapropel correlations, indicate that the hominid fossils have an age close to the older limit. Our preferred estimate of the age of the Kibish hominids is 195 ± 5 kyr, making them the earliest well-dated anatomically modern humans yet described.

This work has been challenged on the basis that the material which was tested cannot be absolutely proven to be contiguous to the Omo I and II fossils, but the other Ethiopian Great Rift Valley site firmly dates a subspecies, *Homo sapiens idaltu,*from the Afar region at about 160,000 years ago.

John Compton in *Human Origins* (2016) proposes that *Homo sapiens* evolved on the Cape coastal plain through stimulus from a seafood diet during the interglacial period 246-186 thousand years ago. During later climate cycles, whenever the coastal plain was extended by sea level changes, these modern people migrated north, reaching the northern ends of the Great Rift Valley by the dates of the Ethiopian fossils. Compton :

> .... a relatively small group would have found themselves trapped on the coastal plain at the southern tip of Africa by the Cape Fold Belt mountains. .... Those groups of our predecessor species who adopted a habitual seafood diet may have then evolved into us, *Homo sapiens*, over the up to 60 thousand years (equivalent to 24000 25-year generations) that they remained isolated on the southern coastal plain during the MIS 7a-e interglacial period 246-186 thousand years ago.

Homo erectus migrated throughout Africa during many climate cycles during the previous two million years. *Homo erectus* migrated out-of-Africa during at least two or three major exoduses and settled northern China and the far reaches of Sundaland of the Indonesian islands at least a million years ago. I do not understand how Compton includes this scenario in his book. It seems to me that he is presenting a partisan opinion favouring the South African southernmost coast as a very special and unique place in the evolutionary story. It is an extraordinary idea to suggest that the most evolved people on Earth at the time were trapped on a strip of coast for sixty thousand years by interior mountain ranges. Wild elephants, let alone people or antelopes, routinely crossed those mountain ranges in the early 20th century. I know that coast well and there is nothing to prevent migrations along it.

I am reminded of Elaine Morgan proposing the Afar Triangle at the northern end of the Great Rift as the seminal place for the evolution of the original hominin line. She believed that a group of early hominids were isolated there and evolved through an 'aquatic' seashore period. This was an unsustainable concept.

Struisbaai lies between the Die Kelders and Blombos Cave MSA archeological sites on the Cape coast.

I am familiar with another important southern site which does not have the added excitement of being at a shoreside location at the Cape with abundant seafood nutrition. This is the Border Cave in the Lebombo Mountains bordering South Africa and Swaziland.

Although it is not at the seashore, it lies no more than 85 kilometres from the present shoreline across flat landscape with rivers which sometimes extend over floodplains. Archaeologist Dr Gavin Whitelaw at the KwaZulu-Natal Museum in Pietermaritzburg has shown that seafood remains have been deposited in Early Iron Age middens up tortuously winding river valleys maybe fifty or sixty walking-kilometres from the ocean. Here is part of a paper on the Border Cave site prepared by archaeologists Leonard van Schalkwyk and Beth Wahl:

> The archaeological deposits at Border Cave date back more than 150,000 years and are evidence of Africa having most certainly been the origin of modern humans. The site was first investigated by Prof. Raymond Dart in 1934 and he demonstrated a Middle Stone Age sequence to be present to [the] bedrock.
>
> In 1941 and 1942 H.B.S. Cooke, B.D. Malan and L.H. Wells returned to the site and extended Dart's excavations ... Theirs, and subsequent excavations, have yielded incredibly rich archaeological material, including the remains of an infant, dating back about 100 000 years, buried in a grave with a shell pendant and red ochre staining suggesting that the body had been sprinkled with ochre at burial. The latest investigations in the 70's and 80's, led by Peter Beaumont, produced the largely complete skeleton of a four to six-month old infant also buried in a shallow grave. This suggests a people capable of abstract and symbolic thought who probably communicated in a fairly complex language. If concern with life after death is taken as a sign of religion, then this is also the oldest record of religion on earth.
>
> Remains of a total of five *Homo sapiens* individuals have now been discovered. Their dating and study has led researchers, including Beaumont, to conclude that the formative processes in the physical and cultural evolution of modern humans took place on the game-rich savannahs of sub- equatorial Africa. All the evidence suggests that modern humans developed in southern Africa and that their descendants migrated northwards ...

194

Border Cave has now yielded more than one million Stone Age implements, as well as the remains of at least 43 mammal species, including elephant and three others that are now extinct. Also discovered in the cave was the Lebombo Bone, the oldest known artefact linked to the basic mathematical activity of counting. Dated to 37,000 BP, the Lebombo Bone is a small piece of baboon fibula which has been carved with 29 notches, resembling the calendar sticks still used by Bushmen in the Kalahari today.

Interestingly, Beaumont, a South African archaeologist, was also suggesting a southern origin for *Homo sapiens*.

*   *

Not directly connected to the Border Cave, but sufficiently coincident geographically to have relevance, is the locally well-known ancient haematite (red ochre) and specularite mine on the top of Ngwenya Mountain [1829m - 6,000 feet] in Swaziland, dated variously to about 40-50,000 BP. I have stood beside the modest remains of a deep excavation where people scrabbled for the precious decorating materials all those thousands of years ago, and admired the exhilarating scene into the depths of the valleys below and far across the Highveld grasslands. It is perhaps of apparent little concern to the dry dustiness of research but I am frequently delighted by the choice of aesthetically enjoyable locations for the activities of the people who were proving their creative awakening in many ways. Why choose the top of a high mountain to mine ochre? There were sources at lower altitudes. It has been suggested because they also wanted specularite (a silvery iron compound) which they found at that place. And how did they find this sort-after material there? I presume simply because somebody climbed to the top to admire the view, just as we do today. Is it so strange that so many archaeological sites are in such sensuously pleasing and attractive places? Because they were exhilarating, they probably also acquired mystical importance and the ochre at the top of Ngwenya Mountain had greater spiritual potency.

It seem clear to me from the evidence of these southern sites, Blombos, Klasies River Mouth, Pinnacle Point and, especially, Border Cave, that the people who moved out of Africa and spread eastwards along the tropical belt of the world were already evolving culturally to what has been arbitrarily defined as 'modern' culture and behaviour. With the emergence of true *Homo sapiens*, before 170,000 years ago, the beginnings of creative activity, linked absolutely to abstract thinking and language, had appeared in Africa, but not only at the Cape.

Anatomically, people have not changed, as a species, since those Middle Stone Age sites were occupied. Divergence in hair, skin colour and stature occurred as we are all well aware, but evolution of our species as a whole has been almost entirely cultural. Our skulls have not changed, it is our minds within our brains which have gone through a major jump.

There seems no obvious reason for mankind to have evolved beyond the level reached at about 80,000 years ago when peopling of the whole planet began. *Homo sapiens* armed with Middle Stone Age technology and culture was able to master all the benign warmer lands close to seas, lakes and rivers in vast Eurasia. It was only a matter of time and opportunity when sea levels were low and population pressures were high for the peopling of the Americas to begin. During the warmer millennia they could explore and settle territory which earlier *Homo erectus* had discovered, living comfortably as far north as 45° latitude. When the cold cycles came, they could retreat to the ideal of the sub-tropics. Surely there was trauma when the retreating had to take place as populations were compressed, but unless there was a sudden shock like the Toba volcanic explosion of 74,000 years ago it was a gradual process lasting centuries.

They had the power of language and abstract thinking, they had refined their tools, they had complete knowledge of their environment and gained nutrients from all the animals and vegetation to which they had access. They knew how to fish, hunt and gather. They had social cohesion and could outwit any predator they were likely to meet. They were producing artifacts which had aesthetic as well as practical value. It seems that they were marking and decorating their habitats and themselves, and presumably their cold-weather clothing, and were wearing simple jewellery. Rituals were being devised to satisfy yearnings for knowledge of the greater Universe and the mysteries of life and death. What more could they need? They were not dissimilar in culture to their close kinfolk, the Neanderthals, who had in their own way mastered the temperate zones of western Eurasia and with whom they shared a common ancestor of maybe three or four hundred thousand years previously.

TEN : *CRO-MAGNON*
Modern humans 'Out of Africa' and extinction of the Neanderthals

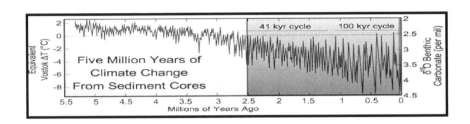

"Far from our biological evolution driving our cultural evolution, it has always been the other way round, and although our brains stopped growing a long time ago, our culture continues to evolve."

Stephen Oppenheimer : *Out of Eden* (2003)

Professor Michael Crawford reminded me in correspondence that Darwin proposed in regard to the progress of mutation and evolution: "... natural selection and conditions of existence, of the two the latter is the most powerful."

Stone and Iron Ages - definitions

The designations of Middle and Late Stone Age as applied to sub-Sahara Africa are different from those conventionally used in Europe. As always there is some controversy as new knowledge is gained and new cultural attributes are discovered. Within professional and academic circles definitions get sharpened and the layperson is easily left behind. Henshilwood and colleagues in their paper on the Blombos Cave archaeological site in South Africa (2001) wrote in their Introduction:

> The origins of "modern" human behaviour are a contentious issue and the subject of ongoing and extensive debate. ... Problems specific to "modern" behaviour paradigms are defining what is "modern", establishing a time frame(s) and place(s) for the behavioural transition and whether the transition to modernity was of a linear or mosaic nature.

In this book, I have assumed a rough guide which I hope will be acceptable to the reader. I have defined the Middle Stone Age in sub-Sahara Africa to be from the emergence of *Homo sapiens* with the refining of tools and early embellishments, with the social changes that these illustrate, from about 190,000 years ago, with clear evidence before 80,000 years ago when the major migrations of modern people out-of-Africa into the rest of the world began. I see the Late Stone Age beginning with the amazing jump to extensive rock-art, wide variations of fine manufacture of tools, weapons and jewellery and a general culture base which successfully prevailed without great change after the last ice-age when agriculture, the rise of urban civilisations and the use of metals began in the Middle East.

My rough-and-ready designations applied to sub-Sahara Africa and used hereafter are therefore:

Early Stone Age : from the beginning of widespread tool-making (maybe 2 million years ago) to about 190,000 years ago.
Middle Stone Age : from about 190,000 years ago to 35-40,000 years ago.
Late Stone Age : from 35-40,000 years ago to the recent present.
Early Iron Age : from first iron-working to about 1,000 years ago.

<u>Late Iron Age</u> : from about 1,000 years ago to the arrival of Western Civilisation.

When using 'Stone Age', I hope it will be clear I am using the definitions I have described for Africa and not the current European delimitations. Inevitably, I may use the term, Neolithic, especially applied to agriculture, and when I do I shall be referring to the last 6,000 years when European Neolithic and 'my' African Late Stone Age cultures coincide.

For easy reference, the stone-ages in Europe are usually designated as follows:
Lower palaeolithic - from earliest tool-making to 120,000 years ago
Middle palaeolithic - 120,000 to 36,000 years ago
Upper palaeolithic - 36,000 to 10,000 years ago
Mesolithic - 10,000 to 6,000 years ago
Neolithic - 6,000 to 2,500 years ago.

The common boundary that sticks out is 35,000 years ago, always a most important transition time. When discussing Eurasia, I tend to merge the Mesolithic and Neolithic, generally referring to it as Neolithic, since I believe that the birth of agriculture and sedentary living at 10,000 BP is the critical marker at the commencement of the era of Civilisation.

Wherever the influence of metal industry and agriculture did not penetrate in Africa, right up to the 20th century, and a hunter-gatherer lifestyle was maintained, I consider that the African Late Stone Age was still active. To confuse this generalisation, it is evident that Late Stone Age agriculture flourished before and in parallel with the Iron Age in Africa.

It is often proposed that knowledge of iron smelting was transferred from the Middle East to sub-Saharan Africa progressively by either diffusion or migrating peoples, or both. New discovery of iron working in the Sahel suggests that iron was smelted and worked south of the Sahara before it became widespread in Egypt. This can lead to all sorts of complex speculations, but I think in general there is a simple explanation. The *knowledge* of metal working may have proceeded by diffusion or with migrants, but once the understanding of the use of high temperatures in smelting metal from ores, and how to recognise the particular rocks, was obtained, then local experts developed the techniques. Copper preceded iron, since it is easier, but the spread of iron working must have depended firstly on the availability of the ores.

There has been a tradition with earliest roots that metal-workers were 'special' people, often also acting as shamans or diviners. In some parts of Africa there were metal-workers who had no tribal affiliation and moved about servicing their clients and keeping their knowledge secret. Smelters lived apart from villagers, by mutual agreement, whilst smiths were often local people.

Besides copper and iron, tin and gold were smelted. It is interesting that there was no African Bronze Age and I have assumed that one did not develop because knowledge of iron came early to Africa perhaps simultaneously to copper, from the beginning of sub-Saharan metallurgy. Gold, such an easy metal to work, was never valued by sub-Saharan Africans because it has no practical use. Copper was valued for jewellery but it also had practical value and was lighter in weight. Gold was sought or worked to provide an important trade good with outsiders. Iron and copper were also traded with foreign seatraders on the Indian Ocean shores.

~~~~~~~~~~~~~~~~~~

Until quite recently there was a hazy area in the story of the last hundred thousand years. It was as if there were two quite separate investigations into the evolution of modern mankind, *Homo sapiens*. One stream of effort was occurring in western Europe and the other was mostly being pursued in southern Africa. In the 1990s the haze began to clear with a number of new archaeological sites being explored and verified throughout Africa, in the Caucasus region and across Europe. Genetics became perhaps the most important tool for tracing movements of modern people. A sharper vision of how climate changed in that time also provided new insights.

It was known that modern people had crossed the Suez land bridge into Palestine before 100,000 years ago because their fossils had been discovered there. In the last twenty years fossil finds have shown that starting from 50 000 years ago, when there was a warmer period following a short ice-age, modern people gradually accumulated in a swath across the temperate latitudes of Europe, from the Black Sea to

200

the Atlantic. These 'anatomically modern people', of the *Homo sapiens* species, are often commonly referred to as Cro-Magnons after the definitive fossils found in a simple cliff side shelter near the Vézère River in the Dordogne. Although not an academic description, I have used that term here.

The Cro-Magnon shelter is within walking distance of the famous rock-art caves in the limestone of the Vézère valley. I have spent time there, marvelling at the enormous significance of that place in the story of our recent origins and taking in the delights of the magnificent paintings and engravings preserved in the caves and tunnels within the cliffs rimming the tranquil valley.

Stephen Oppenheimer has demonstrated the near-certainty that the Cro-Magnon people were not descended from those that crossed into Palestine about 110,000 years ago and whose fossils were found there. It is sure that those people moved no further northward and they expired during a cold dry period. However, genetic trails suggest that it is possible that some people of this outward movement which failed to spread northwards from the Levant were able to beachcomb to the Far East.

The Cro-Magnon people entered Europe much later and the appearance of their fossils at about 50,000 years ago in the Black Sea region, spreading westwards, coincides with genetic traces.

*

Homo sapiens bands of the African Middle Stone Age began moving out of Africa, probably across the Strait of Bab el Mandeb about 80,000 years ago, island hopping across the strait. If the oceans were low, it was much narrower than today because it is possible to find a wandering path with maximum depths of ± 50 fathoms (300 feet) today, which is within the fluctuation range of ocean levels during ice-ages. They beachcombed along Asiatic shores and began colonising up the great rivers of Mesopotamia, the Indian sub-continent and Indo-China. They crossed into Indonesia and moved across to Australia in dugout canoes or on log rafts. These were modern people and had African Middle Stone Age equipment and culture. They learned as they travelled. When they met relics of earlier migrations, including earlier *Homo erectus* descendants, they either interbred or supplanted them.

201

The Toba Volcano in Sumatra exploded in an enormous eruption, expelling 2,800 cubic kilometres of dust and ash into the atmosphere estimated about 74,000 years ago, thickly covering a swath of South Asia with ash, wiping out entire populations of people and animals. Prof Stanley H. Ambrose of the University of Illinois wrote:

> Volcanic ash from Mount Toba can be traced north-west across India, where a widespread terrestrial marker bed exists of primary and reworked airfall ash, in beds that are commonly 1 to 3, and occasionally 6 meters thick.

This caused a temporary separation between modern people who had already moved as far as south-east Asia and those who were in the Middle -East. The destruction of populations by the ash desert and a bried volcanic winter delayed the colonisation of Europe by several millennia.

There was a temperature spike about 60,000 years ago and a period of somewhat warmer climate until the last ice-age increased in severity after 40,000 years ago. During these ten thousand years or more, modern people recovered their numbers and expanded their range. The colonisation of Europe began when populations along the Indian Ocean shores of southern Asia and the Far East had increased again and the ash desert was ameliorated by millennia of weathering. New migration up the Mesopotamian rivers and then westwards from centres in the Black Sea region added to impetus. Complex genetic trails detail these conclusions. These migrations were an early precursor of the invasions of Europe from central Asia which swamped the Roman Empire and changed the culture of Europe in the Middle Ages of our own historical time.

The Cro-Magnons, modern *Homo sapiens* of the African Middle Stone Age, with sophisticated stone and bone tools and new intellectual attributes, appear in the European record about 50,000 years ago and reached western Europe probably around 45,000 years ago when the Neanderthals were arguably at their most developed and successful stage. Stephen Oppenheimer :

> ... there is a climatic reason for the late colonisation of Europe ... from the Gulf region, and we can find it in cores drilled from the seabed off the Indian coast, in the submarine delta of the Indus. ... Access between Syria and

the Indian Ocean was always blocked by desert during glaciations. Almost exactly 50,000 years ago, however, there was a brief but intense warming and greening of South Asia, with monsoon conditions better than today. ...

For a short while that narrow green corridor opened allowing migration from the Arabian Gulf to Syria, and the great-granddaughters of Asian Eve went north-west up the Fertile Crescent to the Levant. The original South Asian source for these European migrants is revealed by the genetic trail ...

* *

The spectacular rock-art of the Dordogne region of France is like a lens focussing attention on the inward migration of the modern Afro-Asiatic people who came to be commonly called Cro-Magnon. It is also a focus on the fate of Neanderthal people living in Europe and parts of western Asia at the critical time of about 35,000 years ago. The Neanderthals did not decorate cave walls. The prolific and outstanding rock-art of the Dordogne and associated caves scattered about southern France and northern Spain was the work of new people, the people who displaced the Neanderthals, and it is the evidence of their rock-art which clearly demonstrates the interface.

The Dordogne is a powerful river that rises in the Massif Central and flows generally west to join the Garonne below Bordeaux to form the Gironde estuary. Together with its major tributary, the Vézère, it has carved its way through the limestone deposits of the Cretaceous period to sculpt cliff-begird valleys. The valley bottoms of alluvial soil are today cultivated farmlands relieved by poplars and willows, but the sides and shoulders of the valleys are densely covered by holm-oaks with pockets of chestnuts and pine. The Vézère, which flows through the village of Les Eyzies, and its local tributaries, the Grande and Petite Beune, have created the cliffs in which are the caves and shelters which Stone Age people found attractive.

During an ice-age the climate and therefore the vegetation were probably similar to that of present-day Scandinavia. There were extensive coniferous forests inland and the populations of large mammals which are illustrated in the paintings would have been thin. Animals such as bisons, horses, ancient cattle and reindeer, which lived in large herds, migrated with the seasons. The rigours of the winters kept their numbers down and restricted the population of their predators, including Neanderthal people. Northern Europe, including most of the British Isles, was covered either by permanent glaciers and ice sheets or was marginal land where trees could not survive and large herbivores could find nutrition only in a short summer season.

By 50,000 years ago, Neanderthal people had evolved to survive up to the interface of the frozen lands during several ice-ages, as the cold moved southwards across Europe. They had experienced several climate cycles during the previous 500,000 years which had provoked this.

The men made better and finer stone and bone tools for tasks that were required by the challenging environment; the women steadily accumulated a wider knowledge of foods to gather as the vegetation changed. There is evidence of a complex social lifestyle, dour and introverted as it may have been. Decoration of the finest of their artifacts proves that they were as capable of creative mental processes as their contemporary *Homo sapiens* relatives.

There is a picture of hardy, extremely tough, quiet people living hard lives in coniferous forests beside icy rivers, often malnourished, frequently anxious, husbanding their energies. They hunted well and there is no doubt that they survived principally because their hunting abilities enabled them to clothe themselves sufficiently to combat the endless cold of long winters. Their skins were certainly white in a climate which required that they were almost continually covered with warm clothes of skin and fur.

They sharpened their skills for survival under the climatic stresses and pressure, but Neanderthals were held in cultural limbo by the general severity of that climate in their northern homelands. The very harshness of the climate and lack of a varied diet for long periods sapped their ability, and indeed their need, to innovate. Survival was an enduring struggle. Neanderthals had learned to survive, but their story illuminates the fate experienced by earlier, less advanced, hominins who endured similar harsh climate.

Also within the limits of the modern village of Les Eyzies in the Vézère Valley of the Dordogne is the Cro-Magnon shelter where five skeletons surrounded by jewellery were discovered in 1868. The skeletons are clearly similar to today's people and distinct from Neanderthals. They were tall, about 1.8m, and had high-domed modern skull shapes. They were distinct from the short, stocky Neanderthals (averaging 1.6 m in height) with heavy brows and low foreheads. The site itself is not impressive : a low overhang protects a long shallow shelter with a plaque to distinguish it.

The French National Museum of Prehistory perched above Les Eyzies is sited in the reconstructed ruins of the 13th century castle of the Barons of Beyac. On its terrace is the often-maligned statue of primitive man sculpted by Dardé from an interpretation of a Neanderthal skeleton found at La Chapelle aux Saintes in the neighbouring Department of Correze. The statue, bulky and heavy-limbed, gazes quizzically and sadly down the valley. Perhaps the feeling of sadness and nostalgia the statue evokes is because one senses that he knew that new people were coming to disrupt a lifestyle that had been stable for so many thousands of years.

It was the Cro-Magnons who painted and engraved on the walls of the caves and shelters in the Dordogne and far across Europe where their other equally significant relict artifacts have been found. These are the fine stone tools and jewellery with regional variations which have been defined in several industries. The paintings of the Dordogne, in Aquitaine, the Midi-Pyrénées, Altamira, Brescia and elsewhere in France, Spain and Italy may receive a more immediate emotional response from us, but the finely crafted knives, axes, scrapers, arrowheads, grinders and sewing-needles illuminate practical daily life. Their craftsmanship and aesthetic appeal is equally noteworthy. What is striking is that these objects were obviously made with an eye to their beauty as well as their utility. Even more importantly, Cro-Magnons made jewellery and ornaments. They painted and engraved on stone and we may be sure that they carved wood, ivory and bone and decorated their animal-skin clothing. Surely they used mineral washes and ochre pastes to colour themselves and they may have tattooed their own skins, perhaps with tribal markings.

The conventional explanation for the demise of the Neanderthals and the flourishing of the Cro-Magnons is that the Cro-Magnons came with the improved hunting technique essential to survival and, especially, to expand in the environment of southern Europe. In the conditions prevailing in the Dordogne, for example, Neanderthals were presumed to eke a precarious living where vegetable foods obtained by gathering were at a minimum and prey animals were scarce. Neanderthal expertise was sufficient for survival only in scattered bands. The modern migrants from Asia had by then refined hunting techniques suitable for the temperate regions of

205

Europe and with better weapons and expertise they were more successful. They gradually pushed the Neanderthals aside into impossible territory where they expired, or were eliminated by accidental genocide. Hunting in the wintery forests became the key to success and the Cro-Magnons were better hunters with better weapons.

It would be surprising if from place to place and at different times, during the early arrival of the new people, there was no interaction. It is not unreasonable to surmise that Neanderthals became clients and there is undouibted interbreeding. The two groups hasve been defined as different species but genetics have shown that this is a grey area. Indeed, fossils in Portugal and Gibraltar are showing both Neanderthal and modern human attributes, illustrating the furthest reach of both peoples, at the end of the European continent.

Evidence, given publicity in science magazines in November 2006, shows that a gene which may affect the brain (the haplogroup D variant of *microcephalin*) which was recently detected in Neanderthals only appeared in modern humans at about 37,000 years ago. The announcement was made by Dr. Bruce Lahn of Chicago University who led a team of researchers. Michael Balter reported in *Science Now* of 6th November 2006:

> The Lahn group concluded that the most likely scenario was interbreeding between prehistoric modern humans and a now extinct hominid that carried haplogroup D – most likely Neandertals. The haplogroup was probably beneficial enough to spread quickly in modern human populations, says Lahn. But he's not sure what advantage it offered. Because most researchers agree that Neandertals were not as cognitively advanced as modern humans, Lahn and his coauthors suggest that the haplogroup might have made *Homo sapiens* better able to adapt to the Eurasian environments that Neandertals had occupied long before modern newcomers arrived.

This is a very ancient gene which seems to be largely absent from Africans and probably emerged by a mutation in *Homo erectus* in Eurasia at about a million years ago. Its appearance in modern humans through hybridisation between Neanderthals and Cro-Magnons is possible although the mixing may have occurred with any other late descendants of *Homo erectus* along the seashores or interior of Eurasia. It should not be forgotten that folklore legends of troglodytes, gnomes and trolls of the forest have persisted in Europe until today. I do not believe that any story in legend and superstition lacks ancient origin or explanation.

Another important factor needs to be considered regarding the extinction of the Neanderthals. I am sure that Cro-Magnons introduced diseases to which they were immune but to which Neanderthals were vulnerable. This has happened in modern times often enough during similar colonisation, as described in numerous historical records. The Khoisan of southern Africa almost disappeared in the 18th century because of plagues of the common measles and small-pox viruses brought unwittingly by relatively immune colonists from western Europe. They were lucky to have survived and to have exponentially increased their numbers since.

The ending of the last Ice-age, starting with a short warming at 14,500 years ago with dramatic changes in climate from cold to warm and back again, finally stabilising with the long warm period leading to the present at about 11,000BP, precipitated the next great upheaval in our evolution. The upheaval was the birth of agriculture and the beginning of urban civilisation. What is fascinating is that the change to culture can be seen to have occurred almost entirely in the northern hemisphere.

Professor Roland Oliver in *The African Experience* (1991) describes the process of gaining improved tools, weapons and hunting technique in Africa during the progress of the Middle Stone Age, provoked by climatic turbulence in the tropical environment, and established from a number of archaeological sites. This occurred before evidence of similar progress in Europe and although he does not describe or date the migration of Afro-Asiatic people into Europe carrying advanced African expertise, (the genetic trails were not established when he wrote), he observes amongst other conclusions:

> Somewhere around 35,000 years ago, human communities throughout the Old World entered upon the final phase of a hunting and gathering existence, which was to end with the gradual adoption of farming and stockbreeding. ... In Africa, as in Europe and Asia, all men now belonged to the single genus Homo sapiens sapiens. The difference is that in Africa some at least of the Middle Stone Age populations had already long reached this stage. In the Cape Province of South Africa, we have seen that Homo sapiens sapiens was

207

present well over 100,000 years ago - even before the Neanderthal period in Europe.

Roland Oliver was satisfied that hunting techniques and the necessary refined weapons and equipment were honed and developed in Africa during diverse climates and environmental changes. Africans were able to achieve these changes because they were already on a suitably advanced Middle Stone Age platform. In Europe, Neanderthals, battling to survive in their sub-Arctic territory, could not make this jump.

Oliver examines evidence from the Klasies River Mouth cave on the Cape seashore, the Kalemba rock shelter in Zambia and the Haua Fteah cave in Cyrenaica, Libya. He suggests a period of transition to Late Stone Age technology from about 40,000 years ago and its dramatic acquisition throughout Africa by 20,000 years ago. He suggests that this jump was promoted by climatic change, by an increase in rainfall preceding this period in the African tropics which had particular effect on the East African savannahs and the Sahara. Deserts became grassland, grassland became woodland, woodland became rainforest. Hunting technique had to change to tackle the smaller mammals and birds of forested zones and weapons and tools became finer and specialised. This change to Late Stone Age industries did not coincide with the migration of people, it was continent-wide and occurring within widely-separated peoples. Middle Stone Age Africans had a technical competence which could be promoted by environmental challenge through the jump to the Late Stone Age.

Oliver is firm about the effect of wet climate in archaeology:

> It would seem that from about 125,000 to 30,000 years ago, when these industries [Middle Stone Age] flourished, the northern third of Africa was experiencing a moister climate than usual. Game animals typical of the dry savannah were thus able to graze over much of the Sahara, and men naturally followed in their wake.

When writing in 1991, Oliver was not aware of more recent clarification of climatic changes, particularly of the Sahara. It has been determined that according to the evidence available in 2005, there was an almost complete hiatus of human occupation of the Sahara during the last ice-age, 20 - 12,000 years ago. In the millennia running up to this peak, conditions not unlike today's prevailed over large parts, especially to the east. In the last 50,000 years, the whole of the Sahara was habitable savannah only for limited periods from about 40 - 25,000 BP and 10 - 5,000 BP. These 'wet' periods are largely mirrored in the Kalahari Desert of southern Africa.

Professor David W. Phillipson, of Cambridge University, in his 1993 revision to his *African Archaeology* wrote:

> By at least 40,000 years ago steadily increasing aridity made much of the Sahara progressively unsuited to human settlement and few Arterian [stone tool industry] sites are significantly later than this. Neither the Nile nor the Niger at this time attained their present courses or extent: the upper reaches of the Niger flowed north-eastwards into the present inland delta where its waters were lost by evaporation. Lake Chad was probably almost dry [as it often is today] These conditions, which coincided with the most severe period of glaciation in northern Europe, continued in the Sahara until about 13,000 years ago.

Hunting for meat and skins became the key to progress in southern Eurasia in the closing millennia of the last ice-age and migrants descended from Africans, the Cro-Magnons, had the expertise. Gradually over the next several thousand years the great herds of European cattle and bison became extinct. The woolly rhinoceros and mammoths disappeared together with other, lesser species.

Jared Diamond in his editorial introduction to a *National Geographic* special edition on Africa in September 2005 suggests that the extinction of large herbivores in Eurasia may have occurred because they were not afraid of human predators, as the herds of plains animals of Africa had become in previous millennia. Superficially, this seems to be a reasonable proposition. Certainly, the bison of North America were selectively extinguished by 19th century buffalo-hunters. But there is a simple flaw in the idea. Those buffalo had been hunted by native-Americans for millennia before the arrival of European colonists and were well-aware of humans as predators. The difference in their case was that instead of hunting with spear and arrow, the new hunters used magazine rifles and rode horses. And in Eurasia, mammoths, horses, buffaloes and deer had been hunted for many millennia before the Cro-Magnons appeared. They were well aware of human predators. There is evidence that Cro-Magnons herded their prey over cliffs and into swamps in massive and unnecessary overkill. However, there is also evidence that earlier *Homo erectus* herded their prey into swamps. The 'overkill' hypothesis has gaping holes in it.

Massive depletion of herbivorous mammals in the northern hemisphere is more likely to have occurred because of sudden climatic shocks. There is the evidence of mammoths and other supposedly warm-climate mammals dying instantly and being frozen in swampy areas of Siberia. The corpses of these many hundreds of animals were so quickly frozen that their meat, hides, stomach contents, horns and tusks were perfectly preserved. Dr. Anthony Hall-Martin wrote in *Elephants of Africa*, by Paul Bosman & Anthony Hall-Martin, (1986) that:

> The remains of entire mammoths, frozen in the Siberian ice, have been found, some with flesh preserved so perfectly that it was edible. Throughout the eighteenth and nineteenth centuries mammoth ivory kept Russia in the forefront of the ivory trading nations and even today it is still a valuable source of ivory.

This is yet another example of the effects of sudden, chaotic climate, whether triggered by a short-lived local disaster such as massive continent-wide seismic and volcanic activity or a brief but catastrophic cosmic event, which people and all other life had to combat for survival. 'Overkill' by Neolithic hunters on foot and using spears is unlikely to have had extinguishing effects. Apart from the determined efforts of practised Neanderthal and earlier hunters for a million years, the efforts of modern Cro-Magnons in Europe from 40,000 BP onwards did not result in massive large mammal extinctions until this occurred at the end of the ice-age at about 11,000 BP. Hunting did not cause the extinction of mammoths, woolly rhinoceros, sabre-tooth cats, and European bisons. It was cosmic forces and the resultant sudden and catastrophic climate changes at the end of the Pleistocene.

By 35,000 years ago Cro-Magnos had successfully colonised all parts of the 'old world' which was compatible with their technology. The Neanderthal people of Europe and parts of western Asia were becoming extinct. With pockets of exceptions, other 'primitive' people in tropical eastern Asia, similarly handicapped by genes from an older era, directly descended from *Homo erectus*, were also disappearing from the fossil record. Cro-Magnons and their equivalents in Asia had survived where others failed. The jump to the Late Stone Age was occurring everywhere.

*   *

Nutritional 'driving forces' from prolonged dietary changes have been discussed at great length with reference to the evolution of humans from their ape ancestors, but nutrition has many general effects apart from brain growth promoted by seafoods. The somatic evidence of the divergence of the descendants of so-called Cro-Magnon settlers or colonists of Afro-Asiatic origins in Europe away from modern Africans is glaringly obvious today. One can wonder at how this happened in such a relatively short time. Europeans, especially north-western Europeans, are the most different in physical appearance in every way to their African brothers and sisters.

A discussion of the differences between all the population groups of modern people and the story of their divergence over the last 80,000 years is beyond the scope of this book. But attention can be given to some particular observations and it is the obvious difference between north-western Europeans and tropical Africans, at opposite ends of the human spectrum today, which seems most relevant. The situation of Africa today is most often regarded in the light of its colonisation by the maritime nations of western Europe in the late 19th century.

The physical difference between Europeans and Africans can be superficially understood. Climate is easily attributed for the obvious. 'White' skin, pale eyes and hairiness can be seen as trends promoted by a great difference in the amount of sunshine received in the wet and cold maritime regions of higher latitudes. But there is more to the environment of western Europe than grey skies and cold winds; there is the effect of nutrition which is perhaps the most important theme of my book.

Crawford and Marsh wrote in *The Driving Force* (1989):

> As human populations increased, man exploited inland regions and plants and animals came under pressure. Early man then learned to domesticate plants and animals. This change in the method of getting food was of the greatest importance. ... The 'Neolithic Revolution' that produced agriculture was the basis of civilisations that followed ...

211

Nutritional dependence on cultivated grains and fruits, a narrowing of the food spectrum often to complete dependence on one major crop, results in physical change and often to degradation.

Hunter-gatherers in an abundant environment were physically superior to agriculturalists, taller and less disease prone. Hunter-gatherers did not fight territorial wars like those waged by civilised nations tied to land or cities. Where was the advantage in converting to urban society for successful hunter-gathering societies? They had leisure and they had art and abstract thought from at least 35,000 years ago. Agricultural and urban society did not 'invent' these desirable lifestyles. The jump to agriculture was maybe a mix of genetic divergence and different nutritional driving forces. The reduction of prey animals which resulted from sudden and dramatic climate change and thence the evolutionary cultural and social path taken by resultant disadvantaged people in marginal geography was a complex combination of these factors.

Neanderthal skeletons show that they were short 'troglodytic' people, males averaging 5'3" [1.6m], whereas the Cro-Magnons averaged close to six feet [1.8m]. In Africa, there have been short people in historical time, the Pygmies of the central rainforests and the Khoisan of the south-western semi-deserts. Did they have anything in common with Neanderthals? Physically, the Neanderthals were more heavily built which was the result of the cold climate, but in some respects there may be similarity. Crawford and Marsh pointed out that European Neanderthals, Congo Pygmies and Kalahari San-Bushmen lived on a diet which was protein deficient. Congo Pygmies are also lacking iodine and other minerals because of leaching of rainforest soils and the shortage of meat in their diets.

Nutritional deficiency, it must also be remembered, inhibits reproduction and women often cease menstruating. Thus, nutrition may control population levels in a natural balance. All higher mammals experience these same physical inhibitions to reproduction. Allied to poor nutrition is food poisoning. There was growing concern in the 1990s at the decline in reproduction amongst humans in 'first-world' countries because of the effect of poisonous chemical additives in food inhibiting the production of sperm in many males. Deficiencies in trace elements following from mono-cultural diets increase non-invasive disease such as cancer and heart failures, and contribute to poor immune systems limiting the power to combat viruses and bacteria. Prof Michael Crawford in a personal communication ruminated on the possibility that the 21st century will be dogged by increasing mental illness resulting partly from nutrition deficiencies. We see the trends already.

Letten F.Saugstad in *Nutrition & Health* (2006) reviewed work by himself, Michael Crawford and several colleagues on the pressing matter of dietary deficiency of Omega-3 fatty acids, obtained primarily from seafoods. Increasing evidence shows a relationship between deficiency in Omega-3 and increases in Alzheimer's and Parkinson's diseases, schizophrenia, extreme excitability, epilepsy and problems with olfaction and vision. In this review reference was made to the enormous growth in the brain during the evolutionary period when mankind was most at home migrating around seashores. Saugstad:

> Notably, there is now good mitochondrial DNA evidence that the migration out of Africa was around the coastlines, testifying to a long prior acquaintance with a marine coastal habitat. Recognising our marine heritage, the necessity of abundant sea food availability as crucial in the evolvement of our great brain, we have to admit that a superior brain function has been replaced by brain dysfunction with our high protein [red meat] diet of the last century, neglecting food for the brain.

The point that nutritional scientists are increasingly making is that the role of seafoods in human evolution and modern health has been neglected in recent time. Much research has been devoted to protein deficiency and palaeontologists and anthropologists frequently suggest that it was the availability of red meat and high protein diets from hunting on the savannah which promoted human evolution. Protein certainly affects growth of the body, but it is seafood nutrition which is critical for the brain, and a good seafood diet provides both protein and Omega-3 fats.

Over and over again, we return to the seashore as the most beneficial habitat for the *Homo* genus.

Professor Phillip Tobias of the University of Witwatersrand showed that Khoisan of Botswana and Namibia significantly increased in median height over just a couple of generations during the first half of the 20th century when their protein intake increased considerably during absorption into 'Western' society. There are many San-Bushmen in Namibia and Botswana and Khoi types in

213

South Africa to-day who have become indistinguishable in stature from Bantu-speaking black Africans. Tobias in *S.A. Journal of Medical Sciences, 40 [4]* (1975):

> ... two populations of hunters and gatherers who are in the process of changing to a more settled mode of life and to a more secure basis of subsistence both show the positive trend [of median height]. These are the San and the aboriginal Australians.
>
> Both groups have been changing from the most borderline subsistence levels, the palaeolithic economy, to settlement and a food-producing economy. The San have shown an increase in the past 20 years ranging from 10,0 to 20,0 mm per decade, while the aboriginal Australians settled on a Commonwealth Government settlement at Yuendumu in the Northern Territory have shown an average increase of some 15,0 mm per decade between the thirties and the sixties.

Described in this and other papers, Tobias' considerable research amongst Khoisan and Bantu-speaking Africans in southern Africa shows that protein nutrition has a dramatic effect on physical size. The effect he described on San-Bushmen was not repeated in most Negro peoples, suggesting to me that the San-Bushmen of the Kalahari Desert were rapidly recovering height previously lost through many generations of poor nutrition, returning to a stature imprinted in their genes. Ancestors of San-Bushmen who did not live in the harsh Kalahari Desert into which they were driven by advancing Bantu-speaking agriculturalists fifteen hundred years ago may have been tall. *Homo erectus* people, over a million years ago, living on a protein-rich environment in East Africa stood tall. Modern animal herders, deriving most of their protein from abundant milk and milk products, and short of starches, in eastern and northern Africa were universally tall and slim. Protein intake togetehr with energetic vegetable foods affect stature and physical swell-being, but not the complexity of wiring within the brain.

The cave paintings of the Dordogne concentrate on ancient cattle, bisons and horses amongst other large mammals including mastodons and rhinos. Perhaps the Cro-Magnon males, who were the artists, felt the lack of prey in the forests of winter-bound Europe to be agonizing. Maybe that is why these Afro-Asiatic colonists painted animals more than people. They were obsessed with hunting for essential clothing and to provide the protein they were accustomed to.

Aggressively innovative modern humans, Cro-Magnons, were obsessed with their prey and the relative absence of people in their rock-art indicates a change in cultural bias. This almost-desperate concept of hunting for meat and hides was quite radically different to methods used in the warm African environment. The Cro-Magnons were learning a ruthlessness, reflected in later Eurasian histories of civilisations, that sub-Saharan Africans did not exhibit for another several thousand years.

The terrible forces of warlike Eurasian tribes which have dominated our planet until the present were probably forged in the harsh climate of the northern hemisphere during the last ice-age 24 - 12,000 years ago.

Continuing climatic change and several millennia of a high red meat diet in Anatolia, Mesopotamia, Palestine and North Africa until game became scarce could have been the trigger for an increasingly deprived people to convert to husbandry and cultivation, followed by fixed territory and urbanisation. It certainly must have been a time of great turmoil which laid the foundations for territorial wars and exponential advances in technology.

Samuel Kramer, a Mesopotamian scholar, wrote a review of the *Cradle of Civilisation* for Time-Life Books (1967). I find his conclusion interesting:

> How did this changeover from parasitic behaviou to productive farmer occur - and why? Psychologically, it seems curious and anomalous for a footloose hunter to surrender his heritage of free roving mobility and let himself be bound to earth and hearth, all for a mess of peasant's potage.
>
> In all probability, however, it was not the confident, self-sufficient and well-adapted among the nomads who let themselves be beguiled by the dubious promise of sedentary life. Rather was it the dissatisfied, the weak and the despised who broke away from their more successful and oppressive fellows...

There is some truth to be seen in this idea; maybe it is always the lazy, physically disadvantaged or eccentric who have been the innovators, forced when faced with final disasters to find a new path.

Maybe it is those who have been behaviourally or genetically modified by extraneous components of their time.

*   *

Where has that led us in the 21st century? J.M. Coetzee the Nobel prize-winning South African novelist, wrote in *Elizabeth Costello* (2003):

> ... the civilisation of the West is based on belief in unlimited and illimitable endeavour, it is too late for us to do anything about that, we must simply hold on tight and go wherever the ride takes us.

If we of 'the West' can hang on tight for this accelerating ride into the increasingly uncertain technical future, what of the Africans who are not of 'the West' but are being dragged along in the dust of this furious passage?

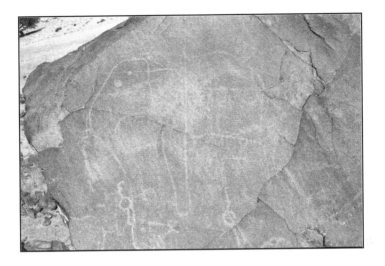

An elephant in the Hoggar of Algeria, 1985
(23°13'N. 5°24'E.)

The famous lion of Twyfelfontein in Namibia, 2001
(20°34'S. 14°22'E.)

Photographs by the author.

ELEVEN : *THE GREAT CULTURE JUMP*
The particular flowering of creativity at about 35,000 years ago.

The urge to decorate seems to be one of the defining characteristics of modern human populations (i.e. Homo sapiens sapiens). There are odd pieces of 'art' known from earlier contexts such as the ground and polished mammoth tooth from Tata in Hungary and possibly dating between 78,000 and 116,000 years, but art does not appear as part of a coherent, visual system until after 35,000 b.p. This is associated with human evolutionary and technological changes in Europe, Africa, and Asia, and the late Pleistocene colonisation of America and Australia. Since this time, people have consistently decorated themselves, their implements and, where available, rock surfaces.

The implications of this artistic watershed for advances in the ability (or need) for new types of social communication are still being argued.

M.J.Morwood and C.E.Smith : *Contemporary approaches to World Rock-art. - 1996*

There are many places where examples of prehistoric rock-art can be seen by casual tourists in Africa, when political turmoil permits, mostly in mountainous regions: paintings in the Matopos of Zimbabwe, the Drakensberg of Natal, the Erongo of Namibia, in Lesotho, the Cedarberg of the Cape, in Malawi and Tanzania, Acacus of the Fezzan in Libya, the Hoggar and Tassili mountains of Algeria, the savannah corridor west of the Congo forests; engravings everywhere where there are no mountains, and examples of both paintings and engravings in many museums from Nairobi to Cape Town. Similar rock-art from recent historical time can also be seen where the artists survived without cultural degradation.

Professor John Parkington of the University of Cape Town has a particular interest in the African Late Stone Age, especially the San people of southern Africa who are direct descendants of the ancient *Homo erectus* lineage. He wrote in *The Mantis, the Eland and the Hunter* (2002):

> Southern Africa is one of the richest regions of rock-art in the world, with an estimated 30,000 or more sites from the Cape to the Zambezi. In the mountainous fringes of South Africa there are usually only paintings, whilst in the arid interior there are engravings and sometimes paintings as well, partly a reflection of the underlying geology and the availability of different kinds of canvases.

Notably, it is people of Late Stone Age culture, whether millennia ago or in the recent past, who generally created rock-art. Iron Age black African people in sub-Sahara Africa preferred to create art or decoration in the form of ivory or wood carvings, elaborate masks for rituals, much pottery, sculptures, decorated skins or cloth, jewellery and beadwork and metal castings or wrought wares. Iron Age people all over Africa have decorated themselves with permanent scars and tattoos and temporarily for ritual ceremony with mineral wash or paste designs. Elaborate hair styles and permanent or semi-permanent metal bracelets and bangles fall into this category, usually denoting clan or totem affiliation which can be extended to a badge of ownership of slaves or clients. Masks and animal heads used to denote a temporary assimilation into an animal totem during intense ceremony have been used for thousands of years in all African cultures, and illustrated in old rock art as well as being lavishly described in modern travellers' tales.

It has been noted that when Iron Age people painted on rock, it was often an embellishment or addition to older Stone Age images. Proposals have been made by archaeologists in South and East Africa that when this was done it would have been through respect for or a desire to evoke the ancient mystery or power of the sacred places associated with particular rock shelters. This makes sense to me. The relationship between rock-art, especially geometric designs, and psychic or spiritual experiences achieved by shamans or healers all over the world is increasingly recognised, especially through the work of David Lewis-Williams.

The Late Stone Age resulted in most sub-Saharan rock-art, and certainly the most sophisticated, but there are zones where Iron Age Bantu-speaking people have been associated with it. Whether this activity was provoked from within their own culture, or whether it was following examples of existing Late Stone Age traditions, is a nice subject for debate. The problem always lies with the lack of dating possibilities in the great majority of African rock images. There is no doubt that some of the southern African art is of the Iron Age period, but San-Bushmen artists were still living within the Late Stone Age culture in separate geographic areas coincident to Iron Age Bantu-speaking agriculturalists for fifteen hundred years. Pictures of Europeans on horse-back or firing guns, Bantu warrior parties with shields and assegais confronting San groups and similar modern paintings are often quoted, but these were produced by San-Bushmen as illustrations of recent changes around them, and often of the people who were harassing them.

Audax Mabulla of the University of Dar es Salaam in his paper in *Azania* (2005) reports on a particular survey in the Mara region of northwest Tanzania. It seems that in this area where nine sites with 14 painted shelters or overhangs were examined some of the art was produced in recent time, probably by Iron Age agriculturalists. It is mostly geometrical with a variety of images, especially concentric circles, ovals, 'uterus-like', 'cross-like', rectangular and so on. Some seem to be depictions of cattle kraals. Mabulla concludes that they are related to rain-making, fertility and puberty initiation ceremonies and an elder of one adjacent village described ceremonies held in his lifetime.

Interestingly, when describing Late Stone Age artifacts found in these Mara shelters Mabulla concludes:

> Although Mara Region rock-art can be attributed to hunter-foragers, it is quite different from the San rock-art found south of the Zambezi River.

Latest genetic research shows that modern Hadza of northwest Tanzania and San-Bushmen of southern Africa were not closely related in recent time, say the last 20-30,000 years. Other researchers who had investigated the culture of the Hadza people have also maintained that the original culture of rock-art comes from their hunter-gathering period. Survivors of the Hadza had no doubt that their ancestors had created the tradition of painting on rocks, especially the geometric designs.

The conclusion I reach is that in East Africa, rock-art which might be older than about 5,500 years, was undoubtedly produced by Late Stone Age people who had been isolated genetically and geographically for maybe thousands of years. But since they were infiltrated by Negroid Late Stone Age pastoralists and then mixed Iron Age agriculturalists, their art like their genes becomes increasingly mixed in style and purpose. Impossible to date, paintings, often overlying one another, cannot be properly identified with one culture or another. I have the impression that in this part of Africa, the savannah and woodland immediately east of the Congo rainforest, there has been too long a time of mixing between the older people and modern Negroid Iron-Age migrants for there to be a clarity of style or subject. Like their genes, cultural styles are blurred and the purposes have been widespread, but in recent time their rock-art was almost always associated with secret or religious activity. Maybe, the locations became sacred within later Iron Age farming communities because of earlier rock-art which was associated with the spirituality of the shy and mysterious hunter-gatherer people who were there before them with origins far back into misty time.

The fact that pockets of Hadza, Sandawe, Dorobo, Njemps and other hunter-gatherers maintained a discrete existence in East Africa, some even until recent time, compared to San disappearance in land fully-occupied by Bantu-speaking, cattle-oriented people in southern Africa, maybe results from the different environments. In tropical East Africa, along the line of the Great Rift Valley there could be tolerant or cooperative co-existence.

The climate was lusher and there were tsetse-infested belts where cattle-herders could not penetrate and hunter-gatherers could continue an undisturbed lifestyle. But climate changed over thousands of years and those zones moved with it. But, the harsher conditions of the southern grasslands made it impossible for hunter-gatherers to keep to a discrete existence except in arid zones where cattle could not survive or in mountains where it was difficult for the tending of herds and flocks. The mixing of rock-art subject and style in Tanzania and the Great Lakes region, on the one hand, and the clarity of style and separation of cultures and peoples south of the Zambezi, on the other, is an interesting manifestation of the events and movements of people in this period of several millennia, for maybe as long as 10,000 years ago when the last ice-age came to an end.

Despite these remarks about the detail of some East African art, I have often been struck by the general affinity of subject and style between the Late Stone Age rock-art of northern and southern Africa. I have compared particular paintings in the Hoggar and Tassili of Algeria and the Fezzan in Libya, with any number of paintings in Namibia and the Drakensberg of South Africa. The art-littered Erongo mountains of Namibia lie about 21½° S latitude, the Hoggar of Algeria is on the Tropic of Cancer, 23° N latitude; a geographical African mirror asserts itself constantly. Throughout the Sahara in mountainous regions there are elaborate paintings, depicting a complex society and that style and content is mirrored in southern Africa.

In 2005 I was able to attend a course at Cambridge University to bring myself up to date on latest developments in the study of rock-art in the Sahara, especially in Libya. Numerous examples of paintings were examined and in my eyes the similarities were reinforced.

This extraordinary coincidence of style, forty five degrees of latitude apart, equidistant from the great geographical barrier of the equatorial Congo rain forest, has puzzled and intrigued experts for decades. My own view, reduced to simplicity, is that there was a common African Late Stone Age culture linking north and south via the core population of East Africa.

As each ice-age pulsed, people retreated back to and then advanced outwards from the harmonious tropics of Africa. The most recent outsurge occurred in both directions during the warm-wet phase after the last ice-age, hence I formed a view that this resulted in similar rock-art at both lines of the Tropics in what is now almost uninhabitable desert in southern Africa and the Sahara.

This is not to suggest that there was some kind of great mass movement of people, a great tidal wave of migration. Rather, it was an expansion over centuries into lands which bloomed as rainfall increased. In southern Africa occupation had not ceased entirely because the proximity to warm seas on the eastern side always provided substantial homelands for Late Stone Age people. The Kalahari and Karoo alternated between desert and savannah, as did the Sahara, but the Kalahari and Karoo are surrounded by mountains which caught whatever moisture was available.

In the Sahara, the mountains of the Hoggar, Tassili, Air, Ennedi and Tibesti are isolated clumps of really ancient volcanos lost in the middle of the broadest part of the continent. There was no friendly warm Indian and Atlantic Oceans nearby. In southern Africa, aridity never reached the extremes experienced across the wide and vast Sahara region. In the Sahara, as archaeology has shown, for thousands of years there was little evidence of people outside the Nile corridor. The continent had a great broad band of desert along the northern tropical zone lasting for thousands of years. After about 40,000 years ago aridity increased and reached a desolate maximum from about 20,000-12,000 years ago.

*   *

Rock-art blossomed around 35,000 years ago, but simple decoration preceded it. During the African Middle Stone Age (about 190,000 years ago to 40,000 years ago) modern people began decorating their artifacts and there are some speculative examples of the first abstract decoration on rocks.

In 1996, Australian scientists claimed that they had proof of rock-art in the form of concave circular shapes chipped or ground out of rock faces in north-west Australia at Jinmium, older than elsewhere. Low sea levels at about 70,000 years ago show when modern people first had an opportunity to migrate through the islands of Indonesia and cross the straits from Timor. More certain and less controversial is dating of a skeleton at Lake Mungo in southeast Australia at about 60,000 years ago. The earliest occupation of Australia by people was therefore established and they were modern people, the ancestors of the Aborigines. These migrants began beachcombing their way to the Far East and Australia at about 75,000 years ago.

The Klasies River Mouth site on the Cape coast of South Africa was a defining location of the Middle Stone Age. More recently, at the Blombos Cave site in South Africa, archaeologists found examples of what is proclaimed as art in the widespread use of ochre, finely made tools and geometric engraving on pieces of ochre which have dates before 70,000 years ago. Later work at Blombos by Henshilwood and his colleagues revealed a collection of perforated shells which have undoubted evidence of being part of a necklace dated to 76,000 years ago. In *Current World Archaeology* of May/June 2004 it was remarked:

223

It is generally believed that full syntactical language is a requisite to share and transmit the symbolic meaning of beadworks and abstract engravings such as those found at the [Blombos] cave.

Eight thousand pieces of ochre were found in the Blombos Cave which indicates an enormous use of this colourant for creative decoration of one kind or another over time. All of this material was carried to the site from sources some distance away and there can be no doubt of the great importance ochre had in the culture of the people who lived there 60-80,000 years ago.

For some time, the parts of a necklace at Blombos were seen as the earliest proven example of jewellery, but earlier examples have been discovered in North Africa and Israel. The general trans-African cultural connections remain true. *Current World Archaeology* (No. 19, October 2006) reported on seashells discovered earlier in the 20th century but freshly dated to between 100,000 and 130,000 BP. They were found at Es-Skhul near Mount Carmel and Oued Djebbana in Algeria. Dr. Marian Vanhaeren of University College, London, led the new dating analysis.

The Israel find is interesting because it confirms the abortive migration out of Africa at that time described by Oppenheimer in *Out of Eden* (2003). It was pointed out in the article that the shells used for jewellery were transported some distance from the sea (200 kilometres in the Algerian case) which requires planning forethought and particular effort, similar to that made to get the ochre from distant sources to Blombos. It is known that stone raw material was transported over distances to be made into handaxes, and probably traded, at Olorgasailie 500,000 years ago, but tools were essential to Early Stone Age people. Jewellery is a luxury.

I cannot resist remarking on the universal attraction of seashells as items of value. I believe that it is all part of the Seashore dynamic in all humans and here is proof at least from 100,000 years ago in North Africa. Cowrie shells were prized as jewellery and currency throughout the western Indian Ocean and across Africa until the 20th century. Cowries had semi-official exchange rates with coins in the older trading regions of Nigeria in British colonial time.

*   *

224

Between 40,000 and 35,000 years ago something formidable happened. The apparently stable Middle Stone Age culture of *Homo sapiens* all over the world leapt over a giant hurdle. Their close relatives, *Homo neanderthalis*, fell into the pit of extinction.

There is a variety of Late Stone Age rock-art all over the world, but according to the certain dates available to us at present, it seems to have emerged in Africa about 35,000 years ago (Apollo XI in Namibia) and flowered in the millennia which followed. Almost coincidentally, rock-art appeared in Europe (Grotte Chauvet in France). It appeared as far away as north-east Brazil (Pedra Furada) and Australia at roughly the same time. This was a worldwide culture jump which apparently happened absolutely outside of any migration of peoples or diffusion through propinquity or trade. Though the themes are eerily related, the styles of this universal art are often distinct and dictated by geography.

In the early 1970s, Dr. C.E. Wendt, working with the University of Cologne, had one of those remarkably lucky breaks that strangely happen to archaeologists from time to time. Wendt was exploring in the Hunsberge north of the Orange River and east of the dusty mining town of Rosh Pinah. Wendt and his assistants worked in a cave which he called Apollo XI because that space mission was proceeding when their work began there. They discovered slabs of rock with paintings that had fallen face down on the detritus of an inhabited period. On top of the slabs, other detritus had fallen over a long time with successive periods of occupation and abandonment. In the layers above and below, there were dateable items of organic material and several separate tests were carried out in Pretoria and Cologne. Wendt wrote in the *South African Archaeological Bulletin* (31: 5-11. 1976):

> The conclusion is reached that this 'art mobilier' was created between 30,000 and 25,000 years B.P. and that with a probability close to certainty even an age between 27,500 and 25,500 years B.P. can be assumed, thus making it by far the oldest dated art known on the African continent [in 1975].

Kathryn Cruz-Uribe and Richard Klein in the SWA Scientific Society *Journal* (1983) wrote:

Apollo XI not only contains one of the longest archaeological sequences in southern Africa, it also has provided some of the oldest art in the world. This consists of schematic animal figures painted on rock slabs sealed in the deposits. Radiocarbon dates on associated charcoal indicate the slabs are at least 19,000 and perhaps as much as 27,500 years old.

B.H.Sandelowsky, writing in the *American Scientist* (1983):

Although Wendt's material remains to be corroborated by further work, it can be assumed that rock-art in southern Africa dates to the very beginning of the LSA [Late Stone Age], 30,000 B.P. Such an early date calls for some new thinking about human cultural development. The implications of highly developed art found in societies with extremely simple technology and at sites far removed from centres of ancient civilisation are considerable. These finds raise questions about conventional notions of the achievement of civilisation.

At Apollo XI, together with various antelope fossils there were bones of the giant Cape horse (dated at 14,000 B.P. and earlier) which became extinct about 12,000 years ago during the trauma of the ending of the last ice age. Traded glass and copper beads from recent centuries add to the story of this remarkable cave site.

From the website of the National Museums of Namibia :

As part of a project with the University of Cologne, Dr. Wendt excavated to obtain a dating of the rock-art of southern Africa through test digs in various regions of Namibia. The excavation of Apollo 11 failed to provide dates for the paintings on the walls, but the material remains of the cave floor could be dated. It had built up over time to a depth of over 2 metres. This depth indicated that the cave had been in use for over 70,000 years. The time sequence of Apollo 11 extends from the Middle Stone Age to colonial times; it reflects more completely than any other site in the country the key phases of Namibia's prehistory....

The oldest painted art was recovered from square A9 at the Apollo 11 cave. It is possible that this layer could be from a later period in the Middle Stone Age. The slabs on which the art was painted are loose fragments and definitely do not represent exfoliations from the cave walls or ceiling.

226

This has led to the proposition that the art was some form of prehistoric mobile art - ART MOBILIER - the French term for loose portable objects of art. As excavations continued and more pieces were found, an age of 27 000 years Before Present was obtained, making it the oldest rock-art to date in Africa. But this date cannot be considered completely conclusive as the carbon material in the paint of the slabs cannot be tested without destroying the art. The date obtained for the art came from analysing the organic material in the same horizon that the art was found. Therefore if the art is considered to be an example of "art mobilier", then it is possible that the art could be older.

Carbon-dating technique has improved and dates have often been pushed back when evidence is re-examined. The problem is that the quantity of carbon in the atmosphere is not constant and earlier dating was based on an assumption of constant levels. The Apollo XI paintings are now reckoned to be maybe as much as 35,000 years old, or even earlier.

Suddenly, there was a yardstick for African Stone Age paintings. There might be older paintings, but here was a solid anchor in time. At the other end of the time spectrum, paintings of sailing ships, men on horseback, battles with Europeans firing guns or war parties of Bantu-speaking tribesmen with spears and shields are scattered from the south-west Cape of Good Hope to the Drakensberg. Stone Age men decorated rocks in southern Africa for more than 30,000 years until the 20th century.

Apart from paintings which fade and are washed away, engravings litter the veld of South Africa, Zimbabwe and Namibia. Researchers G.J. and D. Fock, for example, recorded some 4,500 engravings on just one farm, Klipfontein, and 2,400 at another, Kinderdam A, in South Africa. Dr D. Fock has recorded vast numbers of engravings, many with elaborate geometric patterns, across a swath in South Africa following the course of the Orange River. Nobody knows how many sites there might be (or have been), let alone how many individual images there were. Undoubtedly the numbers reach millions from the Cape to the Sahara.

I corresponded with Dr. Wendt and met him in 1989. I found him to be a charming man with a wry sense of humour who lived in a small apartment in the centre of Windhoek, filled with piles of books and papers and maps papering the walls. He told me that engravings predominate in the Twyfelfontein and Fish River Canyon areas and in a broad track across the country where the geology is suitable. Paintings are more common in the Erongos, the Brandberg and in the south of Namibia. Engravings are found in exposed places and in horizontal sites, whereas paintings are found in shelters where they have been protected. Sometimes paintings are found in extraordinary 'secret' places, difficult to find and difficult to paint in.

He believed that engravings may have had a purpose for the community as a whole, whereas many paintings seemed to be 'private'. Geometric designs were generally confined to engravings.

When I met Dr. Leon Jacobson, who had worked for years in Namibia, at the MacGregor Museum in Kimberley, South Africa, we spoke at length about rock-art.

"Paintings have had all the publicity," he said, "because they are more dramatic in their way. I suppose they are also more interesting to the layman, especially those which are multicoloured. Everybody has heard of the 'White Lady' of the Brandberg and the 'White Elephant' at the Phillip's Cave and so on."

He continued. "There are many thousands of paintings in Namibia let alone the rest of southern Africa: the Cape, Drakensberg, Orange Free State, across Zimbabwe, Mozambique, Malawi and elsewhere. But there are probably many more engravings than there are paintings. Hundreds of thousands? Who knows? Much of southern Africa is vast flat plains and the only places where you can see paintings are where they are protected by good shelter from the sun and the rain. That's obvious. But engravings last for as long as the rock does not break up and crumble.

"As Dr. Wendt told you, there are geological zones across the land where you can see engravings where there are suitable rock faces which the artists liked and which have not weathered away. One stretches from Namibia through the northern Karoo into the Free State, south of the Kalahari sands. There is an amazing wealth of engravings still to be surveyed and recorded. Who knows how much more we still have to learn about the life of those people through their engravings?"

"Are there any noticeable differences between engravings and paintings?" I asked, thinking of what Wendt told me.

"Yes, sure there are," Jacobson replied. "Painting requires more skill, technology if you like. Anybody with a couple of hard stones can scrape or hammer out engravings on softer rock faces. Children may have done many of the engravings. There is a greater variety of engravings than paintings in terms of aesthetic and technical quality. And more of them, as I've said. As to subject, they painted or engraved anything and everything: every animal they knew, depending on where they lived and the environment of the time. They portrayed their own activities in detail. That's why they are so important ... And lots of geometric designs: circles, spirals, grids."

Andrew Collins in his voluminous and detailed work on the several psychic and intellectual influences on Neolithic peoples is much concerned with the artwork of shamans or medicine men. In his book, *The Cygnus Mystery* (2006), he concludes that what Wendt called the 'secret' paintings were always created during deep trance. The trances were pursued by shamans in order to discover the greater meanings of Life and the mysteries of the extraordinary night sky. This obsession was the dawning of modern religions which have been the most important influence on civilised mankind.

We who live inside houses and spend almost all of our nights indoors, isolated from the strange mystery of night-time and the stars above, glued to our television programmes or indulging in social pursuits, have lost our awe of the sky. Most of us have also lost interest in the quest for spiritual enlightenment. Twenty or thirty thousand years ago, and until today in so-called primitive communities, the sky and its greater mysteries are ever-present.

Really old pottery is rare in Africa; that found in the sub-equatorial region is from the last five thousand years, and most from much later. A mostly tropical climate with recurring wet and dry cycles has to be the problem of its survival. The oldest known pottery in the world has been found in Japan. It is generally known as *Jomon* which means 'cord-marked', which is a description of its decoration. Over 70 sites have been recorded with Jomon pottery. Japan was not covered by ice sheets during the last ice-age, but it would have been tundra with glaciers from the mountains; marginal land for people. But it was connected to mainland Asia by land bridges during ice-ages. People were in Japan after a previous glacial time ± 50,000 years ago and settlements of 30,000 years ago have been identified. The sites with Jomon pottery were settled after the last ice-age and many are dated between 12,000 and 10,000 years ago.

Pottery in the Sahara itself is another matter entirely. Earliest examples have been dated to about 9,000 years ago, not much different to the Japanese tradition. Presumably, it is because the

Saharan climate has always been drier than that of East and Central Africa that easily-found pottery relics have been preserved there. Nomadism and the abandonment of temporary and casual settlements has allowed pottery to survive disturbance by later occupation. It has been claimed that earliest Saharan pottery relics are older than examples from the Middle East and it is tempting to draw extravagant conclusions from this. But I am certain that the age of preserved pottery which has been found in this range of time is not relevant to a sequence of invention, but rather to the conditions which have prevailed locally since the pottery was made.

Suggestions that Saharan pottery is of better quality, thin-walled and polished, than early material from the Middle East has resonance with what John Kinehan told me at the Windhoek Museum in Namibia some years previously. Earliest Saharan pottery was apparently made by hunter-gatherers and I cannot forget being told by Kinehan that earliest pottery in Namibia made by Late Stone Age people was finer than that of later Iron Age agriculturalists. Is this because hunter-gatherers and transitional nomadic herders lived a 'simpler' lifestyle than agriculturalists, and had greater esteem for their few possessions on which they lavished greater care? It makes sense to me.

It may be asked why hunter-gatherers needed pottery at all since they did not store cultivated grains and I suppose the easiest answer is that in the Sahara, the Namib Desert fringes and the open savannah people needed to carry water from wells or waterholes and store it, and cooking coarse grains is necessary whether they are cultivated or harvested from the wild. Maybe wild grains were more important to hunter-gatherers in the Sahara and the southern semi-desert savannah than to those living on seashores and in lusher pastures of eastern Africa.

*   *

The rock-art of the Drakensberg mountains in KwaZulu-Natal is prolific and well known to local residents, ramblers and mountaineers. The Drakensberg art is believed to be mostly from recent millennia, but the amazing similarity of style from the Sahara southwards is easily remarked. Dr Lyall Watson, author of many books on life from *Supernature* (1973) to the recent *Elephantoms* (2002) wrote :

Southern Africa is the home of the largest open-air art gallery in the world....

In form, line and composition, they astound. In number, they exceed anything to be found anywhere else. The Rock-art Register at the South African Museum now lists nearly five thousand separate sites with over 100,000 subjects, and more are being discovered every year. All of which is exciting, but it is in intellectual content that this southern tradition excels.

Like the Saharan scenes, they include subtle portrayals of animal and human figures involving careful foreshortening, a skilful use of perspective in red ochre, orange and yellow earth colours, white lime and black charcoal ... The southern works also involve complex overlay and superimposition, extraordinary mythical figures, caricatures and elaborate geometric designs.

Professor David Lewis-Williams in his illustrated book, *Images of Mystery* (2003) writes about the Bushman art of the Drakensberg:

The sheer quantity of the art is breathtaking. In some valleys, hardly a single habitable shelter has not been embellished with at least a couple of paintings. A few large shelters, such as the one known as Sebaaieni (KwaZulu-Natal), contain over a thousand individual images. Moreover, important sites are still being discovered; the treasure trove seems to be inexhaustible. But sheer numbers are not everything. The quality of the Drakensberg paintings is no less remarkable than their quantity.

Drakensberg art does not merely astound with its quantity and quality. It is unique in that it is perhaps the only art of hunter-gatherers which has been explained by living people of that culture, unaffected by Bantu-speakers or Europeans. In the Drakensberg itself in 1873, Joseph Orpen was appointed British Resident in what is today known as East Griqualand. In the course of his duties, Orpen travelled extensively in the Drakensberg and obtained a particular rapport with his San-Bushman guide named Qing. Orpen was entranced by the prolific images and recorded them, and at the same time sought their explanation from his Bushman companion. Coincidentally, a philologist, Wilhelm Bleek and his research assistant, Lucy Lloyd, were working on the /Xam-Bushman language with a number of these people in the Cape. Using Orpen's copies of Drakensberg images,

Bleek was able to obtain further insight from his /Xam informants. As Lewis-Williams describes:

> Bleek ... and Lucy Lloyd took down 12,000 pages of verbatim /Xam language texts and prepared line-by-line English translations of them. The Bleek and Lloyd Collection is one of the most important collections of information on nineteenth-century hunter-gatherers, not just in southern Africa but in the world.

From these bases, research into San-Bushman rock-art, both pictorial and symbolic, proceeded with great strides in southern Africa. An understanding of the San-Bushman's psyche has been obtained which, though it can never be complete because the people have increasingly and irrevocably lost their culture, is more complete in that part of Africa than anywhere else.

I was shown 'Bushmen's Paintings' for the first time while on holiday in the Drakensberg in 1941 when I was seven years old. Later, I grew up within sight of those mountains and was privileged to be able to roam the veld and took shelter in caves where there was rock-art, and where direct descendants of the oldest people on Earth had sheltered and painted for hundreds and thousands of years before me. The existence of Late Stone Age African rock-art was a normality of the land I knew as a boy. I have enjoyed its purity and variety in many places since then.

In 1985 I visited the Hoggar in Algeria and wrote shortly afterwards in my book *The Reflected Face of Africa* (1988):

> ... We were taken to two sites close to each other in a small wadi with jumbled, rocky walls. Some of the slabs of rock and giant boulders had slipped and crashed down during centuries of erosion and there were several old paintings amongst the chaos of stone. They were unimportant sites and much damaged by nature therefore suitable to show casual tourists. Nevertheless, I was enchanted. Crude but unmistakable outline drawings in pale, aged ochre illustrated elephants, ostriches and birds which I was satisfied were kori bustards. I examined them carefully and took photographs. The style and the animals were identical to other neolithic paintings I had seen and photographed in the desert mountains of Namibia, especially at Twyfelfontein and in the Erongo.

In the Tassili and Hoggar mountains of Algeria no very early dates for rock-art have been determined but that is because Late Stone Age people were not living there in the cold-dry period before 11,000 years ago. The general style seems to me to be remarkably similar to the art of southern and eastern Africa, but there are also some that are reminiscent of the Dordogne and Altamira in Europe: more 'impressionistic'. The expert Henri Lhotse, in his article in *National Geographic* (August 1987), stated:

> ... this remote massif in Algeria [the Tassili] is enlivened by some 4,000 paintings and many more engravings. I consider it the world's greatest collection of prehistoric art.

Studying photographs of the early Tassili paintings, from before cultural transfers from the Nile and Middle East civilisations, convinced me that there was quite remarkable similarity between pictures of people of the Sahara and southern Africa between10,000 and maybe 5,000 years ago. There is that matter of 'style', but it is more than that: the illustrations show similar people. Their jewellery and body decorations are similar, particularly of their legs with strings of seed rattles and grass or fur fringes; their dance postures, the weapons they carried, the way movement was depicted. Much has been made of the 'roundhead' period in the Sahara, about 7,000 years ago when people were portrayed with blobs for heads. Blob-headed people are also common in the Drakensberg.

*   *

In Europe, the magnificent art of Lascaux and the other sites in the Vézère valley of the Dordogne, together with those in the Altamira caves near Santander, the Valcamonica engravings in Brescia and in many lesser known sites such as Levanzo Island of Sicily, represent what many believe was the epitome of European palaeolithic and mesolithic art. Because some of the European art was in caves occupied by people of clearly defined culture for limited periods some time precision is possible, and dates of 24-11,000 years ago are variously applied to paintings in the Dordogne (the late Gravettian and Magdalenian periods).

In 1994, a cave was found near Avignon with fine pictures of lions, bears, rhinos, horses and deer. To my eyes, the lion portraits are outstanding in their faithful detail and sympathy. It was named the

Grotte Chauvet and has been dated between 34-30,000 BP although this was subject to some academic discussion. The stylistic similarities between art at Chauvet, Lascaux and elsewhere suggested to some that the Chauvet paintings are not as old as has been generally accepted. If style is seen as the dominant determinant and chemical analysis at Chauvet has been somehow skewed by an unknown factor, then the Chauvet art is possibly no earlier than maybe 24,000 years ago. Interestingly, the Chauvet art can be seen to be divided into two distinct periods of style, also characterised by colour, the red being older than the black. The later paintings are rather more sophisticated and some seem surreal.

However, Chauvet was caught for posterity in a perfectly pristine state, and not damaged by an influx of visitors over many years as happened to Lascaux. The floor with Palaeolithic and Neolithic remains, even the charcoal of fires, was undisturbed for researchers to work painstakingly. The date of 32,000 BP can be determined with confidence, whereas a similar date for Apollo XI in Namibia is rather more hazy. Chauvet is stated to have the earliest cave paintings in the world based on this certainty, but I am not concerned. Clearly, rock painting began to be created all over the world in the same time scale. What fascinates is that it was relatively simultaneous, while differing in style (and some would say in sophistication) between Africa and Europe.

One has to remember, of course, that the artists were living during a cool period and there was great difference in climate. One has also to keep remembering that the European artists were Cro-Magnon and descended from people who had left Africa maybe forty thousand years previously, while the African art was created by those who stayed behind. This is portentous.

In the valleys of the River Beune before it flows into the Vézère, are the deep cave sites of Font de Gaume and Combarelles. At both, a cave opening lies up a limestone cliff surrounded by holm-oaks and patches of willow scrub. Within, there are twisted and uneven passages leading into the heart of the hillside. Late Stone Age men must have crawled through with sputtering tallow lamps to light their way. On the walls there are marvellous portraits of extinct bulls, mammoths, sheep, reindeer, horses, goats and rhinoceros. At Combarelles there is a particularly fine engraving of a horse's head with ears perked forward brightly and intelligence shining from its eyes. There are some strange faces or 'masks' of people, somewhat grotesque, like caricatures. An immediate response could be that they are some kind of effigies of mystical beings because of their contrast with the animal portraits which are real and executed with considerable sympathy and skill.

At the Cap Blanc site the art takes the form of a great frieze of wild horses carved deeply into the rock. They are wall-sculptures, not engravings, and show that over the several thousand years during which people were decorating the caves and shelters of the region every art form had been produced with the available media and technology.

At Lascaux the cave system has been closed to the general public since 1963, but a replica of the most important section was created with care and opened in 1983. The real cave's walls were covered with more than fifteen hundred paintings and engravings dated to about 17,000 years ago, at the beginning of the so-called Magdalenian culture. It has been determined that the cave was then open to the outside but a rock fall and deluge of mud sealed it until boys, searching for their pet dog in 1940, broke in. Being sealed up for all those thousands of years, the paintings were in pristine condition and astonishingly clear and beautiful. I have marvelled at them.

What has exercised investigators of Lascaux, and the lesser cave sites such as Combarelles, is the sophistication of the art. There is, of course, the technical competence that has to be admired; the use of several methods of painting, sketching, engraving and sculpting and the discovery, selection and refining of different naturally-occurring mineral pigments. Beyond that, however, there is the style that impresses with its 'modernity'. Perspective is widely used to vitalise the pictures. Jean-Philippe Rigaud, writing in *National Geographic* (October 1988), comments:

> Study of the works themselves shows that Magdalenian artists had great experience. Engravings were made with incomparable sureness; drawings executed without erasures, without 'repentance'.
>
> Some animals were drawn on irregular surfaces so that it was impossible to see the head while drawing the tail. This implies a complete vision of the animal by the artist. ....The use of undulations in the wall is frequent, and they give a surprising volume to the paintings...
>
> .... to give a third dimension, the artists have detached - by means of a blank or uncolored area - the legs

that are the most distant from the spectator from the rest of the animal.

The large pictures, life-size, are outlined with thick, bold rough strokes. Some animals are dotted with black spots, often seen in southern Africa as well. Horses, extinct cattle and bisons constitute 80% of the figures and it is shown from associated fossil deposits that they were the most sort-after prey. But there were also bears, cats, hares, boars and goats. There are few people except for crude stick-figures with blobs for heads, like a modern kindergarten picture. There are more of the mysterious dots, lines, squares and grids scattered about.

Dr Jean Clottes, the Conservateur General of the Grotte Chauvet makes these important remarks about European rock art which appeared so abruptly at about 32,000 years ago at Chauvet and was practised until about 11,000 years ago, at the end of the Ice-age, when sculpture and megalithic culture spread rapidly. From an article in *Adorant* Magazine in 2002, and published on line by the Bradshaw Foundation :

> Contrary to a well-spread idea, [European] Paleolithic rock art is not merely a 'cave art'. In fact, a recent study showed that if the art of 88 sites was to be found in the complete dark, in 65 other cases it was in the daylight (Clottes 1997). Three main cases can be distinguished : - the deep caves, for which an artificial light was necessary; - the shelters which were more or less lit up by natural light ; - the open air sites. The latter are essentially known in Spain and Portugal. Only one case has been discovered in France (the engraved rock at Campome in the Pyrenees-Orientales). The art in the light and the art in the dark: those two tendencies have coexisted for all the duration of the Paleolithic. The art in the dark was preferred in certain areas (the Pyrenees) and at certain periods (Middle and Late Magdalenian). The low-relief sculptures are only to be found in shelters. On the other hand, the paintings which used to exist in shelters have for the most part eroded away and only very faint traces remain, contrary to engravings which could in many cases be preserved in them.
>
> In the shelters, there have most often been settlements next to the wall art. People lived there and went on with their daily pursuits close to the engravings, the paintings and low-relief sculptures. The case is quite

different for the deep caves which usually remained uninhabited. This must mean that the art of the one and that of the other were probably not considered in the same way: in the deep caves the images were nearly never defaced, destroyed or erased, where as in the shelters the archaeological layers - i.e. the rubbish thrown away by the group - often ended up by covering up the art on the walls (Gourdan, Le Placard). The art inside the caves was respected, while the art in the shelters eventually lost its interest and protection.

I suppose the most notable difference between the paintings I have seen in the Dordogne and those I am familiar with in Africa is the relative absence of human figures. In Africa, people proliferate, in the Dordogne and Chauvet they are rare, but it is interesting that in both Europe and Africa animals are painted with greater care and fidelity whereas people are depicted in stylised form. In general, African rock-art tends to be subtly different in style to the 'impressionistic' art of Europe. A.R. Wilcox wrote in *The Drakensberg Bushmen and Their Art* (1984):

> The Bushman artist ... painted animals as he saw them, subordinating detail to the whole. His painting is a visual image recreated, though he might slightly stress characteristics such as the length of an eland or the bulk of an elephant. These remarks apply to the paintings of animals only .... not to the Bushmen's paintings of human figures which are stylised ... Observe the heads [of people] - almost always featureless, often mere blobs.....
> .... the human figures seldom appear singly; they occur in groups, almost always in some kind of individual action or group activity .... whereas animals, though often shown in groups, are commonly shown singly and may be in quite static attitudes.

Lyall Watson, in *Lightning Bird* (1982), states it clearly:

> The cave art of Europe is composed almost entirely of animals and abstract signs. Human figures are rare and descriptive scenes almost nonexistent. Prehistoric African rock-art, on the other hand, teems with people and narrative scenes. It is alive with animals, humans, and mythological

mixtures of the two. All are involved with, or superimposed on, each other in meaningful ways.

Watson quotes Credo Mutwa, a renowned South African 'diviner' and oral historian:

"Cave paintings are our [African] archives. Every one is either a record of a particular historical event, usually in symbolic form, or it displays certain aspects of legend, custom, and ritual. These are the illustrations to our oral history."

In Africa, from the Tassili, through eastern Africa down to the Cape of Good Hope, and down the western side seaward of the Congo rainforest, people are everywhere on rock walls: often dancing but also hunting, marching somewhere, disputing, sitting together. This, to me, especially differentiates the earliest African from European art. The African art seems to me to be influenced by the 'whole' of communal activity whereas European art seems to have concentrated on the hunting activities of the region.

The simplest explanation for the difference in style between European and African art is that the people were indeed different. The artists who painted in the Dordogne and elsewhere were descended from those that had migrated out of Africa about 80,000 years ago. There had been divergence of culture between them and Africans for a very long time. What is absolutely astonishing is that despite this, the very appearance of rock-art, and the similarities that do exist, was almost contemporary. It seems almost miraculous.

There is a clear common denominator amongst all Late Stone Age art and that is the variety of geometric designs and symbols. Everywhere in the world, from the Amazon to Australia, Late Stone Age people used zigzags, spirals, circles, patterns of dots, grids and cross-hatching to decorate walls, tools, totem poles, ivory implements, jewellery and, particularly in the later Late Stone Age periods, pottery. In early African rock-art strings of dots, zigzags or lines connect different figures in a frieze, or surround groups or particular animals or people.

Much thought and speculation has been given to motives behind the appearance or 'invention' of rock-art and parallels of decorating tools, jewellery and small artifacts. Most often, the explanation has been that it has been a religious activity symbolically binding the prey to the hunter, a visual prayer. But the variety of paintings preclude any one reason and, in the fashion of categorising that we often tend to, there has been opposing argument between those who think that the motive was a spiritual imperative and those who think it was creative impulse or drive; 'art for art's sake'. Indeed, the two are not mutually exclusive and it must be that rock-art was executed for a number of practical reasons, whether religious or for recording, instruction and learning, as well as for the pure joy of creativity.

Professor David Lewis-Williams and Thomas Dowson summarised these difficulties and the neglected importance of southern African rock-art in the Preface to their book, *Images of Power* (1989).

> Today research is coming full circle. Armed with what we know about Bushman religious experience and the ways in which it is emblazoned on the rocks of southern Africa, we are returning to the dark caverns of western Europe. Contrary to the received archaeological wisdom of decades, we are finding that important clues to the great enigmas of Upper Palaeolithic art have been awaiting discovery in an entirely unexpected place: southern Africa. .... we outline our new understanding of this art in the exciting knowledge that it points to the very origin of artistic activity and thence to some of humankind's greatest triumphs. Bushman rock-art stands at the centre of research into the origins of religion and aesthetics.

I believe Late Stone Age people painted and engraved for all the many reasons and impulses that people create today and the evidence is there. I have seen many images that must have been created by the finest artists of the community next to some which must have been done by young children or an untrained mind. There is a vast variation of subject. A few, clearly, were done deliberately by medicine-men or shamans in a spiritual tradition of visual prayers for the hunt, rain, recovery from illness or famine. But as modern people doodle on a telephone pad, decorate a dinner plate, paint great religious masterpieces or record events, for all the reasons that the human mind can conceive, so did people 35,000 years ago.

Sensory deprivation also induces trance and if a lamp was doused in the depths of caves with narrow, crawling tunnels deep in mountainsides the sensory deprivation would have been severe.

Working with the guttering light of a primitive lamp fuelled by animal fat, with no immediate source of kindling should it fail, requires exceptional motivation. This is especially applicable to the limestone caves of the Dordogne, where I have felt the sensation of claustrophobia and was immediately reminded of Dr. Wendt's remarks about particular 'private' and 'secret' paintings in places with difficult access in Namibia.

Could shamans or diviners have deliberately sought out such places to practice their art with personal religious symbolism because they were able to experience trance states in them? The universality of geometric designs which appear to have undoubted relationships to trance or ecstatic experience all over the world in the Late Stone Age indicates not only the universal experiences but a universal seeking for them.

Andrew Collins, who has made a study of the deep cave paintings and their artists in Europe, described to me in correspondence that there must have been particular powerful and pressing reasons for the artists, whether shamans or other gifted people in a clan-group, to seek these extraordinarily difficult and psychically painful places to execute their art. It is probable, suggests Collins, that the artists used mind-expanding drugs, such as certain varieties of mushroom or herbs. Collins also suggested that perhaps it was the acoustic qualities of certain deep caves that attracted them, where chants and sounds from musical instruments would have strange psychic effects.

It has been remarked by Lewis-Williams that San shamans in southern Africa, according to their own oral traditions, used cannabis to enhance trance states, especially animal transformations featuring snakes, and it was used to strengthen 'weak' shamans. It is usually assumed that cannabis was first domesticated in China and its use for fibre, food and drugs spread from there through India to eastern Europe by Neolithic agriculturalists in the last 5,000 years. Its use by Late Stone Age artists in Africa cannot be proven except during historical time, when it was certainly cultivated for drugs by all southern African indigenous people.

The assumption is that cannabis cultivation was brought southwards by agriculturalists in the last three thousand years. But cannabis is not the only source of mild hallucination. There is no reason to think that other sources of other mind-changing drugs were not known within hunter-gatherer society for many thousands of years. After all, the gathering of all plants and their parts, and their varied usefulness, was the mainstay of their lives and survival. Discovery could easily have occurred by accident when effective herbs or bark were thrown on a fire and the smoke was inhaled.

Professor David Lewis-Williams presented a TV documentary by the BBC in April 1989, when he was able to expound his views widely. He had examined research by neurologists which establish that when people enter a trance state they see geometric patterns: spirals, circles, dots, zigzags, grids and so on. This is a function of the electro-chemical state within the brain and I do not suppose it matters how the trance is induced. Epilepsy causes a form of trance and my daughter who suffered from mild epilepsy as a teenager always knew when an attack was coming on: "Windmills are starting!" she would cry. Epileptics are universally revered in Africa, because of their being forced into trance states by their particular affliction and it is reasonable to assume that most people were unable to distinguish between an epileptic seizure and an autonomous trance-state. Adrian Boshier, whose depth of experience in explorations of African lore is described by Lyall Watson, was an epileptic and this enabled him to gain particular confidences of learned tribal elders and healers or shamans.

Lewis-Williams saw the geometric symbols in rock-art as being the depictions of those entoptic (within the eyes) patterns which appear when entering a trance state. The pictures could be executed by medicine-men after a trance-dance when they were still emotionally excited by their experience, still more-or-less in a trance state. Many paintings in southern Africa and in the Sahara, show people linked to each other and to animals by 'ropes' of dots or enclosed by zigzags and other geometric figures. In the Drakensberg the animals are mainly eland antelopes, who are the noblest of African antelopes and the height of desire and respect by hunters. Although there are few people in the paintings of the Dordogne, there are the same geometric symbols which have puzzled researchers.

A number of native Africans, like Credo Mutwa, have written or stated that the symbolic images seen in rock-art have meanings. Whether they were painted by diviners still in the throes of a trance experience, executed by artists on the instructions of medicine-men or for specific purposes of their own, or by initiates or even children practising and 'doodling', there was a purpose. These symbols, it is said, were a simple means of communication. Each symbol had a

241

common interpretation which was understood by people across cultural and language groups. A hand imprint on a cave wall could simply mean: "This is my place, please do not disturb!" Hand imprints can evolve into stylised 'U' shapes. A sunburst sign can be part of a rainmaking ritual or represent a Sun-god, evolving to spirals, and so on. Many interpretations have been made and the move to scripts described.

Prof. Felix Chami of the university of Dar es Salaam is quite definite in his opinion that geometric designs are an early form of script. In his book, *The Unity of African Ancient History 3000 BC to AD 500* (2006) he devotes space to this theme. Symbols are written language in its simplest form and have clear examples in our modern world in international road signs, recognised from Chile to China. In any airport across the planet, a running figure tells where an emergency exit can be found or a symbolic man or woman shows where we may find a toilet.

In Africa and in Europe, or South America and Australia, a system of icons seems to have been in use long before the cuneiform writing of Mesopotamia or the *quipu* of the Caral civilisation of Peru. Modern computer programmes such as the one I am using as I write make essential use of common symbols or icons. But geometric symbols, perhaps described as icons, are only a small part of those profound changes which occurred 35,000 years ago.

Professor David Lewis-Williams, together with David Pearce, both of the Rock Art Institute of the University of the Witwatersrand, published an important book, *Inside the Neolithic Mind* (2005), in which they explored their latest conclusions as to why artists in Europe and elsewhere about the world painted and engraved so prolifically during the period 35,000 to 11,000 years ago, and then in Eurasia changed to widespread sculpture and megalithic structures. They explore the culture of this period when abrupt changes occurred in the human psyche, and relate it definitely to latest neurological research on the brain. Their work is soundly based on science. I cannot begin to précis this book properly here, but hope to expound on some of the points which I found most relevant to my thesis.

Lewis-Williams' principal theme is concerned with the extraordinary changes to creativity at about 35,000 years ago with the coincidental flowering of spectacular cave art particularly in Africa and Eurasia, which then abruptly changed in Eurasia to sculpture and the appearance of megalithic constructions, founding of settled villages and towns and the birth of agriculture and civilisation from 11,000. I have described Lewis-Williams' earlier investigation of the neurological explanations for the wide use of geometric designs in rock art: the entoptic images created within the brain and visualised by a mind entering a trance state. The use of trances by shamans or medicine-men of the San-Bushmen people, in particular, was the specialist field of study which he pioneered.

In this latest published work, he pursues this theme with detailed reference to the European and west Asian evidence. The difference between that and the art of Africa has already been mentioned; the difference in the style and content of paintings and engravings, and the transformation to sculpture at the end of the last Ice-age. He goes much further in examining the psychic mechanisms at work, but remains convinced of the scientific reasons. He sees that trance and altered consciousness is directly related to the emergence of formality in religion, all coupled together with changes in the physical workings of the brain itself which is the engine of the mind.

Altered states of consciousness, culminating in the passing into trance, progress through three stages: the visualising of entoptic spirals, grids etc (geometric images), moving through some kind of vortex often described as a tunnel or tunnel-like analogy sometimes with a sensation of flying, and ending in deep trance with vivid dreams and hallucinations. Probably an accomplished shaman could direct his hallucinations or follow paths previously experienced or regularly practised.

One can understand that this process occurs naturally with all people today when deep sleep is achieved. I often hover briefly in what Lewis-Williams calls the hypnogogic state of half-sleep when it is possible to consciously pull oneself out of an unpleasant dream, or when one is aware, however fleetingly or instantaneously, of passing from an alert wakefulness to unconsciousness. Most of us remember dreams of flying or whizzing along paths or tunnels. Occasionally, it is possible to re-enter a dream if one is not roused to be fully alert, pausing in the hypnogogic state.

Lewis-Williams and Pearce write in *Inside the Neolithic Mind*:

> ... We are agreed that they [the sensations of flying, travelling through tunnels etc.] derive from the sensation of passing through a vortex that is wired into the human nervous system, a functioning of the brain that recent

neurological research has located in a precise spot in the brain.

He extensively examines and analyses the use to which shamans put these neurological processes. He is particularly clear as to the way in which Late Stone Age people understood or employed this working of the brain from wide-awake alertness to deep trance dream state, and how this differs from ours today. Then, people valued all states of the mind, shamans being most concerned with an ability to enter deep trance deliberately for specific purposes. The range of psychic experience was seen as a 'whole'. Today, we have become most concerned with the alert, wide-awake state and dreams are seen to have no practical use or importance.

From about 35,000 years ago the dynamic explosion of artistic creativity exemplified the extraordinary changes in the workings of human minds. After 11,000 BP this process went through another gateway in the northern hemisphere. Along the Nile and in Eurasia, the awareness of the wholeness of life reflected in the extended range of psychic activity became formalised in religion which increasingly became entwined more firmly with daily affairs. It was a cultural template based on changes in the neurological system in the brain; it was a genetic imperative. This mind-set persisted well into the Christian era. Greek philosophers wrestled with the problem and it remained potent right through to the Middle Ages in Europe, and in parallel in other societies.

Lewis-Williams and Pearce:

> In summary, we can say that both neuropsychology and world ethnography show that the new universality of belief in a tiered cosmos [a structure of all religions], and in movement between the levels [of consciousness] may be ascribed to the function of the common nervous system in a variety of altered states. The vortex [the transition from a conscious to an unconscious state] leads through a tunnel or some construct down to a nether level, while flight leads up to a realm in or above the sky. ... Those who do [consciously experience this vortex] thereby acquire high status and are in a position to 'naturalize' their experiences, to proclaim their irrefutable reality. Those who do not , ... manage to glimpse in their dreams something of what the visionaries experience. That is their reassurance.

Later, in explaining the certainty of the 'truths' conceived within trance, usually by shamans or priests:

Because the levels [states of altered consciousness] are created by the nervous system ... people who experience these 'visions' believe that they can actually see the levels.

Confirming what I had surmised and described earlier, they outline the process of painting in the European caves from about 35,000 years ago.

Some visions of these preternatural animals [experienced while hallucinating in a trance] were 'fixed' with a few deft strokes painted or engraved on the walls onto which the functioning of the brain projected them. This 'fixing' was done either in a lighter altered state of consciousness or, after having been returned to an alert state, as they sought to re-create and control their fleeting visions.

At the beginning of the European Neolithic at 11,000 BP there is a paradigm shift from rock art to sculptures and elaborate burials with sacrifices requiring megalithic structures and temples. Lewis-Williams and Pearce, again:

Neolithic people did not - could not - challenge the tiered nature of their universe [the underworld, the Earth, the heavens]: it was wired into their brains. Nor could they ignore notions of passing through a vortex and flight: these experiences were 'hard-wired'.

They propose that there is a difference between the 'hard-wired' understanding of the cosmos in the Neolithic of the Nile and Eurasia and that which is maintained in the Late Stone Age of sub-Saharan Africa. Whereas the tiered imagery of religion, manifested in art and creativity in the northern hemisphere, was consolidated into vertical social and political structures, the nomadic hunter-gatherers of Africa, (and Australasia and the Americas) retained a 'horizontal' structure. In the northern hemisphere, society became increasingly formalised in the grand and classical civilisations where the Pharaoh or King often had god-like status with a complex descending hierarchy and a variety of megalithic structures and other material attributes to support it. This is the essence of the connection between

245

the shamans or medicine-men (or priests and preachers) with their particular psychic abilities, the art they generated and the emergence of religions and their power within modern mankind's culture and civilisation.

This 'hard-wired' tiered, vertical structure of the cosmos, manifested in the real world as a feudal socio-political structure, did not occur south of the equator. There was no shift away from painting and engraving in African Late Stone Age society. This only appeared coincident to the advent of metal-working and agriculture as it spread southwards. Rock-art was practised by shamans and their imitators by Late Stone Age, nomadic San-Bushmen in South Africa until after the European colonial period. The political aspect of this 'lag' behind cultural evolution in the northern hemisphere was the retention of a 'horizontal' social structure where the shaman or medicine-man was a respected and revered member of the community but without special political status.

It is extraordinarily important to notice that this clear division of the nature of art, which is the physical manifestation of psychic imagery, between northern and southern hemispheres, was parallelled by the different social and political structure of their societies. This absolute division emerged quite abruptly at about 11,000 years ago at the culmination of the last ice-age.

Lewis-Williams and Pearce see this 'lag' as being a result of the constraints of the savannah environment in sub-equatorial Africa; that hunter-gatherers had to keep to a nomadic life which inhibits a tiered or formal social and political structure. The 'hot-wiring' of southern Africans had occurred, but this did not force the adoption of a sedentary life and conversion from rock-art to sculpture because the environment dominated. Itinerant painting and engraving on natural surfaces continued with continued nomadic life. To an extent, I agree. But it is noticeable that a tiered or formal structure spread quickly enough southwards in the same environment with the migration of Iron-Age agriculturalists at about the beginning of the Christian era. These migrants brought with them a culture which had spread outwards from the Nile and been honed and improved in Nubia and along the Sahel.

These Iron-Age agriculturalists were semi-nomadic where their environment required it for the husbanding of cattle, but they settled wherever it was possible because their economy was based on cereal cultivation. Later, with other influences, such as trade, permanent megalithic towns were built such as Great Zimbabwe. They are known to have painted on rocks, but their main artistic expression was in sculpture, carving, decorated clothing and jewellery and, most obviously, with pottery. The 'hot-wiring ' was in place. Modern nomadic herders such as the Masai or Samburu of East Africa were of the iron-age but did not develop a tiered society, and this supports Lewis-Williams' proposal that an environmentally-induced nomadic culture is inhibiting. The Khoi-Hottentots of South Africa were Late Stone Age nomadic herders, economically halfway between hunter-gathering and semi-nomadic Iron Age agriculturalists, and also shunned a tiered society. This shows, once again, that there are no black-and-white rules to human behaviour.

A formal, tiered, hierarchical society - civilisation - spread southwards through Africa on the wings of agriculture and metal-working. This enormous change in sub-Saharan African society and culture did not reach the far south until the beginning of the Christian era. The rumblings of this truly sizable shift from horizontal to vertical structures might be what continues to disturb and ravage sub-Sahara African politics today.

It is in the last five hundred years that the spark of rationalism born in the European Renaissance increasingly caught fire, separating the everyday from cosmic awareness formalised in religion. This caused enormous conflict between the spiritual and the worldly which was strong even into the 20th century, and remains a troubled area today. In our modern technical civilisation formal religion has a small place in our lives, if it has any relevance at all, and we thrash about trying to order society with a huge burden of laws and multifarious regulation imposed by the secular state.

It is almost impossible today to understand fully the importance of the spiritual universe in the ordering of life for the Greeks, or even that of medieval Europeans, let alone in the earliest civilisations of the Egyptians or Mesopotamians in the misty far-distance of the Neolithic period.

Professor Nicholas Humphreys in *The Inner Eye* (1986) wrote:

> Yet in our own culture shamanism, as such, has evidently all but died. Admittedly, pockets of the old tradition persist in other guises: notably in the world of psychoanalysis where the training of an analyst closely resembles a traditional initiation, with its emphasis on transformation of the self, confrontation with dark forces, sexual confusion and so on -

all of it guided by an elder shaman who has trod the thorny path before. But such practices remain at the margin of our own society. At first sight it seems that Western culture neither encourages nor recognises the role of the dream journey, let alone prescribes a particular regime of fantasy.

In African and other tropical and southern hemisphere native societies, the roles of shamans or 'traditional' medicine men and women, and the malevolent activities of witches or wizards, are not only still recognised and employed, but are often on the increase under the onslaught of our technical, materialist civilisation. And within our Western Civilisation, 'alternative medicine' is gaining respectability as conventional medical practice increasingly relies on technology.

We are all still 'hot-wired' with brains which resulted in a psyche which ranges from alert to deep trance states, with a tiered cosmological structure first evident 35,000 years ago and then strengthened and defined 11,000 years ago. Like the hunter-gatherers and nomads of the past, the integration of this phenomenon with daily living has become inhibited by our environment, but in our case the environment is increasingly altered and controlled by our own artificial activity.

I am reminded that a significant part of this artificial environment is the nature of our limited and processed nutrition which worries medical scientists, because of increasing mental disorder and disease. Mental disorder and bizarre social behaviours must also be manifested by the underlying conflict between the 'hot-wiring' of our brains, which resulted in the first civilisations, and the inhibiting materialist environment of the Civilisation which we have recently created, and whose complexity we continue to extend and complicate. It often seems to me that these are dilemmas which we will not easily resolve and a global catastrophe, a rising of a Phoenix from the ashes, seems the only salvation for our species.

*   *

I have often pondered the appearance of music in Africa. Music and dancing is essential to the life of African people. The rhythm of African music has conquered the contemporary world in the guise of rock-and-roll. That conquest is not only of present time; all tropical tribal societies who chant and dance as an integral part of their culture developed similar style to Africans. Whenever I watch TV documentaries these days which show genuine, 'un-modernised' tribal music and dancing, from native Americans to Papuan Aborigines, I am impressed once again at the strange conformity with that of the San-Bushmen and other African music with ancient roots.

The particular cadence, pitch and tone of Pygmies of the Congo forests chanting and singing is similar to that of San-Bushmen of the Kalahari Desert and being lucky enough to have recordings of both, made before tourists intruded on their activities, I have listened to them sequentially and, to my untrained ear, they could be the same people. The singing and chanting of Central African Bantu-speaking people, without modern western influence, has similar cadence, melody and tone, but the differences can be easily detected. The Pygmy and Bushman singing has, for me, a simpler 'feel' to it, more emotional perhaps; while the Bantu-speaking people sang songs with more variation and technical sophistication. West African singing and music-making, whilst having an 'African' style seems to have greater influence from the Middle East, which is obviously because of the infiltration of people and culture across and along the Sahara, especially during the last twelve hundred years. Those particular influences did not penetrate the interior of central and southern Africa to any significant extent even after the 19th century surge in Swahili-Arab trading activity from the Indian Ocean coast.

The fossil record cannot give much evidence of ancient musical instruments apart from possible stone 'clappers' and stone gongs. In Africa there are places where great rocks show evidence of being used as gongs. Lyall Watson in *Lightning Bird* (1982) describes rocks in South Africa where there are places which must have been struck repeatedly by clappers and which produce clear resonating notes of pure tone. He describes how archaeologist Adrian Boshier was shown such a rock gong and heard its melodious ringing by an old man in the Limpopo Province of South Africa in the 1950s.

Stone gongs were used in savannah country to carry territorial and other messages in the same way as wooden drums were used in the forests. Henry Morton Stanley described how awesome were the great drums, hollowed-out from giant trees, of the Congo when he traversed it in 1876-77. I saw them myself, precisely as illustrated in Stanley's book *Through the Dark Continent*, and listened to their booming language when I traversed it in 1985.

Other than reference to stone gongs and wooden drums probably of very ancient use as communications media, any discussion about ancient music has to be speculative. But most modern percussion instruments have their origins in traditional African music. Drums come from forested regions and are particularly related to people of central and western Africa and those Bantu-speaking migrants who had most direct descent from West Africa. Marimbas are perhaps the best known traditional African instruments, apart from drums, but there is the bow with attached gourd sound box whose string is lightly struck and presumably had roots with the San as ancient as the bow itself. Bantu-speaking people took it over from the San and it voyaged to Brazil with slaves from Angola. In Brazil it is a central pillar of samba music culture and is known as the *birimbão*.

The Zulu regiments in their war dances created terrifying rhythmic sound by beating their spears on their cowhide shields and stamping their feet to accompany their booming war-chants. Handclapping is used throughout Africa and was the common group dance percussion sound accompanying singing of the Kalahari San-Bushmen and Congo forest Pygmies. Various combinations of seeds and nuts in gourds, pods and artificial containers were used for shaking and rattling.

When watching young people singing in a formal choir, live or on the TV, I am enchanted by the entranced expression on their faces as they concentrate on their singing. There is something special going on in their brains.

Rhythms were used to assist long epic songs or repeated chanted mantras that accompanied dancing. There is a link between trance-dancing and geometric rock-art proposed by David Lewis-Williams which suggests the simultaneous flowering of music and visual art at the dawn of the Late Stone Age in Africa. Since chanting is linked to poetry and language, it may be that music preceded rock-art but I am sure the two flowered together anyway, around that magical 35,000 years ago. Andrew Collins suggested that one of the attractions of deep caves in Europe for creating the psychic state helpful for inducing trance and the execution of geometric rock-art may have been the special properties of resonating sounds in such places. Equally, there is the special property of absolute silence in total darkness.

The uses of music and dancing have been observed often enough amongst the San-Bushmen of the Kalahari when a medicine-man either wished to communicate with the spirits of ancestors or when he was carrying out a particular healing task for one of his community. Holy trances and visions were frequently the reason for sanctifying people by the Roman Catholic Church and trances are used regularly in religious activity today in all societies. Music is used to facilitate all religious worship across the world. Monotonous chanting and fatigue-inducing postures and activities are regularly used triggers to trance. Espionage agencies and the police use them as aids to force victims to reveal secrets or to brain-wash them.

In the culture of the San-Bushmen, as has been examined above, there were no compartments or divisions, no dogmas or classes or definitions. Life and every individual's unique understanding and position as part of Life was within the *whole* of the Universe. Without people in South Africa like Joseph Orpen, Marion How, Wilhelm Bleek, Lucy Lloyd, Elizabeth Marshall Thomas and David Lewis-Williams himself, our knowledge of the psyches of the purest ancient lineage of the world's people would have been lost. How much more would be known of the culture of their far ancestors, going back to before the 'out of Africa' diaspora, if they had been given the proper attention they deserved before it was too late? Perhaps we would today understand more about why we of the 'out-of-Africa' peoples are different to Africans, what we could have learned from them, and how we could have controlled and guided our destined assault on African civilisation in the 20th century with greater care and caution.

What is tragic is that post-independence African governments in countries such as Botswana and Tanzania acquiesced in local efforts to expunge hunter-gatherer culture, or have actively harassed and forcibly re-located hunter-gatherers in the name of converting them to a sedentary 'modern' lifestyle. That this is being done by native Africans is bad enough, that it is being done without effort being made to record their culture is sad. Aggressive Christian organisations, such as the New Tribes Mission of Florida, continued to undermine or actively destroy ancient indigenous culture despite sustained criticism and opposition. This is scandalous.

I was lucky to be able to observe !Kung and GiKwe groups, still living outside the embrace of Western Civilisation and protected then by the *Apartheid* regime, dancing all through the nights of the

251

full moon on the banks of the Okavango River at Andara in 1975. Henry Francis Fynn, who often sojourned with the Zulus of Natal in the 1820s, described their endless dancing and singing all night and into the next day until people collapsed from exhaustion.

Those who have been lucky to have camped out in the remote African wilderness away from radios and music machines will have heard singing that has not ceased until dawn. In the late 1950s in Nigeria it was still possible to hear the endless drumming and chanting of village celebrations in the Niger River delta region. It is sad that, with the almost universal proliferation of electronic reproduction, traditional music produced by all the people in a community is disappearing fast. I watched Owambo village elders in Namibia trying to reproduce a traditional rain dance as long ago as 1975. After a while they gave up after shambling about hesitatingly, shamefacedly saying that they had forgotten how; and then proceeded to dance in universal disco-style 'boogie' to music from a radio station.

All people are dancers, Africans especially so, and dancing and enjoyment of repetitive music are part of being human. Maybe it is a genetically implanted behaviour, together with the need to scribble and draw, and to talk, to enjoy tropical seashores and swim in warm seas. Criticism of modern popular music and night-club dancing displays ignorance of the ancient common heritage of mankind. Only some of us can compose orchestral symphonies and paint masterpieces, but we can all respond to disco-music or military marching bands, and doodle on scrap paper or in the dust at our feet.

*   *

Rock-art pictures of people which abound in Africa illustrate the development of clothing. Decorative clothing and adornment, beyond what is needed for simple covering, is portrayed in rock-art and perhaps appeared at the same time. A continuity of style over thousands of years was also illustrated. People of different totems, age-sets, tribal groups or cultures, separated by thousands of miles and years, decorated themselves similarly whilst using variations to define their own group.

Henry Morton Stanley, often derided as a brutal colonialist transgressor when making his epic exploration of central Africa from the Indian to Atlantic Oceans, was a sensitive and admiring recorder of African culture when it was still without any local influence from Asiatic or European civilisations. He was astonished at the perfection and detail of adornment, extraordinary hairstyles, clothing made from every naturally available material and in the skilled production of everyday utensils, especially weapons and other ironware. He was awed by the dancing and singing, and the disciplined orderliness of the clans and communities he met. I believe that Stanley's memoirs have been sadly neglected by anthropologists. This is often true of the Congo region as a whole.

For many years the western side of the Congo forests was not thought to be important for rock-art. The rainforest comes close to the ocean there and as climate has swung from wet to dry and back again, the forest has encroached and retreated within the narrow band of savannah which forms a corridor along the Atlantic seaboard. Today it is drier than it was 2,500 years ago when the corridor was narrower, or even non-existent in places. At other dry times, especially during severe ice-ages, the pathway would have been wider and an easy route and a good settlement zone for people. It is not surprising that rock-art has been recorded in this region by researchers looking for it.

Dr Richard Oslisly of the Institut Paléontologie Humaine in Paris published a map of main rock-art sites. Peter Robinson of the Bradshaw Foundation wrote on their web site after interviewing Dr. Oslisly in 2002:

> This region appears to have been a major conduit for migration over a long period of time and therefore important in understanding the overall picture of population migration and cultural influence in Africa. The Western Central Africa section is categorised by location rather than by style or age : Gabon, Central African Republic, Cameroon and Congo.

The map shows one site in Cameroon, eight in Central African Republic scattered around the northern edge of the Congo rainforest, twelve along the Atlantic savannah corridor and four in northern Angola on the southern edge of the rainforest.

There seems to be no part of modern culture which cannot be related backwards to the culture-jump which occurred, seemingly spontaneously everywhere, but which is most noticeable in Africa. The possibility of a genetic influence becomes increasingly questioned.

Because Late Stone Age people lived a simple lifestyle compared to ours, we tend to assume that they were simple people. All writers who have spent any length of time with Kalahari San-Bushmen groups have described how complicated their intimate relationships were. As much time as was necessary was used to resolve conflict between individuals, no stress was left unresolved. The ultimate solution, where no internal solution was possible, was for individuals to move away. After exhausting efforts by the community, those in conflict either conformed or left, but efforts were always made.

Unresolved conflict or stress was intolerable. The need to maintain the integrity of the group created social stability and great patience with the eccentric or aberrant personality. Indeed, eccentrics were tolerated for their special talents and contributions and often revered. Interestingly, the typical San-Bushman band under stress in the desert numbered twenty-five, which is the sort of number that many gregarious mammals such as hunting dogs have found to be the ideal in sparse environments. It is the number which many school-teachers say is the maximum for a class. In more congenial environments, a band would number about a hundred.

Ancestors of the San reached a level of intellectual integration with the environment about 35,000 years ago which I believe has not been improved since. Probably they also achieved a level of group social and personal psychic happiness that will never be seen again.

!Kung San-Bushmen with temporary grass shelters at Andara, Namibia, 1975 Photograph by the author

Photograph: : Katie Hale

Pygmies by their shelter in the Ituri, Congo, 1985.

TWELVE : *THE "CYGNUS EVENT"*
Speculation on possible effects of cosmic radiation.

I have no expertise justifying an examination of cosmic radiation, in whatever form having an effect on genes and therefore on evolution. Having made that clear, I have included this chapter as a stimulus to thought, and because I devoted much time to understand the particular problem of the worldwide, spontaneous and almost coincidental explosion of rock-art. This phenomenon has intrigued and excited me for many years.

~~~~~~~~~~~~~~~~~~~~~~~~~~~~

There is a magic that continually emerges around the period of about 40,000 to 35,000 years ago. Without any doubt there was a particularly significant global event at about that time, lasting several thousand years perhaps. The flowering of creative aesthetics touching all of mankind's activities began then, exemplified in the rock-art, jewellery and decorated tools they have left us.

It is the usual order of time that I use to define the beginning of the African Late Stone Age in which this artistic creativity was developed. That is also when the Neanderthals of Europe and the Middle East disappeared from the fossil record. For many years in my reading and thinking, and listening to archaeologists talking, 35,000 years ago kept cropping up as a kind of evolutionary watershed. I *knew* that something extraordinary happened about then.

The universal culture jump to the Late Stone Age everywhere and the extinction of the Neanderthals could not have been coincidence. By then, Neanderthals had weathered several prolonged ice-ages. So climate does not seem to have been a major factor in their demise although it has often been suggested as the reason. Other large mammals had also been affected and some sub-species disappeared although there was no mass extinction. Indeed, it seemed that some species had seized opportunities.

As the 'out-of-Africa' scenario was proposed in scientific circles during the 1980s, I was comforted that my reasoning was being demonstrated by a growing volume of evidence. However, no clear explanation was available. Increasingly I thought about some strange worldwide mutation or genetic imperative but could not imagine what it was.

And then, on 21st December 1991, I was astonished to read a report by Adrian Berry in the London *Daily Telegraph* and I quote it in full:

> The ozone layer was destroyed 35,000 years ago in a disaster which lasted 2,000 years. At that time, people were nomadic hunters, and it helped rather than slowed human evolution. The cause was the closest supernova explosion in known history - the disruption of a star 150 light-years away - which ripped away the ozone layer and bombarded Earth with violent shock waves of cosmic rays.
>
> Evidence comes from the discovery of the element beryllium-10 in the Greenland and Antarctic ice caps. Prof Grant Kocharov, vice-chairman of the Cosmic Ray Council of the Soviet Academy of Sciences, said: "The explosion must have unleashed violent showers of cosmic rays which smashed into nitrogen and oxygen molecules in the atmosphere, producing beryllium-10."
>
> He and colleagues at Arizona University found beryllium-10 in ice that formed about 35,000 years ago.
>
> Dr Paul Damon of the University said: "From the density of the beryllium we have calculated that the supernova must have been within a distance of 150 light-years, a number in miles of only 900 million million."
>
> Mr Ian Ridpath, editor of the British journal Popular Astronomy, said: "For several months, the exploding star would have been brighter than the full Moon. It would have been painful to the eye to look at. It would have cast shadows and turned night into day."
>
> Dr Paul Murdin, director of the Royal Observatory at Edinburgh, said: "It is possible that the surviving relics of the explosion may have formed what is now one of the most beautiful objects in the sky, the Veil Nebula in the constellation of Cygnus."
>
> The physical effects on our ancestors would have been cataclysmic. "In successive shock-waves that would

have lasted for more than 100 human generations, the Earth would have been bombarded both by cosmic rays and by ultraviolet radiation from the Sun as the ozone layer was ripped away," he said. "Those who were prone to cancer would have died prematurely, but descendants of the survivors would have developed immune defences."

I spoke to Adrian Berry who told me that he had detailed conversations with the scientists concerned from which he had summarised his brief quotes.

I looked for some confirmation elsewhere of a close supernova in astronomically recent time and was pleased to find it from a study of radio waves. I.S.Shklovskii and Carl Sagan in *Intelligent Life in the Universe* (1966) wrote:

> There is one other curious circumstance which may be related to supernovae. For a decade, an unexplained detail has remained in our picture of the distribution in the sky of cosmic radio noise. ...
>
> A hypothesis of the English radio astronomer Hanbury Brown and his colleagues concerning the nature of this anomaly [a 'tongue' of isophotes, of similar luminosity, in our Milky Way galaxy] deserves special attention. They believe that it may be the radio envelope of a supernova which exploded very close to our solar system several tens of thousands of years ago.....

I was much excited by this. It seemed that an extraordinary cosmic event had occurred which could have precipitated major changes to life on Earth about that magical watershed of time.

Dr. Paul Murdin in 1991, quoted above, was correct in suggesting the Veil Nebula was the remnant of a supernova, but subsequent observations with the Hubble Telescope and instruments designed to observe specific radiation have given better information. The Veil Nebula is indeed the remnant of a supernova, but it has been determined that it occurred at about 15,000 years ago and was about 2,500 light years away. This is very far in terms of an effect on life on our planet. This supernova is generally known as the Cygnus Loop. But it is interesting that the constellation of Cygnus was noted for a number of large stars which usually terminate in supernovae, and in 2001 F. Mavromatakis and R.G.Strom published their proposal that there were two supernova remnants in Cygnus Loop. Uyamker,

Reich, Yar, Kothes and Fürst published a paper, *Is the Cygnus Loop two supernova Remnants?*, in the journal Astronomy and Astrophysics in 2002.

There seemed to be no indication available of age or distance of this possible second stellar explosion and there may have been no connection with the event which concerned me. I was now beset by doubts, but there was the evidence of the beryllium. Something strange and apparently random had occurred which had caused the surge in cosmic radiation, first brought to my attention by Adrian Berry's article.

Regarding beryllium, much work with deep ice cores in Greenland and the Antarctic continued after 1991. The focus of investigation into evidence provided by ice-cores is these days tuned to the problem of global warming which is politicised and for which funding is available. Beryllium 10 is an important marker in this particular research because its existence in precipitation also has correlation to sunspot activity, which in turn is related to the power output of the sun and its warming effect on the Earth.

From time to time I trawled through the Internet seeking references and found the paper, *A tentative chronology for the EPIC Dome Concordia ice core* by Jakob Schwander and others in Geophysical Research Letters v.28 no.22 of 2001. Although the examination was principally concerned with recent observations of various types to establish the accuracy of dating in ice cores, one of the bench-marks used was the 'high peak' of beryllium 10 deposition dated to 41,000 BP. Elsewhere, I found a date of about 40,000 BP with variation of 2,000 years noted.

I found an older report from the American Geophysical Union's *Earth in Space* in November 1995 which was useful though vague confirmation, briefly stating:

> Beyond their use as dating tools, ice cores convey specific geochemical information. Variations in 10Be concentrations are caused by factors other than accumulation changes. The existence of peaks in 10Be around 35 and 60 kyr B.P. have been attributed to increased production of 10Be.

The additional reference to a peak of Beryllium 10 at ± 60,000 BP, which indicated an unusual event could have had relevance to earlier advances in creative thinking and expression. The whole matter of subtle mutations, reinforcing environmental pressures, aiding or provoking jumps in culture, coinciding with extraordinary periods of extra-solar or cosmic radiation bore deeper examination. Scientific support was sparse, but my intuitive thinking about some kind of mutation-driven, speeded-up intellectual evolution between say 80,000 and 30,000 years ago remained active. The logic seemed sensible, but the physical data seemed to be wisps of cobwebs floating just outside my reach, brushing at my fingertips.

A severe blast of extra-solar or solar radiation would have caused extinctions amongst marginal species throughout the range of life. Hairless humans would have suffered and those who lived outside the tropics, the ones who were 'white', would have suffered most from strange ultra-violet solar peaks and other hard radiation. The demise of the Neanderthals could have been accelerated quite simply because they were pale-skinned. Dark-skinned races of Africa, tropical Asia and Australasia would have been least at risk from unrestrained ultraviolet radiation, but those bursts of cosmic radiation may have caused random mutation in all lifeforms.

If the Cro-Magnons had not yet become 'white' they would survive when Neanderthals succumbed. Intense, unobstructed ultra-violet light maybe killed those Neanderthals most subject to it and there would have been genetic defects affecting subsequent generations. The species was weakened and unable to withstand the challenges of the colonising Cro-Magnons encroaching on their territories, the rigours of an ice-age, or combat new parasitic diseases.

Drastic climatic surges, caused by extraordinary seismic activity from rapidly melting glaciers and ice-caps, inter-acting with the cosmic onslaught, some very short-lived as the atmosphere sought stability, no doubt results in the disturbance of many species. Ice core analysis shows that the end of the last ice-age about 12,000 years ago was abrupt, probably taking place in a matter of decades. There were more detected coincidental extinctions amongst larger mammals at the end of the last ice-age than at any time during the two million years of the Pleistocene.

The demise of larger variants of common species (such as mammoths, rhinoceros and cats in the northern hemisphere, the giant horse in Africa and a giant kangaroo in Australia) and the widespread expiration of herd herbivores in Eurasia and the Americas were probably caused by these sharp geographical shocks to a greater extent than any increased hunting by expanding Late Stone Age human populations. Late Stone Age people, and their predecessors,

261

had been hunting these prey animals for many millennia before their sudden decimation or extinction at about 12,000 years ago.

If hunting caused extinctions, then there must have been a most extraordinary increase in human populations! Modern elephants and plains antelopes in Africa, and buffaloes in North America, survived in vast numbers until the invention of the breech-loading rifle in the 19th century. I have never accepted the conventional explanation held by some anthropologists that hunting by Late Stone Age people caused extinctions.

*

The London *Daily Telegraph* gave me another piece of information which was relevant to extra-solar radiation. Robert Uhlig in late 1996 wrote an article based on interviews with Prof. Aman Dar of the Space Research Institute of the Technikon University in Haifa and Dr. David Schramm of the University of Chicago. Following the apparently cyclical reoccurrence of disasters resulting in mass extinctions, they had investigated probable local phenomena which could be the cause. Rather than subscribe to the idea of a regular invasion of comets or meteors, such as the one at Chicxulub in Mexico which must have been the final straw for the demise of the dinosaurs, they thought that supernovae, or the collision of binary stars, close to us may have been a cause of a number of extinctions. The merging of stars or nearby supernovae explosions would not account for all the extinction events, of course, but could be the cause of some.

Robert Uhlig went on to write:

> Prof. Dar said this theory [meteor crash] did not explain the great leap in biodiversity following the mass extinctions. He argued that the vast amount of radiation produced by a neutron star collision explained why the number of animal and plant species increased so quickly after mass extinctions.

Dr. Schramm said of Prof Dar's theory on the probable effect of star explosions and their influence on Earth: "We do know that there is at least one known pair of neutron stars [near Earth] which are spiralling closer together and will indeed collide."

I would say that the 'great leap' in biodiversity also happened as the natural result of nature abhorring a vacuum, but an increase in biodiversity can obviously result from accelerating mutations caused by external radiation. There is no doubt that our small and insignificant planet is occasionally buffeted by extraneous radiant forces, randomly, that enhance or retard evolution of life.

Other reports from deep drilling in ocean floors were concerned with the discovery of layers of iron isotopes which show evidence of there being a close supernova or other cosmic event sometime in the last 5M years, perhaps at the beginning of the Pleistocene, 2M years ago. The lack of time definition is typical of the problems scientists still encountered in pinpointing past events of this kind. Although I am considering another context here, it is notable that it is at the beginning of the Pleistocene that the *Homo* range of hominids first appeared and the *Australopithecines* began fading away to extinction. Other estimates place the supernova which caused the iron isotope deposits to have been only 100 light-years away which could have caused massive extinctions and mutations and suggest that if it occurred at 5M years ago it could explain the extinction of some hominid species and the emergence of the new hominin variants.

In 2008, A.M.Soderberg and forty two other scientists published an article in *Nature* describing their "serendipitous discovery" of the "extremely luminous X-ray outbursts at the birth of a supernova".This particular aspect of a supernova explosion had not been known before the extraordinary good luck in catching this evidence of particular cosmic radiation. It shows, once again, how massive energy outbursts occur during common galactic events, some of which can be very close to Earth according to the random chance of our chaotic universe. It also shows that we are still learning about the Cosmos.

Professor Richard G. Klein of Stanford University was a lone voice amongst scientific authorities proposing mutation for the cultural revolution exemplified by the explosive flowering of rock-art and other aesthetic developments. He used the example of computers to explain this evolution, explaining that Late Stone Age people's brains had somehow become "re-wired" or re-programmed, or its 'operating system' had been upgraded, while the hardware remained the same. I like this simile. His arguments have been attacked and his thesis had been muddied by creationists seizing on the concept as being further evidence of intervention by a Supreme Being. Klein has been unable to give an explanation for this mutation and the "re-wiring" of brains, and his hypothesis was seen as a lame duck. The 'Cygnus Event', or similar, provided the possible explanation he needed. I contacted Prof. Klein and his colleague, Prof. John Parkington of the University of Cape Town, an authority on the Late Stone Age, but was unable to get their attention to my ideas.

*   *

In late 2005, on a whim, I contacted Adrian Berry whose article in the London *Daily Telegraph* had started me off on this speculative track away back in 1991. He had become a much-published scientific writer and author and had a regular column in the journal, *Astronomy Now*. His interest was stirred and he wrote a follow-up piece in *Astronomy Now* of March 2006. After this article I received an email from Andrew Collins. He generously gave me much information he had acquired during his own researches and directed me to important sources. We met and talked in 2006. My enthusiasm for my proposals was abruptly re-awakened.

Firstly, as I had already discovered, Collins pointed out that the supernova in the Cygnus Loop had been shown to be recent and too far away to have had any effect on Earth. There may have been another supernova in that part of space, but there was no firm evidence.

That a supernova in the Cygnus Loop could not have caused the coincidental mutation in humans and other mammals at ±35,000 years ago was a disappointment, but other more important and specific alternatives were possible. Not only that, but there might be the possibility of a more general hypothesis emerging to engage the strange coincidence of universal cultural 'jumps' all around the world.

Cygnus X-3. Andrew Collins generously gave me the draft of a paper he had prepared, and provided numerous references. Whereas a supernova has to be very close (within 150 light years or less, as discussed earlier) to provide sufficiently powerful cosmic radiation to affect the molecules of the genes in sperms or ova, and thus cause mutation, other possible sources have been discovered and identified. Close supernovae are extremely rare and their peak of radiation lasts a short time in the region of months. But other extraordinarily powerful sources radiate gamma and X-ray bursts, and neutral particles at speeds approaching that of light.

264

These sources may be neutron stars or black holes in a close binary relationship with red super-giants or the massive and hot Wolf-Rayet stars which generate clouds of gas particles and radiation. These clouds are collected and projected in a concentrated narrow jet of enormous energy by the neutron star or black hole partner at right angles to its rotation plane, and they are active in varying strength for hundreds of thousands of years. They are increasingly identified in our own galaxy and others throughout the near universe. As our galaxy ponderously rotates and its spiral arms change shape, in a time-scale of tens of millions of years, the jets from neutron- and black hole-binary systems swing achingly slowly in relation to our own solar system. It has been determined that Cygnus X-3 is one of these binary systems in our own galaxy which lies at a distance of 30,000 light years. The power of its 'blazar jet' touches Earth.

Andrew Collins prepared a paper in 2006 explaining his support of Cygnus X-3 as a critical source of cosmic radiation affecting Earth. He refers to a number of scientific observations and enters into discussion of astrophysics, some of which I have omitted. I quote from a portion:

> Cygnus X-3 is today known to be a high mass X-ray binary, consisting of a compact star, either a neutron star or a black hole, and a companion star, most probably a Wolf-Rayet with huge weight loss. Discovered in 1967, Cygnus X-3 has been monitored across the electro-magnetic spectrum, from X-ray to infrared, radio, optical, gamma (γ)-rays and cosmic rays. It is one of the brightest galactic X-ray sources, and is the outright brightest during radio flares associated with the production of relativistic jets. ...
>
> Cygnus X-3 (RA 307.6 dec 40.8) has been identified as a source of high-energy γ-rays of an extremely energetic nature. Indeed, their initial discovery in the 1970s was responsible for a complete reassessment of particle acceleration in compact stars. As early as 1973 the SAS-2 satellite reported γ-radiation with a narrow phase interval of 4.8 h, noted separately in connection with x-ray and infrared observations of Cygnus X-3, estimated to be at 11.6 kpc. This periodicity is caused either by the eclipsing of the compact star by its companion, or the precession of a relativistic jet (Hillas, 1984). Cygnus X-3 is also thought to be a sporadic 12.6 ms pulsar (Chadwick, 1985) with γ-rays produced at or near the maximum (phase 0.6) in the 4.8 h X-ray cycle (Bowden et al, 1992)....

... The extremely energetic γ-rays from Cygnus X-3 were early considered to be 'the products of interactions between even more energetic particles within the source, mainly protons', leading astrophysicists to conclude that Cygnus X-3 was 'the first astronomical object to be identified with reasonable certainty as a source of cosmic rays', i.e. any cosmic radiation above 10^8 ev (Cordova, 1986), or, indeed, a 'cosmic accelerator' (Dar, 1986). Moreover, γ rays from Cygnus X-3 indicated that 'only a very small number of sources of like nature would be required to produce most of the observed high-energy cosmic rays.'(Cordova, 1986).

Among the suspected method of production of γ-rays were two popular models. Either they were protons accelerated by the electric field induced in the accretion disk held in the magnetic field of the neutron star, or they were accelerated by shocks in the matter accreted on to a neutron star or black hole.

... it was concluded that Cygnus X-3 accelerated particles to at least 10^{16} eV (i.e. PeV and over), and that if these were electrons, then protons might reach a higher level still (Hillas, 1984). Indeed, at Kiel the EAS reached energies near 10^{18} eV (Cassiday et al, 1989; Sommer and Elbert, 1990).

At the same time two underground nucleon-decay detectors set up originally to observe proton decays, Soudon (Marshak et al, 1985) and NUSEX (Battistoni, 1985, Baym, 1985), reported excessive muon fluxes either with a time modulation of the 4.8-h period of Cygnus X-3, or coincident to its daily transits. The flux from single-muon events was greater than several orders than that expected from high energy photon flux, suggesting most probably either a primary of unique characteristics, dubbed the 'cygnet', or a new mechanism for very efficient muon production in high energy photon-initiated air cascades (Dar, 1986). ...

On the Internet there are a number of sites discussing the extraordinary nature of this object and supporting the information that Andrew Collins gave me. For example, the Department of Physics and Astronomy of Georgia State University published this useful description of the phenomenon on its website in 2005.

Cygnus X-3

Located 37,000 light years away in the constellation Cygnus, which straddles the galactic plane, is a powerful x-ray source named Cygnus X-3. Although it is only the third brightest x-ray source in the constellation after the famous Cygnus X-1, it is much further away on the far side of the galaxy and is obscured by intervening interstellar gas and dust near the galactic plane. When this is factored in, it appears to be one of the two or three most luminous objects in the galaxy in intrinsic brightness. It has received attention because it is one of the few sources of ultra-high energy cosmic rays with energies in the 100 - 1000 TeV range. But its most unique aspect is the production of anomalous cosmic ray events in a proton decay detector deep in Minnesota's Soudran iron mine. These events have defied analysis and have led to questions about whether Cygnus X-3 is a standard neutron star or perhaps something more exotic, like a star made of quarks. Cygnus X-3 is a compact object in a binary system which is pulling in a stream of gas from an ordinary star companion.

Cygnus X-3 has distinguished itself by its intense X-ray emissions and by ultrahigh energy cosmic rays. It also made astronomical headlines by a radio frequency outburst in September 1972 which increased its radio frequency emissions a thousandfold. Since then it has had periodic radio outbursts with a regular period of 367 days. These flares are of unknown origin, but they are exceedingly violent events. Naval Research Laboratory observations in October 1982 using the Very Large Array detected the shock wave from a flare; it was expanding at roughly one-third the speed of light.

Cygnus X-3 has an orbital period about its companion of only 4.79 hours. Intriguing underground events in the Soudron iron mines in October 1985 included 60 anomalous muon events in a cone 3¡ around Cygnus X-3 with a precise period of 4.79 hours, so they clearly came from that source. But that requires a neutral particle travelling at almost precisely the speed of light, and there are no reasonable candidates for such a particle.

The most exciting discovery of these strange and exceptional radiations from Cygnus X-3 were described by the highly respected scientist France Anne-Dominic Cordova in her article *Cygnus X-3 and the Case for Simultaneous Multifrequency Observations* in the journal *Los Alamos Science* of Spring 1986. This was a report on the number of specially focussed observations at different locations of Cygnus by herself and colleagues in October 1985, mentioned in the article above.

Investigation of exceptional cosmic rays from the direction of Cygnus continue to be reported. (David Shiga in the *New Scientist* of 19 October 2006 reported on exceptional radiation recorded from the direction of Cygnus by a Japanese team lead by Michihiro Amenomon of Hirasaki University).

The latest information I have found on the Internet is an article posted to the Chandra X-Ray Observatory (NASA) blog by Dr Michael McCollough who has been involved with observing the phenomenon for years. The information he provided is unchanged from that available ten years ago.

Chandra X-Ray Observatory blog, 21 November 2016
Michael McCollough

Cygnus X-3 is a high-mass X-ray binary that consists of a compact object (either a black hole or a neutron star) in orbit with a type of massive star called a Wolf-Rayet Star. A Wolf-Rayet star has evolved to the point where strong winds have already ripped off the outer hydrogen envelope and the star is now made up of helium and heavier elements. The compact object is very close to the Wolf-Rayet star, orbiting it every 4.8 hours. Cygnus X-3 is a bright X-ray source because material that is pulled away from the Wolf-Rayet star by the compact object – in a process called accretion becomes hotter and shines in X-rays.

Cygnus X-3 is also a bright radio source producing jets that travel close to the speed of light (i.e. relativistic jets) and powerful radio flares that at times make it one of the brightest radio sources in the Galaxy. This makes Cygnus X-3 part of a class of objects known as microquasars. A quasar is powered by a supermassive black hole with millions or billions of solar masses that produces relativistic jets by accreting material. A microquasar, on the other hand, is powered by either a black hole weighing 5 to 30 times the mass of the Sun or a neutron star that produces relativistic jets by accreting matter from its companion.

In 2000, Chandra made an observation of Cygnus X-3 to study its X-ray spectrum, that is, the X-ray intensity measured at different energies. In this observation an X-ray source was found 16 arc seconds away from Cygnus X-3 (this separation is roughly the angular size of a penny observed from the distance of three football fields). Chandra is the only X-ray telescope we have right now that has high

268

enough resolution to see both of these close objects. In 2006, another Chandra observation was made to study its X-ray spectrum during a brighter state and make a more detailed study of the nearby source to Cygnus X-3. We found the source to be extended (not a point source) and that it varied in X-ray intensity with the same 4.8-hour period of Cygnus X-3 (but delayed in time). Because of the location of the feature relative to Cygnus X-3 and the similar variability, we started calling it the "Little Friend".

There is no doubt that Cygnus X-3 is an exceptional source of cosmic radiation, both of the range which is well understood, but of new types which demand further study. Perhaps there are more kinds of electro-magnetic forces and very high energy sub-atomic particles which have yet to be identified and which bombard Earth from enormously powerful sources. Collins and others point out that Cygnus X-3 is not in any way unique. A number of similar binary systems have been recorded. The relevance of Cygnus X-3 is that its blazar jet happens to be aimed directly at us. (The term 'blazar' applies to a stellar source with a jet pointing our way.) Andrew Collins dramatically described it to me as: "Looking down the muzzle of a gun!" There is nothing at all simple about the constituents of the Universe; it is its laws that are simple

Nevertheless, knowing that my 'Cygnus Event' was not a near supernova, but perhaps something of even greater significance, does not end my quest for a solution to the enigma of ± 35,000 BP. Indeed, new doors were opened, for the bombardment from Cygnus X-3 did not occur during a short and specific time, as would that from a supernova, but has been going on for a long time, maybe as long as 700,000 years, with fluctuations caused by its own position in the galaxy and the effects of other activity on it. Maybe both cosmic effects have been experienced: bombardment from Cygnus X-3, or a similar galactic source, and a supernova.

Beryllium isotopes. At the beginning of this chapter, and this train of speculation, beryllium [10] was the isotope which was important to the discovery of cosmic radiation effects in Greenland and Antarctic ice-cores. Other isotopes, such as beryllium [7.8], are also used to detect them.

Andrew Collins directed my attention to a paper presented by Aden Meinel, distinguished Emeritus Professor of Astronomy at the

University of Arizona, during the TAG Conference at Sheffield University in December 2005. Prof. Meinel and his colleagues had been researching several relevant avenues and in his paper he published several graphs illustrating results from ice-cores. He showed, for example, that the cores confirm the fluctuations of temperature which have caused the warm interglacials and severe ice-ages between the generally cool state of the Earth during the Pleistocene.

What Meinel's graph showed, however, is that the average planetary temperature proceeds in a series of irregular jumps downwards after each high peak and that every warm period starts with an abrupt upwards leap. All the jumps both up and down appear abrupt and there are no long periods of stability. Of course, one is dealing here in long periods of years and my use of 'sudden' and 'abrupt' must be interpreted accordingly. (More precise details of temperature change from Antarctic ice-cores were published by Dieter Lüthi and colleagues in *Nature* of 15 May 2008.) There are two sources of temperature change: random catastrophes such as volcanoes or meteors and cyclical change in the quantity of energy received from the sun.

The abrupt melting of ice at the beginning of the present warm interglacial has been detected at the end of the last ice-age, but it was thousands of years before the climate stabilised and the Sahara dried. Catastrophic floods resulted from the melting, but the Earth has great inertia and the force which causes acute atmospheric temperature change is followed by the expenditure of energy in warming or freezing ice-caps, stabilising the ocean currents and climatic structures of winds and rainfall in the atmosphere. An event which instantly freezes mammoths in Siberia or melts the northern hemisphere glaciers in decades must be followed by a sustained increase or reduction of energy for centuries and millennia for a generally warm or cold period to follow.

This inertia of the Earth creates what seems to be endlessly long periods of stability to humanity with a life-span of a mere seventy years. If it were otherwise, our core-ancestry would not have survived. Professor Meinel's paper proceeded to discussion on detailed analysis of the ice-cores and the importance of beryllium isotopes. He wrote:

> It was during this work [research on intrinsic luminosity of the sun] that we became aware of something in the archives

270

that caught our attention and that led us to today's topic. What caught our attention were two additional data archives. 1) the data on the annual variations flux of cosmogonic beryllium during the last 200,000 years, and 2) the data on the annual accumulation of ice, both measured at the same depth in the ice core.

Meinel correlated beryllium deposits, which is a measure of cosmic radiation, and temperature evidence and found no agreement. Cosmic radiation and atmospheric temperature variation were not precisely related. He wrote:

> There is no apparent correlation between cosmic rays and the course of temperature. There are many gaps in the cosmic ray data archives where a core segment simply was not measured for its beryllium content, especially where a sampling showed nothing interesting was happening.
>
> ... [but] There are two separate epochs in the cosmic ray record. The flux remains essentially constant until about 80,000 years ago whereupon the nature of the curve dramatically changes. Sinusoidal oscillations begin. ... It immediately looked to us like something was precessing. Could it be the source - or could it be the Earth? We measured the oscillation period as 22,000 years and immediately recognized that oscillations had the same period as the precession of the Earth. But what about the lack of any effect of the Earth's precession on the curve earlier than 80,000 years ago? ...
>
> The encounter [with a cosmic radiation source] began about 80,000 years ago and apparently ended only 11,000 years ago.

It is not possible to ignore the enormous implications of those dates.

The graphs that he created to illustrate these statements show that cosmic radiation fluctuations increased above a 'normal' level at 80,000 years ago with a sudden peak, experienced a more sustained peak at about 60,000 years ago and a substantial one at 40,000 years ago. They tapered off at about 11,000 years ago. It will be recalled that in references I obtained in earlier years and quoted in the first part of this chapter, the periods of excessive radiation around 60,000 and 40,000 years ago have been known for some time, but no professional scientist had apparently seen their significance in relation to changes in human culture.

This directly concerned my thinking regarding the planet-wide flowering of rock-art and decoration of artifacts from about 35,000 years ago. It also raised another important question: is there evidence of cultural change following the periods of 80,000 and 60,000 years ago?

And the answer is clear. At about the 80,000 years ago event, there are two significant changes to modern human behaviour. Firstly, there was evidence of abstract artistic creation proven from the South African seashore cave sites; and secondly there was the out-of-Africa migration from the Horn of Africa leading to the colonisation of the whole planet by modern people. An obvious question is why it was that African people with a strange new and advanced culture began moving so purposefully about the planet at that time? The conventional reason that I considered was that there was population growth following good times in eastern Africa and climate change; followed by a prolonged drought period which precipitated a nomadic thrust. I have referred to Stephen Oppenheiner and his book *Out of Eden* (2003) and Christopher Stringer & Robin McKie in *African Exodus* (1996) in previous discussion on this particular problem.

At around 60,000 years ago, I see a new surge beginning: migrants crossed the seas to Australia and explored far beyond the apparent previous limits of about 45ºN latitude in Eurasia. Colonisation of western Europe by Cro-Magnons began. It is possible that island-hopping and coastal migration began from northeast Siberia to the northwest coast of North America.

Is it possible that this behaviour may have been precipitated or facilitated by subtle mutation in these Middle Stone Age people's brains, caused by cosmic radiation?

Here, I have been examining the periods of around 80,000 and 60,000 years ago coinciding with radiation bursts described by Aden Meinel, but the importance of this concept has to be taken backwards into far reaches of time. I speculate that the major jumps in evolution which have resulted in modern mankind may have been stimulated by similar cosmic ray bombardments. Significant increases in cosmic radiation over a fairly prolonged period of tens or hundreds of thousands of years will not have been the sole cause of evolutionary jumps. That could be absurd. But the combination of climate change forcing great environmental alterations, which in turn forced migration and changes in diet and nutrition, especially prolonged seashore living and seafood eating, and combined with periodic mutations in soft tissue caused by cosmic ray bombardment, all coincidentally acting with feedback through natural selection may have been the magical combination of ingredients we have been seeking.

Meinel's paper examined mutation. He wrote:

> During our JPL [Jet Propulsion Laboratory] days we encountered this issue concerning whether astronauts could sustain genetic damage from cosmic rays during long space missions. Astronauts had reported seeing bright streaks of light whether their eyes were open or closed. This was concluded to be caused by cosmic rays. ...
>
> ... these various reports were limited to opinions from medical experts. But there was insufficient medical data to hazard more than a best guess how cosmic rays might cause DNA fragments within the ova or sperm. They also needed to know how these fragments could recombine to create new genes, whether these changed genes are inheritable, remain silent, or are lethal.

NASA was aware of the problem of cosmic ray damage to astronauts and conducted experiments to investigate. Here are the conclusions, posted to the NASA official web site (www.nasa.gov) in the Space Station Research and Technology section on 22 November 2016.

Anomalous Long Term Effects on Astronaut's Central Nervous System (ALTEA),
Developed by Italian Space Agency.
Project leader : Dr Livio Nanci

Posted to NASA (www.nasa.gov) 22-11-2016

Since the Apollo flights to the moon, it has been known that most astronauts experience sudden visual light flashes during spaceflight. Described in early reports as occurring in darkness and typically before falling asleep, these light flashes are thought to originate as an effect of high-energy particles, abundant in space, interacting with the eye and/or the visual anatomy. The ALTEA project, active on ISS [International Space Station] since August 2006 and currently investigating the ISS-US Lab radiation environment (ALTEA-DOSI, ALTEA-SHIELD/survey), has also been studying the risks of possible damage to the brain from particle radiation in space (ALTEA-CNSM). It is proposed that these interaction effects may go well beyond light flashes and could constitute a new kind of risk for longer space voyages. One study focus was on these abnormal visual perceptions and the impact on retinal and brain visual structures. ALTEA, with its 6 double detectors covering most of the astronaut's head, permits a 3-dimensional reconstruction of the energy released in the brain by ionizing particles. In addition, ALTEA monitors the functional state of the optical pathway in order to interpret the biophysical mechanisms generating abnormal perceptions. A survey was conducted in 2003 with 59 astronauts on the perception of light flashes, or "phosphenes", during missions. It was found that 80% of space explorers experience light flashes at some point (mainly before sleep when the eyes are night adjusted). As many as 20% of the respondents thought that light flashes sometimes disturbed their sleep. Light flashes are predominantly white, but other colors are mentioned, in particular yellow (10%). Most light flashes have an elongated shape, like stripes or comets, and are associated with a perception of motion. The motion is left-right or in-out, but never up-down, and about 8% of light flashes have a "blob" shape. There is a positive correlation between light flashes and radiation flux, and the majority of light flash in space is most likely produced by a direct interaction of an ion with the retina, although there is indirect indication that light flashes can result from interaction between particles and brain structures as well.

Solar Particle Events (SPEs) could represent a high radiation hazard for the ISS crew. During most of the December 2006 SPE, the ALTEA detector collected continuous data inside the U.S. Lab module. Results indicate that a SPE significantly affects radiation energy levels in the ISS, producing a substantial increase of low energy radiation rate, which reaches the highest values in quite short periods. This confirms the need to consider SPEs in those biological processes for which radiation rate plays an important role. These results provide the first information for charged radiation risk assessment in space habitats during a SPE.

When considering mutations caused by cosmic radiation, this principle must be always before one's eyes. Living cells may be changed by radiation, and the greatest concern is that they then develop into cancers. Research on male airline pilots in Canada and the United Kingdom and on female airline staff in Scandinavia show increased rates of prostate and breast cancer among them. But, those malevolent changes are within a living entity and do not survive their death. For mutations to succeed in changing the genes of a population, they have to occur in reproductive cells before conception, and the resulting offspring must survive to reproduce itself, and so on.

It is evident that many authorities disregard the probability of major genetic change through the action of cosmic radiation simply because the possibility of many similar mutations in sperms and ova in large populations seems remote with normal levels of radiation, normally protected by Earth's ozone layer and magnetic field. However, we are considering in this chapter recent evidence of extraordinary levels of radiation, particularly those strange peaks at times coincident to worldwide change in human behaviour. These high levels of radiation were also coincident to the extinction of the Neanderthals.

Aden Meinel ges on :

> If there were genetic changes induced by that surge of cosmic rays [at 40,000 years ago] they should have become evident relatively soon after the 40 Ky event. Thus we noted with interest the frequent appearance of 40 Ky BP in connection with the new species, as reported in recent issues of *Science* and *Nature*.

He then proceeds to speculate on possible scenarios resulting from probable mutation. He suggests:

> ... The transformation would be imperceptively slow, yet accomplish physiological and mental changes to yield the capabilities of modern humans. It could have been so gradual that it neither induced social stress nor heightened the normal level of inter-group hostility. Life simply went on as though nothing was happening.

Here, for the first time, I was reading material from an academic scientist with much experience in astronomical disciplines who linked proven bursts of exceptional cosmic radiation to possible evolutionary mutation.

Dr. Paul LaViolette and his theses. Stimulated by Andrew Collins' material and casting about on the Internet, I found Dr. LaViolette's website and discovered that he has been researching cosmic radiation for many years. He is Director of an independent research institute in the U.S.

LaViolette is the author of an alternative theory of the origin of galactic energy sources and therefore his research may be viewed with scepticism by many scientists, but it is his work on cosmic radiation effects on Earth with which I am concerned here.

His thesis is that massive blasts of gamma radiation originate from the region of the centre of the galaxy caused by the continual production of energy at that location. He asserts that this is true of all galaxies and nebulae. The physics argument for this is beyond the scope of this chapter. As part of this phenomenon, these gamma ray bursts are preceded by a gravity wave which propels gas and dust particles outwards from the galaxy centre.

The local effect of these events are that, firstly, gas and dust particles are blown into our solar system and a principal result is that the sun's surface is activated causing unusual solar flares and increased activity which can extend as far as the orbit of Earth. Gas and dust intrusions interfere with the magnetic fields of the planets and the solar system as a whole. Interference with the sun increases its radiance and its solar flares can 'scorch' nearby bodies. The spectrum of the sun's radiation is shifted towards both infra-red and ultra-violet during different phases of activity and both have major effects on our climate and the health and survival of animals. Visible light may be 'dimmed' by these spectrum shifts. The phenomenon of extreme solar flares is generally accepted and is not particular to LaViolette's thesis.

The arrival of a massive burst of gamma and other cosmic radiation has less obvious results. Normally, gamma radiation is mostly absorbed by our atmosphere. However, when LaViolette's postulated bursts arrive, they are hugely in excess of any 'normal' background radiation and when coincident with other anomalies resulting from the gravity wave and dust intrusions overwhelm Earth's defences. The searing effect of gamma radiation itself may be life-threatening and cause mutations and extinctions.

276

LaViolette is certain that a particular 'starburst' event with a gravity super-wave and intense gamma radiation occurred, maybe several times, at the end of the last ice-age. Relating such an event to our present time, LaViolette predicts the shutdown of electronic devices, damage to power systems and widespread disruption and chaos to our civilisation.

In the abstract to his paper, *Evidence for a Global Warming at the Termination I Boundary and Its Possible Cosmic Dust Cause,* he wrote:

A comparison of northern and southern hemispheric paleotemperature profiles suggests that the Bölling-Alleröd Interstadial, Younger Dryas stadial, and subsequent Preboreal warming which occurred at the end of the last ice-age were characterized by temperatures that changed synchronously in various parts of the world, implying that these climatic oscillations were produced by significant changes in the Earth's energy balance.

These globally coordinated oscillations are not easily explained by ocean current mechanisms such as bistable flipping of ocean deep-water production or regional temperature changes involving the NW/SE migration of the North Atlantic polar front. They also are not accounted for by Earth orbital changes in seasonality or by increases in atmospheric CO_2 or CH. On the other hand, evidence of an elevated cosmic ray flux and of a major interstellar dust incursion around 15,800 years B.P. suggest that a cosmic ray wind driven incursion of interstellar dust and gas may have played a key role through its activation of the Sun and alteration of light transmission through the interplanetary medium.

This is a long and comprehensive paper and, together with much other material, it was available on the Starburst Foundation website. Amongst the conclusions, he wrote:

... the Sun was unusually active during the global warming period at the end of the last ice-age from about 16,000 to 11,000 years BP. It is likely that the Sun was also particularly active at earlier times, particularly during interstadial periods (e.g., 36 - 31 kyrs BP) and during the termination of the previous ice-age (136 - 128 kyrs BP). However since data is lacking on the degree of solar activity during these

277

periods, the data has been adjusted only for the period ending the last ice-age. ...

There was great detail in this paper which was an extended scientific description of the mechanism of the last ice-age. Several tables showing ice-core readings and cosmic radiation calculations corelating to known glacial and interglacial periods were included. The list of references seems equally exhaustive. He wrote at the end:

Ice Core Chronology and the Assumption of Synchronous Climatic Change . The [above] ice core chronologies are derived by correlating climatic boundaries seen in the Byrd and Vostok ice core oxygen isotope profiles with those seen in the well-dated GRIP ice core from Summit, Greenland (Johnsen, et al., 1992). In correlating the ice core isotope profiles, we have assumed that major changes in climate occur contemporaneously in both the northern and southern hemispheres and hence that distinct climatic change boundaries evident in the GRIP ice core may be matched up with similar boundaries in the Byrd Station and Vostok ice cores. The assumption that the Earth's climate warmed and cooled in a globally synchronous manner at the end of the last ice-age is supported by evidence from dated land, sea, and ice climate profiles which show that the Bölling/Alleröd/Younger Dryas oscillation occurred synchronously in both northern and southern latitudes. This evidence has been reviewed above ... The chronology adopted here for the Byrd core is consistent with that of Beer et al. (1992) which was obtained by correlating distinctive 10Be concentration peaks found in both the Byrd Station, Antarctica and Camp Century, Greenland isotope records, some peaks dating as early as 12 – 20 kyrs BP. The Camp Century isotope profile, in turn, has been accurately dated through correlation with the annual layer dated Summit, Greenland isotope profile.

It is enormously important that at about 11,000 years ago, at the end of the last Ice-age, mankind underwent such extraordinary psychic and cultural changes which have resulted in a drastic modification in the natural order of our planet. From that time onwards, instead of mankind being just one species within the envelope of all life, we began to dominate. From that beginning of domestication of other species, especially vegetation, we have proceeded through technical mastery to change vast areas of the terrestrial environment. Our efforts may equal, some suggest potentially exceed, the effects of externally-imposed global change.

The evidence from ice-cores shows that there were external influences at work with peaks of activity at different times, and these may have coincided between 15,000 and 11,000 years ago. It could be that cosmic radiation from Cygnus X-3 coincided with, or stimulated, other sources as described by Paul LaViolette. Undoubtedly, whatever scientific doubts or arguments there may be on this matter, the evidence of dramatic change within our forebears is clear. We do dominate our planet now, and the fate of all lifeforms is in our hands.

*   *

Our skeletal structure did not change between 100,000 and 10,000 years ago and our skulls are the same. It is what goes on inside those skulls which is different. Palaeontology and anatomical studies of skulls cannot provide proof of a mutation within our soft tissues. It is the evidence of abrupt efflorescence of culture and behavioural change, exemplified in the worldwide explosion of rock-art from 35,000 years ago, which is the potent signpost. Another extraordinary efflorescence occurred at about 11,000 years ago with the rapid development of agriculture and urban society in the Middle East.

Andrew Collins in exploratory conversations asked me why I had concluded that cosmic radiation, from whatever source, had contributed to the development of the African Late Stone Age at about 35,000 years ago. I replied along these lines:

"Knowing perfectly well that it is an obvious circular argument, I could not stop thinking that there had to be something beyond climatic or other factors which could trigger such a tremendous change in culture all over the world inhabited by people at that time. We are what we are. And the demise of the Neanderthals by Cro-Magnon impact also seemed too easy and slipshod an explanation. There had to be some extra-terrestrial event, but I could not think of what it would be. It had worried at me for years.

"And then I came across that brief article by Adrian Berry in 1991, purely by chance. How many pages of daily newspapers do you skim through without picking up a small column? Berry's story had been a revelation.

"A burst of cosmic radiation at the right period, which had seemed to eminent scientists specialising in the relevant disciplines to be sufficiently

powerful to blow away the ozone layer and cause extinctions and mutations, was so strikingly obvious. And if it happened in 35,000BP or a few thousand years earlier, what about the other milestones in behavioural evolution? What about the first hominids? What about the first imagining of stone tool-making from chunks of rock and the taming of fire; amazing developments which require forethought and abstract reasoning? And what about those other milestones? The first migrations of early Homo erectus, the second major out-of-Africa migration of later Homo erectus associated with mitochondrial Eve, the first tentative steps to art and decoration and the coincidental out-of-Africa migration of homo sapiens? The development of agriculture, tiered hierarchical society and cities?

"Climate and environment, and most especially seafood nutrition for long periods, were always dominating driving forces in our evolution performing relatively gradual mutation of our genes, working with natural selection. But surely it may be bursts of cosmic radiation with strongly induced mutation which were the triggering mechanisms.

"It's the combination of forces, coming together at crucial times."

Seashore-living early hominins, and later *homo erectus* and *homo sapiens*, had the necessary nutritional regime at the seashore of the Indian Ocean with epigenetic activity at work to be affected by mutation from a cosmic radiation burst. Chimps and the other great apes did not have that nutritional advantage, and they were sheltering within the high rainforests.

The Universe is vastly complex and chaotic, beyond our capacity to understand. Despite our apparent mastery of so many branches of science, there are many of the most important first principles of existence which we still guess at, and try mathematical models to explain what is probably never going to be explained. Returning to consideration of our own small planet and our own extraordinary species, we have difficulty in seeing 'the whole', because even at our level the complexity is enormous. We think about and experiment with bits and pieces. Human evolution has to be examined within the widest possible spectrum of knowledge and speculation.

"What is past, is prologue."

Shakespeare.

Samburu women on the Ewaso Ngiro near Archers Post, Kenya, 1985.

!Kung women at the Okavango River, Namibia, 1975. (Photos by the author.)

THIRTEEN : *MODERN SUB-SAHARAN AFRICAN PEOPLES*
A brief overview of modern African divergence.

Note : there is a problem with naming these peoples. It is fashionable in South Africa to use new variations, but Khoisan is still acceptable. But there seems to be no politically-correct name for the rest of the Sub-Saharan peoples. Negroid was used in anthropology but is discouraged because of possible racist abuse. In this chapter I have used Negroid from necessity to refer to the non-Khoisan, or 'the rest' of sub-Saharan native Africans. Clearly, its use here is not a racist activity.

~~~~~~~~~~~~~~~~

In Africa *Homo erectus* evolved to *Homo sapiens*. In western Eurasia the Neanderthals were the descendants and in eastern Asia there were divergent pockets such as *Homo Floresiensis* which survived until the last ice age. If *Homo helmei* was indeed a distinct species or a significant divergent race in Africa it seems to have been a temporary diversion which did not survive. Africa was the cradle of mankind, the heartland, the core-land, as it has always been.

The Sahara has always been a great geographical boundary between tropical Africa and the rest of the world. The Sahara was the giant portal dividing the tropical core-lands of eastern Africa from the vast spaces of Eurasia for long periods of many thousands of years and this has global importance. Perhaps people first understood something of geography sometime around the prominent warm interglacial centred about 240,000 and a lesser one about 210,000 years ago, when it is assumed evolution was proceeding to *Homo sapiens* in some mysterious jump.

200,000 years ago hard evidence of *Homo sapiens* appeared in Africa. Palaeontologists found skulls in the Great Rift Valley in Ethiopia dated to about 190,000 BP and genetics support this date when mitochondrial Eve's haplogroup R0 split into two main branches in Africa, L0 and L1. Haplogroup L0 is the parent of the Khoisan and L1 is the parent of all other contemporary Black Africans, the Negroids. It is from this latter branch of the genetic tree that modern *Homo sapiens* migrated 'out-of-Africa' to people the rest of the world; merging with or displacing the Neanderthals and the descendants of *Homo erectus* in eastern Asia.

My story of the evolution of mankind along a route dominated by the Indian Ocean littoral of Africa with its abundance of seafoods and their special nutritional advantage for mammals ends here. But, I have succumbed to a temptation to go just a little further, to examine latest discoveries about the divergence of sub-Saharan Africans into their two main branches.

*   *

It would seem that after major genetic change occurred about 200,000 years ago, two emergent populations diverged genetically and occupied distinct areas of the continent. An assumption must be that this differentiation occurred because of adaptation to different environments and it is easy to assume that the differentiation was simple: one group of the new people became adapted and habituated to the eastern savannahs with their vital Indian Ocean seashore, and the other to the forest fringes along the Sahel belt, from which base they learned how to live within the central and western rainforest zone. The Khoisan were the savannah people and the Negroids were the forest people.

But, it cannot have been a simple distinction, because climatic cycles with varying environments would blur the edges and there was the great pulsing mass of the Sahara, from wet to dry, green to sand, and back again as climate swung. The ancestral Negroid people would have been most affected by these pulsations, being pushed back and forth and having to increasingly learn the alternate ways of the deep forest and the limits of desert subsistence in order to survive. Thus, Negroids themselves diverged into those who lived on the fringes and those who became specialised to forests. The genetic trail echoes this for there are a great many more branches to the Negroid genetic tree than there are to the Khoisan.

Whatever happened to the Sahara as climate swung, also happened in the southern mirror, the Namib-Kalahari. But Africa is considerably narrower at the southern tropic than it is across the

Sahara. The Sahara was empty of people for long periods and so was the Kalahari, but there was a broad eastern path around the Kalahari. The severe desert periods broke up the continuity of occupation, populations declined and there were migrations.

In contrast to West Africa where cyclical changes in Saharan climate repeatedly compressed people into constricting geography, whatever rigours changing climate imposed on people in eastern-southern Africa, at whatever stage of evolution and technical development, migration could always find a viable homeland for sparse populations within the greater geographical zone. Eastern Africa is the core-land and its geography has always been the most suitable to the core-people. Over long time, the acceptance by nomadic people in eastern-southern Africa of the necessity to accommodate each other, as climate changed, resulted in a remarkably peaceable trait, infrequently found elsewhere. Together with peaceableness, the particular social mechanism of clientship was perfected. After all, mankind was born and matured there.

The Khoisan people inhabited a widespread range. The savannahs of Africa were their ancestral lands and whereas the Pygmies and the Negroids diverged genetically within the tropical forests and their fringes, affected to a greater or lesser extent by the pulsing Sahara, the Khoisan line of descent remained clear.

According to recent genetic studies, the divergence of the Khoisan from the rest of African peoples had occurred at 150,000 BP with the appearance of the haplogroup L0 which descends from R0, while the rest of African peoples are of the haplogroup L1 with numerous subdivisions over time. This suggests that the Negroid peoples were distinguishable at about that time in central-west Africa whilst the ancestors of the Khoisan thereafter inhabited the eastern savannahs from Ethiopia to the Cape.

Doron M. Behar, and his several colleagues wrote in the Introduction to their important paper, *The Dawn of Human Matrilineal Diversity*, in *The American Journal of Human Genetics* 82, 1130–1140, May 2008:

> Current genetic data support the hypothesis of a predominantly single origin for anatomically modern humans. The phylogeny of the maternally inherited mitochondrial DNA (mtDNA) has played a pivotal role in this model by anchoring our most recent maternal common ancestor to sub-Saharan Africa and suggesting a single

dispersal wave out of that continent which populated the rest of the world much later. However, despite its importance as the cradle of humanity and the main location of anatomically modern humans for most of their existence, the initial Homo sapiens population dynamics and dispersal routes remain poorly understood. The human mtDNA phylogeny can be collapsed into two daughter branches, L0 and L10203040506 (L105),located on opposite sides of its root. The L105 branch is far more widespread and has given rise to almost every mtDNA lineage found today, with two clades on this branch, (L3)M and (L3)N, forming the bulk of world wide non-African genetic diversity and marking the out-of-Africa dispersal 50,000–65,000 years before present (abl).

This entangled pattern of mtDNA variation gives an initial impression of lack of internal maternal genetic structure within the continent. Alternatively, it might indicate the elimination of such an early structure because of massive demographic shifts within the continent, most dominant of which was certainly the recent Bantu expansions [in the last 3-5,000 years] and spread of agriculturist style of living. However, some L(xM,N) clades do show significant phylogeographic structure in Africa, such as the localization of 1c1a to central Africa or the localization of L0d andL0k (previously L1d and L1k) to the Khoisan people, in which they account for over 60% of the contemporary mtDNA gene pool.

These authors clearly identify the Khoisan but do not state where the Pigmy people stand on their tree. Stephen Oppenheimer in *Out of Eden* (2003) quotes a genetic tree which shows that they diverged from the Khoisan at about 57,000 BP, but that diversion would have been on the eastern side of the Congo Basin, the side which bordered the Great Rift Valley and the savannah plains. In the deepest heart of the forest, the climatic pulses were hardly felt. Here, the turmoil which honed the Negroid peoples was stilled and millennia might pass with no indication of change. It is the environment which nurtured the gorilla and chimpanzee who have lived in evolutionary tranquillity.

Pygmies became specialists, experts in rainforest living. Their small size, which is their distinguishing feature today, when they can be found untouched by today's world, was restricted by their particular nutritional regime which is low in protein and short of some essential minerals including iodine. Rainforest living results in most mammals being reduced in size compared to their brothers and cousins who inhabit more varied habitats. Forest elephants are smaller than those living on the savannah; bonobo chimps of the deep Congo basin are smaller than the common chimps who live on the outer fringes. The Pygmy tribal group known today for their particularly small stature are the Mbuti with an average height of the men of 130 cms, which is 4 feet 3 inches. Contemporary examples of forest specialisation can still be observed in the dwindling numbers of Pygmies in the Ituri Forest of the Congo. Today there may be only a few thousand Pygmies left who have unique genetics and live by a rough approximation of their ancient lifestyle.

Obviously there was mingling at the edge of the deep core of the African rainforest. It was where information and culture, and genes, were exchanged between the Pygmies at that edge and those of the diverging Negroid peoples. On the western side of the Congo Basin, there was no geographical border within the forest. There was no exact dividing line, all of the forest dwellers were modern *Homo sapiens* and racial difference never proceeded to speciation. From the central core deep in the Congo to the fringe of the Sahel savannah the genetic and cultural difference was gradual, unstable and never had fixed boundaries.

A delightful book, *Gorillas Were my Neighbours,* by professional hunter, Fred G. Merfield, describes his experiences with gorillas and chimps and the habits of the people of the rainforests of French Cameroon before WWII when that wilderness had not been degraded and forests denuded. His descriptions of the people living as hunter-gatherers, but planting some crops in small far-apart clearings, must be precise snapshots of how it was.

*

A most important fact does emerge from genetic study. It is that the people who migrated 'out-of-Africa' and populated the rest of the world were not of the Khoisan who curried the L0 genetic marker. They belonged in the M and N clades of the group L3 which diverged from L2 at about 115,000 BP, which in turn diverged from L1 at about 165,000 BP which descended from the ancestral 'Mitochondrial Eve'.

All of these people were of the African Middle Stone Age which is observed in its clearest form in archaeological sites from the

Cape, around East Africa and into the Sahara. The people of the savannahs who were least affected by the rigours of changing West and Central African forests kept to the least diluted line of cultural evolution. The 'out-of-Africa' migrants of 80,000 years ago may have descended from the Negroid haplogroup, but the culture they carried was that of the eastern African savannah from where they jumped off into Asia.

*

Another study provides information focussed on the remnant click-speaking peoples of the eastern savannah, the Khoisan, the Hadza and the Sandawe. This is an important study which I had long awaited. It bears directly on the problem of the general structure of the savannah peoples of eastern-southern Africa at the time of the out-of-Africa migrations and in the millennia which followed. Sarah A.Tishkoff and her colleagues published their findings in the Oxford journal, *Molecular Biology and Evolution* 24-10 in 2007, entitled: *History of Click-Speaking Populations of Africa Inferred from mtDNA and Y Chromosome Genetic Variation.*

Here is the abstract to the paper:

Little is known about the history of click-speaking populations in Africa. Prior genetic studies revealed that the click-speaking Hadza of eastern Africa are as distantly related to click speakers of southern Africa as are most other African populations. The Sandawe, who currently live within 150 km of the Hadza, are the only other population in eastern Africa whose language has been classified as part of the Khoisan language family. Linguists disagree on whether there is any detectable relationship between the Hadza and Sandawe click languages. We characterized both mtDNA and Y chromosome variation of the Sandawe, Hadza, and neighboring Tanzanian populations. New genetic data show that the Sandawe and southern African click speakers share rare mtDNA and Y chromosome haplogroups; however, common ancestry of the 2 populations dates back >35,000 years. These data also indicate that common ancestry of the Hadza and Sandawe populations dates back >15,000 years. These findings suggest that at the time of the spread of agriculture and pastoralism, the click-speaking populations were already isolated from one another and are consistent with relatively deep linguistic divergence among the respective click languages.

The statement that "new genetic data show that the Sandawe and southern African click-speakers share rare mtDNA and Y chromosome haplogroups ... " is a welcome clarification for me of the confusion which had been prevailing in recent years. Logic had told me that there had to be a common savannah population at the core of *Homo sapiens* in eastern and southern Africa during the Middle Stone Age while the Negroids were diverging in the specialised environment of the central and western African forests and forest margins. However, there was no consensus, as noted by the authors:

> The presence of Khoisan linguistic groups in Tanzania was earlier considered to support a paleobiological-based model, indicating that Khoisan populations inhabited all southern Africa and much of eastern Africa (as far north as Egypt; Tobias 1964; Bräuer 1978). This model of a continuous distribution of Khoisan populations in southern and eastern Africa has been criticized (Stringer et al. 1985; Morris 2002). Instead, the Hadza and Sandawe are thought either to be population isolates or to resemble their Tanzanian neighbors genetically (Cavalli-Sforza et al. 1994).

Lack of detailed genetic clarity had seemed to conflict with the logic of the common savannah population in the millennia leading to the dawn of abstract artistic expression, a period about 100,000 years ago. I could maintain my acceptance of the logic and support the earlier opinion of Tobias and others, but had to assume that I might be wrong. If I was wrong, then there had to be an equally logical alternative which I was missing.

Within the body of this latest paper, following detailed analysis, is this in regard to mtDNA :

> ... the Hadza and Sandawe cluster more closely with each other than with other Tanzanian populations and more closely with the SAK-speaking [Southern African Khoisan] populations relative to any other Tanzanian populations. The estimated time of divergence between the Sandawe and SAK speakers is 44–50 kya (CI 21–100 kya for the Ju/'hoansi and 29–100 kya for the !Xun/Khwe), whereas the Hadza are estimated to have diverged from the SAK-speaking

populations 56 kya (CI 33–100 kya for the Ju/'hoansi and 40–100 kya for the !Xun/Khwe [Khoisan language groups].

And in regard to Y chromosome groups, I quote, omitting references to tables and diagrams:

> In the Hadza, Sandawe, and SAK [Southern African Khoisan] populations, we observe 3 relatively basal Y chromosome haplogroups: B2b (defined by the M112 mutation),E3b1 (defined by the M35 mutation), and E3a (defined by the M2 mutation). ... The relatively old (>55 kya,) B2b-M112 haplogroup is unreported outside of sub-Saharan Africa and is most common in hunter/gatherer populations across sub-Saharan Africa, notably the central African Pygmies and the SAK-speaking Ju/'hoansi (Knight et al. 2003; Wood et al. 2005). We detected the B2b haplogroup at a high frequency in the Hadza and at a moderate frequency in the Sandawe. Tanzanian populations do not, however, harbor the P6 and P7 mutations that define the subhaplogroups of B2b that are found among SAK speakers and central African Pygmy populations (Wood et al. 2005). The frequency of B2b in the Hadza (51%) is higher than reported in any other population . In addition, the B2b lineages in the Hadza have higher STR diversity than any of the other surveyed populations, and STR haplotypes are shared with only one Datog individual. Sandawe and SAK B2blineages appear to be similarly distinct from those of other populations. STR variation of B2b sub clusters that include primarily SAK speakers, Hadza, and Sandawe indicates that these groups shared a common ancestor 35 (±4) kya.

We are being informed in this complicated description that the remnant people of Africa who speak a click language are divided into three linguistic and genetic groups. The genetic results from analysis of both mtDNA (the female line) and y chromosome (the male line) show that the separation of Khoisan of southern Africa from the two small remnant Tanzanian groups occurred probably about 35,000 years ago but not earlier than an outside date of 100,000 years ago. This coincides with that magical date for the commencement of the African Late Stone Age and covers the time span during which the 'out-of-Africa' migration occurred. The tiny remaining populations of Hadza and Sandawe in eastern Tanzania live very close to each other

(150 kilometres) and are separated from the fairly numerous remaining identified Khoisan by more than 1,500 kilometres.

The Hadza and Sandawe were much later constrained by immigrant Negroid farmers and pastoralists into small pockets where they maintained some integrity while the San were pushed into territory which was unsuitable for Iron Age agriculture. The San survived extinction by the colonists by adapting to the vast semi-desert and mountainous country of southern Africa whereas their Tanzanian cousins were lucky to find pockets which their new neighbours did not covet.

Elsewhere, from Ethiopia to the Limpopo River these indigenous people of the savannah have lost their genetic and linguistic identity under the flood of new peoples in the last 3,000 years. Outside of the south-western arid lands, it is only in south-eastern Africa's mountainous regions where there were substantial numbers in an amenable environment. It is here that their language and genes are discernable in the modern Nguni and Sotho-Tswana people (as described by Tobias many years ago) and where isolated groups were still living in symbiosis with these dominant Iron Age agricultural colonists until historical time in the European colonial period.

It can be remarked that the strange existence of scarce genetic traces of Khoisan genes detected by some researchers amongst people in the Ethiopian region could be evidence that during some similar timescale the indigenous Khoisan of the East African savannah were pushed into marginal lands of the Horn too, just as happened at the Cape 2,000 years ago.

The brief paper, *Ethiopians and Khoisan share the deepest Clades of the Human Y-chromosome Phylogeny*, by Semino, Santachiara-Benerecetti, Falaschi, Cavalli-Sforza and Underhill (2002) details the technical information. In the summary they write:

> The genetic structure of 126 Ethiopian and 139 Senegalese Y chromosomes was investigated by a hierarchical analysis of 30 diagnostic biallelic markers selected from the worldwide Y-chromosome genealogy. The present study reveals that (1) only the Ethiopians share with the Khoisan the deepest human Y-chromosome clades (the African specific Groups I and II) but with a repertoire of very different haplotypes; (2) most of the Ethiopians and virtually all the Senegalese belong to Group III, whose precursor is believed to be

involved in the first migration out of Africa; and (3) the Ethiopian Y chromosomes that fall into Groups VI, VIII, and IX may be explained by back migrations from Asia. The first observation confirms the ancestral affinity between the Ethiopians and the Khoisan which has previously been suggested by both archaeological and genetic findings.

Apart from the assumption that Khoisan people were pushed into the mountains of Ethiopia by population pressures, the existence of their genes amongst modern Ethiopians can also be easily explained by the always open highways of the Great Rift Valley and the Indian Ocean littoral, which is my pervading theme.

*

All of this genetic evidence assembled so far confirms my view that the Khoisan people were the natural direct descendants of the first *Homo sapiens* who lived on the savannahs of Africa. It was after about 120,000 years ago that they began to be displaced by, or merged with, people from the west. It was from that mixture, dominated by Negroid genes of the mtL1 group, that the 'out-of-Africa' migration surged. And it was during the millennia around that period that there were perturbations. It was exponential population growth in the central-western Negroid peoples which drove the out-of-Africa migrations. It seems probable that migrations into Arabia were sufficient to relieve the pressures. They did not migrate southwards, they began 'beachcombing' eastwards. It was the easier path.

*

Thousands of years later during the Holocene after the last ice-age, Negroid peoples expanded to dominate sub-Saharan Africa. Their ability to survive and then exploit the forests which always remained whatever the extent of the Sahara, was reinforced by the acquisition of agriculture and then metallurgy.

It is now increasingly certain that the people of North Africa had begun herding domestic animals of the goat and sheep family, possibly as early as 80,000 years ago, but agriculture and sedentary urban living, which is necessary for farmers, spread across the Sahara in the wet and green times after the end of the last ice-age. The Sahara was empty of people from 24,000 - 10,000 BP but this changed quite rapidly thereafter. Populations expand rapidly to fill niches provided by environmental advantages.

Professor Phillip Tobias wrote in his wide-ranging paper, *The Peoples of Africa South of the Sahara,* as long ago as 1966:

> Bushman-like [San-like] skeletons are known from a far wider area than the present restricted distribution of Bushmen; it is likely that a large part of Central and East Africa, if not also northeast Africa, was inhabited in the earlier parts of the Holocene Period [since the last Ice-age] by people skeletally similar to the Bushmen. On the other hand, little is known of the skeletal ancestry of the Negro; probably the earliest recognizable Negriform material is that excavated at Khartoum and dated to about 6000 years ago. On this prehistoric evidence, it is possible that the Bushman skeletal type represents the ancestral form. Perhaps from this form, with selective pressures and hybridization, the Negroid peoples have differentiated; in this event, we should have to regard the Negro as an offshoot of the Khoisaniform racial stock rather than the other way around!

Improved technical dating methods have since shown that the Negroid skeletons discovered in the southern Sahara lived there about 9-8,000 years ago. Since 1966 when Tobias published his paper, the frontiers of archaeology have been constantly pressed backwards into time and our knowledge of what went on in the Sahara and West Africa has increased. Whether the Sahara was wet or dry since 35,000 years ago, it is not a great uniform sandy or rocky plain, although most of it is like that. There are underground reservoirs and rivers relict from the last ice-age and resultant oases. There are notable mountainous islands of old volcanoes like the Hoggar, Tassili, Tibesti, Aïr and Ennedi. These collections of volcanic peaks and massifs are spectacular and amazing sights, rising from the endless sand and gravels. All reach at least 1500m [5000ft]; the Hoggar rises to 2900m [9500ft] and there are peaks in the Tibesti which top 3200m [10500ft]. All have fine collections of rock-art from the Late Stone Age.

The similarities between rock-art of the Sahara and eastern-southern Africa suggest common origins. Like Tobias, I had assumed for many years that Khoisan people were the clearest direct descendants from Mitochondrial Eve and had inhabited all of the savannah regions of sub-Sahara Africa until the outburst of Negroid people from the West and Central African forests at about 3,500 years

293

ago. But that was before the human genome began to be unravelled in the 1990s.

Cultural similarity, such as seen in rock-art, may be evidence of common cultural characteristics but it is not necessarily so. Today, the great majority of all people on Earth belong to the same industrial and technical culture, but we were at the summit of diversity only a few decades ago before the effect of technical globalisation in the later twentieth century.

It is now quite clear from the genetic evidence, discussed earlier, that the picture is rather more complicated. Khoisan and Negroid diverged somewhere in the region of 150,000 years ago. An examination of world temperatures show that there was a prolonged ice age reaching a peak at about 140,000 years ago and this cannot be coincidence. The Sahara would have been at a maximum of aridity then and populations were severely reduced, pushed away into the forest zone of West and Central Africa and back into the interlacustrine area of East Africa and along Indian Ocean seashores. When the climate warmed and became lush again, there was an outsurge from the Negroid heartlands, precisely similar to what happened 10,000 years ago at the end of the last ice age. The Khoisan and Negroids became clearly differentiated genetically, there was a movement of people across the Suez landbridge which failed and then there was the successful out-of-Africa migration of 80,000 years ago, mostly from the Horn.

I am satisfied that it is the agency of the great bellows machine of the Sahara, pulsing from complete aridity to partially grassy savannah and back in tune with world climate, which acted on people again and again in a similar way. During these fluctuating climatic periods there were incursions into northeast Africa from the Levant and Arabia. They become more easily defined after 50,000 years ago when 'out-of-Africa' people had circled around and began retro-migrations especially into the Nile valley and along the Mediterranean shores. These people have been loosely defined as Afro-Asiatic.

Leaving aside the matter of genetic definition of the increasingly diverse peoples of equatorial and northern Africa, there is the rather more interesting problem of culture. Clearly, in a broad sense, the economic and industrial cultures of forest and savannah are different. The prey animals of hunters and the vegetable foods sought by gatherers are quite different. When agriculture became the

294

dominant economic culture, domestic animals in the forest were restricted to pigs and cultivation to some roots and fruits. Agriculture flourished on the savannahs where there was good rainfall or sources of irrigation where cereals could be grown, until iron tools made forest clearance easier. But forest clearance always required much expenditure of energy and soils become quickly leached requiring onward movement. It was the savannah that was most used by farmers.

It is hardly surprising that since the last ice age, the Holocene, there is evidence of a common savannah culture, as seen from rock-art. Whether people were roughly Negroid north of the equator or Khoisan south of it, they lived with this similar culture until agriculture and metallurgy were introduced.

*

Examining the Holocene, latest climate research indicates that there was variation between different parts of the Sahara which, one has to remember, is the largest desert zone in the world, spreading across Africa at its widest point (more than 7,000 kilometres) and adjacent to similar geography extending through Arabia and as far as the Indus valley. Variation within that great area is to be expected, especially during the waxing and waning stages of a climate cycle.

The University of East Anglia's Fezzan Project (2003) had this to say on its website:

> Over the last few hundred thousand years, the Fezzan [central Sahara zone] has been subject to dramatic changes in climate that have affected the Sahara as a whole. ... These have generally taken the form of hyper-arid periods associated with large-scale ice cover in the northern hemisphere during glacial episodes and wet episodes associated interglacial conditions. Some 135 thousand years ago (ka), large lakes covered much of the Sahara as a result of massively increased rainfall with respect to conditions today. ... After the last glacial maximum at 21 ka, climatic conditions in the Sahara fluctuated in response to the episodic collapse of the northern hemisphere ice sheets and the resulting impact on northen hemisphere atmospheric and oceanic circulation.
>
> The most important wet periods in terms of archaeology and the development of human society

occurred during the Holocene (the last 10,000 years). By about 10 ka, rainfall was plentiful and most of the Sahara was vegetated; in the south, vegetation zones were displaced some 400 km north of their present-day positions, and fauna from the equatorial regions had migrated north into the Sahara. ...

There is widespread evidence that the onset of the hyper-arid conditions that characterise the Sahara today occurred at around 5 ka. It is believed that the dessication occurred in two phases, and was the result of changes in the Earth's orbital parameters ... Groundwater levels remained high in some areas after the onset of hyper-aridity, and lakes are likely to have persisted in some regions [e.g. Lake Chad]. ... Where such oasis refuges did not exist, people would have migrated to the Saharan margins and the Nile Valley; it is plausible that a large influx of Saharan refugees was one of the factors that led to the development of Egyptian Dynastic civilisation; certainly a knowledge of astronomy and various religious themes appear to have been common to Pharaonic Egypt and pre-Dynastic Saharan cultures [e.g. the Dogon people of Mali].

[Sundry discussion on detailed climate has been omitted, and it is known that the early period of the first Egyptian dynasty exhibits the tension between pastoralists from the south and agricultural farmers of the lower Nile and its delta.]

Approximately, the southern Sahara in the vicinity of Lake Chad was wet from 40,000 to 20,000 years ago, then dry, then wet again after that fairly universal date of 12,000 years ago. The eastern and central Sahara was always drier with longer periods of desertification, not having the advantage of the West Africa 'monsoon' bringing moist air in from the Atlantic. In Sudan it was semi-arid from 40,000 to 25,000 years ago before becoming severely arid. The Holocene 'wet' period came later at about 8,000 years ago. By about 2,500 years ago the present drying of the Sahara from the centre outwards had affected most areas.

Rock-art in the mountain fastnesses of the centre of the Sahara provides fascinating information about people in the Late Stone Age. Henri Lhotse, a specialist in Saharan prehistory and an ethno-archaeologist, wrote in *National Geographic* (August 1987):

When the Sahara was green, millennia ago, man hunted buffalo and drove cattle over grasslands where giraffe browsed and hippo wallowed in lakes. ... As the Ice-age waned 12,000 years ago, a shift in weather patterns brought a moist climate to North Africa, making it a far more hospitable place than it is today.

Lhotse described four phases of rock-art in the Tassili, commencing with portraits of 'round head', 'proto-Negro' people about 9-8,000 years ago. They seem related in lifestyle, body decoration and style of rock-art to the Khoisan group of eastern and southern Africa.

Lhotse described the next three phases reflecting cultural and technical advance influenced by events to the north and east and climatic change from about 7,000 years ago. Cattle herding is depicted after 5,000 BC, horse-drawn chariots from about 1200 BC and camels about 100 BC.

His conclusions from Tassili art were that as the climate became wet again after about 12,000 years ago the area became peopled with dramatically changing culture and technology until it dried out in the centuries before Christ and the horse was replaced by the camel. These dates are most important. They were suggested by Roland Oliver whose time scale concluded that all of the Sahara was dry between 20-10,000 years ago and then became wet again in what is known as the 'Holocene Wet Phase' which "had its main effect within the first twenty degrees of north latitude and as far west as the Niger bend."

Oliver draws a picture of the geography of central Africa during the Holocene Wet Phase, peaking between 9,500 and 6,500 years ago. Lake Chad stretched from the Chari river to the Tibesti Mountains and its waters breached the watershed to flow down the Benue and Niger Rivers to the Atlantic. The Sudd swamps of the upper Nile spread vastly as Lake Turkana was raised so that its waters flowed north into the Nile system, creating yet another source. Lakes in the Great Rift Valley merged as the valley was inundated.

Other models suggested that the Zambezi-Okavango-Limpopo river system in southern Africa became interconnected with a network of waterways and flood-plains covering immense territory including the Makgadikgadi salt pans which were a great shallow lake similar to Lake Chad, its mirror in North Africa. In 2008 the Bundesanstalt für Geowissenschaften und Rohstoffe published the results of its project

297

investigating this southern inland lake system. Dr. Thomas Himmelsbach led the research and here are salient points:

> In the late Pleistocene the Okavango Delta and the Makgadikgadi Pan in Botswana were covered by lakes reaching levels of 945 m, 936 m, 920 m and 912 m asl which corresponds to water depths of locally more than 60 m. ...
>
> Already during the early Pleistocene, tectonic movements formed a depression which lead to the nowadays Makgadikgadi Pan. The paleohydrology was controlled by the Okavango- and Zambezi River and the high level stage on 945m asl developed between 40,000 and 35,000 BP, before the connection with the prominent Zambezi water course was disrupted. ...
>
> During the Holocene [the last 10,000 years] both lakes dried up gradually. Since a direct correlation of the lake levels with South African paleoclimate records is difficult, the influence of over-regional tectonic movements for the history of the lakes becomes more and more evident. The ancient lakes had obviously a vast catchment which was gradually cut off with time.

Latest study on these ancient lake systems both north and south, though more detailed, generally confirms Oliver's information and the palaeoclimate of the Sahara is also reasonably certain.

From 12,000 years ago, fishing and its associated sedentary lifestyle became predominant again amongst a wide spectrum of the savannah people in the south-central Sahara and the wettest parts of eastern and southern Africa. Very early pottery from about 9,000 years ago is associated with bone harpoons and with a cultural relationship to people of eastern Africa. This is of principal importance in judging who re-populated the Sahara after the Holocene Wet Phase began.

Professor D.W.Phillipson in his book *African Archaeology*, revised in 1993, described the Sahara during this re-population period. He is sure about the evidence showing that fishing became probably the principal source of protein nutrition for people settled in stone huts around newly formed lakes and rivers. An extended Lake Chad region is typical. Boats are seen in rock-art in the Ennedi mountains which suggests that substantial rivers feeding Lake Chad led from their foothills, 700 kilometres from the present lake. The use of barbed bone harpoons have been traditionally in use around Lake Turkana in northern Kenya from about 10,000 years ago until the present. 'Wavy-line' pottery was manufactured beside the greatly expanded Lake Turkana before 7,500 years ago.

Phillipson wrote of the Sahara, on fishing and artefacts :

> Bone harpoon heads, as described above at Early Khartoum, were the characteristic artefacts indicative of this new development. Pottery is also present at most sites of this type: it usually bears the idiosyncratic wavy-line decoration.

These bone harpoons and wavy-line pottery have been discovered from Lake Turkana, a focus for human remains for millions of years, to the upper Nile, to the Acacus region of the Fezzan, to modern Niger and Mali where, by the 1960s, the pottery style was reported near Timbuktu and the bone harpoons near Bamako.

Although impossible to prove, all this encourages my broad overview that after the departure of the main migration 'out of Africa' at about 80,000 years ago, and the subsequent population collapses and hardships of the cold periods that followed, the re-population of the savannahs was carried out by people with a common African 'savannah economic culture'. The pulsing heart of the core of humanity, tropical eastern Africa, always provided the means to fill the void after natural catastrophe. If the most natural source of re-population was from the savannah of eastern Africa in 12-9,000 years ago, the logic of this having happened in previous similar circumstances is reasonable.

What is now clear, however, is that the people who re-populated parts of the Sahara from a south-eastern source were not Khoisans. They were Negroids. They would have brought with them their fully developed African savannah Late Stone Age culture which is strongly suggested by the similarity of rock-art style and subject from the Cape to the central Sahara. But, the evidence of a common savannah culture within the sub-Saharan African Late Stone Age must be clearly separated from consideration of genetically different population groups.

The appearance of 'roundhead' people in rock-art, suggesting Negroid types, began in what has been termed the Late Acacus period of 9,000 - 7,000 years ago in the Fezzan. But there were other migrants into the Sahara from the fringes. Other people from the north and northeast, Afro-Asiatic, moved into the Sahara maybe two thousand years later and further mixing began. Pastoral agriculture was introduced and the emergence of the Berber-Beduin people began. This coincides with the very beginning of the Early Pastoral period with cattle, sheep and goats from 7,000 to 6,000 years ago. The Sahara became a cultural melting pot as people converged from every direction to take advantage of the huge zone of savannah and grassland being created by relatively rapid climate change.

In a University of East Anglia web site maintained by Nic Brooks and updated in January 2003, there was this pertinent passage which neatly summarises the Holocene period.

> In terms of archaeology, there is a wealth of evidence indicating a fairly high degree of spatial and temporal cultural continuity in the central and eastern Sahara. For example, mummification and the ritual burial of cattle were practised in the Fezzan region of southwestern Libya prior to the Egyptian Dynastic period. Rock-art and funerary monuments exhibit similar styles throughout the central Sahara. Archaeological, genetic and anthropological research indicate that the distribution of modern Saharan (and some sub-Saharan) populations is the result of several episodes of migration, first from the south some 10,000 years ago (at least in the southern Sahara; migrants also entered the northern Sahara from the Mediterranean coast around this time), then from the east between about 8000 and 7000 BP, with further migration from the east occurring in some locations around 3000 BP. Animal domestication appears to have been associated with the second wave of migration mentioned above. The outcome of these migrations was not necessarily the displacement of existing populations; considerable mixing of population groups appears to have occurred. Further migrations within the Sahara and from the Sahara to its fringes undoubtedly occurred as a result of the desiccation of the region after 5000 BP.

Agriculture was developed in Egypt. Cattle were brought in from the Middle-East and metals followed. Hunter-gatherers lived in the central Sahara when it was 'wet' again 9,000 years ago and painted on rocks, but they began to be joined by migrants with sheep and cattle moving in from the northeast. They merged through clientship over time, and formed the ancestors of the present Sahel people, the Beduin, who never penetrated the woodlands where tsetse flies killed their cattle and horses.

When the Sahara dried again in the first millennium before Christ and desertification in settled areas was speeded by overgrazing with herded goats and sheep, and then cattle, social turmoil and outward migrations were precipitated. The pulsing of the Sahara was being repeated once again in relatively recent time when archaeology could illustrate it.

The Negroid people of West Africa and the central forests spread east and south. Nilotic- and Cushitic-speaking people of north-eastern Africa moved south. The migration of Negroid people from the forests into the savannahs of eastern and southern Africa seems to be most easily detected early in the first millennium before Christ, forced by increasing population pressures resulting from the arrival of new techniques and culture and the drying of the Sahara. It could have begun earlier. Indeed, as Professor Felix Chami of Dar-es-Salaam University has proposed there seems little doubt that from the beginning of the Holocene there had been continual interaction between East Africa, especially the Great Lakes region and Rift Valley, and the upper Nile and eastern Sahara. Pottery links assist this hypothesis, and it is entirely logical.

It seems increasingly clear that the transition from the Late Stone Age to the Early Iron Age along the Sahel belt from the Niger River to the upper Nile, bordering the forest zones, has great significance to an understanding of the latest expansion and spread of Negroid people, especially the Bantu-speaking group. Archaeology from several sources has shown that there was sudden population growth in the first millennium BC which coincides with the transition.

The discovery of iron technology may have occurred in parts of this region coincidental to its establishment in Anatolia and then elsewhere in the Middle East. Once there is general knowledge of smelting of metals from ores through sufficient heat, then experimentation with different ways of reduction and refining follows, the recognition of suitable rocks and the provision of sufficient heat with charcoal furnaces must inevitably proceed to iron. The general knowledge of metallurgy may have moved across the Sahara from Egypt together with other cultural transfer, but the specific techniques of iron smelting practised south of the Sahara did not have to wait for this special intelligence to be imported.

At the far end of the geographical and time scales, it was noted by early European colonial observers that the Bantu iron workers of South Africa in the 19th century made a superior steel, the

301

equal of sophisticated industrial production in England. Zulu ironsmiths in the 19th century were able to provide armies of 30,000 men with steel-bladed assegais and rapidly re-equip them after battle, equalling the capacity of an industry of the classical civilisations of the Mediterranean or Middle East.

The significance of the transition from Late Stone Age to Iron Age technology has to be its effect on agriculture in the fringes of the central and western rainforests, and increasingly within it. Iron tools enabled people to clear forests for cultivation at a rate and on a scale never previously possible. The increase in cultivation enabled population explosion, with attendant territorial stress and the need for expansion and migration. Clearing the bush of the eastern and southern savannahs and burning grasslands reduced the risk of disease to cattle from flies and ticks. The general change in societies had to have been dramatic and relatively sudden, and this is demonstrated by archaeology which has found evidence of expanding villages and towns.

The modern language and cultural differences between Bantu and Nilotic speakers in the Interlacustrine Zone, causing such terrible turmoil in our own time, suggests that Bantu-speakers emerged from the Cameroon forests as a result of the introduction of iron tools and burgeoning cultivation, as has been long held by historians, and then impinged on older-established people who were masters of animal husbandry. There has to be the obvious association with the desertification of the Sahara at this same time. The later movement of Bantu-speakers with a cattle cult into southern Africa during the first millennium AD was the natural culmination of these first millennium BC population convulsions.

A Zulu *impi* at a ceremonial celebration in Natal, South Africa, in 1925.

The lights of the city glide within me
but do not pierce through me with their glitter
deep in me there still persists the black depths
of the black history I hear singing.

Mindelense   [Guinea-Bissau poet]

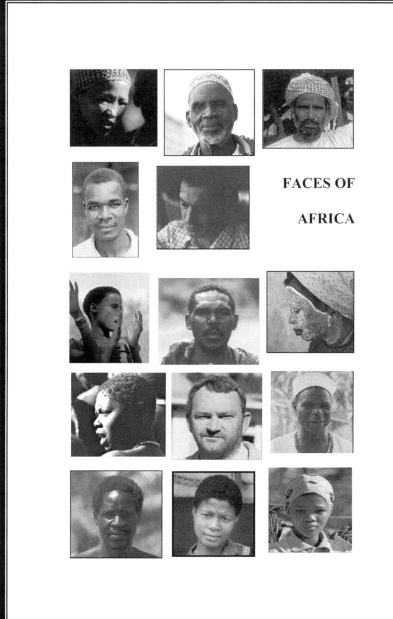

FACES OF

AFRICA

304

BIBLIOGRAPHY and background reading.

Abysov, S.S. et al : *Deciphering Mysteries of Past Climate from Antarctic Ice Cores*. American
    Geophysical Union - *Earth in Space*, v.8 no.3. 1995.
Adams, W.M.: *Definition and Development in African Indigenous Irrigation*. Azania, 1989
Al-Maamiry, Ahmed Hamoud: *Oman and East Africa*. Lancers Books, 1979
-    -   : *Omani-Portuguese History*. Lancers Publishers, 1982
Allen, Anita: *Exciting Hominid Fossils Discovered*. The Star, Johannesburg, 29 October 1993
- - : *Royal Graves Found in Kruger*. The Star, Johannesburg, 7 August 1996
- - : *Fossil Find takes Anthropological Theory into the Desert*. The Star, Johannesburg,
    12 Aug, 1996
- - : *Stone-walled Ruins with a Unique 'Sense of Lightness'*. The Star, Johannesburg,
    24 Sep, 1996
Ambrose, Stanley H. : *Late Pleistocene Human Population Bottlenecks Volcanic Winter,
    and Differentiation of Modern Humans*. Extract from : *Journey of Human Evolution*,
    Bradshaw Foundation, 1998.
Andaman Association (Ed. Weber, George) : *Lonely Islands*, Internet (2006)
Anderson, Andrew A: *Twenty-Five Years in a Waggon*. Chapman & Hall, 1888, (Struik, 1974)
Anderson, David M.: *Agriculture and Irrigation Technology at Lake Baringo*, Azania, 1989
Anderson, Gavin : *Bushman Rock Art, South Africa*. Art Publishers, 2004
Anderson, Julie R. & Ahmed, Salah Mahomed. *Revealing terra incognita: Dangeil, Sudan*.
    Current World Archaeology no. 19, October 2006.
Ardrey, Robert: *African Genesis*. Collins, 1961
-   -   : *The Territorial Imperative*. Collins, 1967
-   -   : *The Hunting Hypothesis*. Collins, 1976
Asher, Michael : *In Search of the Forty Days Road*. Longmans, 1984.
Athena Review : *Levant Suite Yields Oldest Evidence of Cereal Processing*. v 4 (2). 2005
Athena Review : *Oldest* Homo sapiens *Evidence at Omo, Ethiopia*. V. 4 (2). 2005
Axelson, Eric: *South-East Africa, 1488-1530*. Longmans, 1940
-   -   : *Congo to Cape*. Faber & Faber, 1973
-   -   : *Portuguese in South-East Africa 1488-1600*. Struik, 1973
-   -   : *Vasco da Gama*. Stephan Phillips, 1998
-   -   : *South African Explorers*. Oxford University Press, 1954.
Baker, Samuel White : *The Albert N'Yanza*. Sidgwick & Jackson, 1962 (1868)
Barker, Graeme: *Economic Models for the Manekweni Zimbabwe, Mozambique*. Azania XIII, 1978
Barrow, John & Tipler, Frank J.: *The Anthropic Cosmological Principle*. Oxford, 1986
Battuta, Ibn: *Travels in Asia and Africa 1325-1354*. Routledge & Kegan Paul,1929
Beach, D.N.: *The Shona and Zimbabwe 900-1850*. Mambo Press, 1980
Beaumont, P.B. & Boshier, Adrian: *Some comments on Recent Findings at Border Cave,
    Northern Natal*. South African Journal of Science, 1972
Behar, Doran M., et al : *The Dawn of Human Matrilineal Diversity*. The American Journal
    of Human Genetics. 82/5, 24 April 2008.
Bent, J.Theodore : *The Ruined Cities of Mashonaland.*. Longmans, Green, 1896
Berger, Lee : *Sediba - interview with New York Times*. 8 April 2010.
Berger, Lee R., et al : *Homo naledi, a new species of the genus* Homo *from the Dinaledi Chamber, South Africa*.
    eLIFE, 2015.
Bergerot, Sylvie & Robert, Eric: *Namib, Dawn to Twilight*. Southern Books, 1989
Berry, Adrian: *The Ozone Layer Was Destroyed Before*. The Daily Telegraph, London, 21 December 1991
-        -   : *2001 Replayed*. Astronomy Now, March 2006
Bieber, Heidi; Bieber, Sebastian W; Rodewald, Alexander & Christiansen, Kerrin *Genetic study
    of African populations: Polymorphisms of the plasma proteins TF, PI, FI3B, and AHSG in
    populations of Namibia and Mozambique*   (Human Biology, Feb 1997).
Bittner, Maximillian, Ed.: *Das Indischen Seespiegels*. Geographischen Gesellschaft, Vienna, 1897
Blench, Roger. *New paleozoogeographical evidence for the settlement of Madagascar*. Azania XLII, 2007
Böeseken, A.J.: *Slaves and Free Blacks at the Cape 1658-1700*. Tafelberg,1977
Boivin, Nicole; Crowther, Alison; Prendergast, Mary & Fuller, Dorian Q. : *Indian Ocean Food Globalisation
    and Africa*. African Archaeological Review, 2014.
-      -   : *East Africa and Madagascar in the Indian Ocean World*. Springer Science, New York, 2013.
Boonzaier, Emile; Berens, Penny; Malherbe, Candy; Smith, Andy : *The Cape Herders*.
    David Philip & Ohio University Press, 1996
Bosman, Paul & Hall-Martin, Anthony: *Elephants of Africa*. Struikhof, 1986

Bourne, Harry : *The Phoenicians in East Africa.* WWW. 2003
Bousman, C.Britt. *The Chronological Evidence for the Introduction of Domestic Stock
   into Southern Africa .* African Archaeological Review, 1998
Brace, C..Loring: *Background for the Peopling of the New World.* Athena Review, 2002
Brunet, Michel *et al : A new hominid from the Upper Miocene of Chad, Central Africa* .Nature 418, 2002
Broadhurst, C.Leigh *et al. Brain-specific Lipids from Marine, Lacustrine, or terrestrial
   food resources: potential impact on early African Homo Sapiens.* CBP, 2002
Broadhurst, C.Leigh ; Cunnane, Stephen C.; Crawford, Michael A. : *Rift valley lake fish and shellfish
   provided brain-specific nutrition for early Homo.* Nutrition Society 1998.
Brook, Ed. *Windows on the Greenhouse.* Nature, 15 May 2008
Brooks, Nic; di Lernia, Savino; Drake, Nic; Raffin, Margaret; Savage, Tony. *The Geoarchaeology
   of Western Sahara.* Draft paper for *Sahara,* 2003. www.cru.uea.ac.uk
Brown, Mervyn: *Madagascar Rediscovered.* Tunnacliffe, 1978
Cachel, Susan: *The Paleobiology of Homo Erectus and early Hominid Dispersal.* Athena Review. 2004
Campbell, John: *Travels in South Africa,* Black, Parry & Co, 1815
Carr, M.J. & A.C. and Jacobson, L.: *Hut Remains and Related Features from the Zerrissene.*
   Cimbebasia, 2-11, Feb. 1978
Casson, Lionel : *The Ancient Mariners.* Victor Gollancz, 1959
-   - : *The Periplus Maris Erythraei.* Princeton University Press. 1989
Chami, Felix : *The First Millennium AD on the East Coast.* BIEA 1996
-   - : *The Early Iron Age on Mafia Island and its relationship with the Mainland.*
   Azania XXXIV 1999
- - : *The Graeco-Romans and Paanchea/Azania : sailing in the Erythraean Sea.*
   British Museum 2002
- - & Kwekason, Amandus : *Neolithic Pottery traditions from the Islands, the Coast and the
   Interior of East Africa.* African Archaeological Review , 2003
- - : *Kaole and the Swahili World.* Extract from *Studies in the African Past 2.*
   University of Dar-es-Salaam, 2003
-   - : *The Unity of African Ancient History 3000 BC to AD 500.* E & D , Dar-es-Salaam, 2006
Carbonell, Eudald, *et al : The First Hominin in Europe.* Nature, vol 452. March 2008
Clowes, Wm.Laird (Ed.): *The Royal Navy.* Sampson Low, Marston, 1897
Collins, Andrew. : *Gods of Eden.* Headline, 1998
-   - : *In defence of Cygnus X-3 as a Cosmic Accelerator.* Unpublished paper, 2006
-   - : *The Cygnus Mystery.* Watkins Publishing , 2006
Compton, John S. : *Human Origins,* Earthspun Books, 2016.
Connor, Steve : *DNA Tests trace Adam to Africa.* London Sunday Times, 9-11-1997
Cooke, H.B.S.: *Preservation of the Sterkfontein Ape-man Cave Site, South Africa
   .* Studies in Speleology 2-1, 1969
Cordova, France Anne-Dominic : *Cygnus X-3 and the Case for Simultaneous Multifrequency
   Observations.* Los Alamos Science, Spring 1986
Crawford, Michael & Crawford, Sheilagh : *What We Eat Today.* Neville Spearman, 1972
Crawford, Michael & Marsh, David: *The Driving Force.* Heinemann, 1989
Crawford, Michael A., *et al : Brain-specific Lipids from Marine, Lacustrine, or terrestrial
   food resources: potential impact on early African Homo Sapiens.* CBP, 2002
- - *et al: : Evidence for the Unique Function of DHA during the evolution of the modern
   Hominid Brain.* Unpublished
Cunningham, E.P., Syrstad, O. *Crossbreeding bos taurus and bos indicus for milk production in the tropics.*
   FAO of the UN, 1987
Cunnane, Stephen C; Harbige & Crawford. : *The importance of energy and nutrient
   supply in human brain development.* Nutrition and Health v 9, 1993
Current World Archaeology : *Mons Claudianus & Mons Porphyrites.* (Sources : David Peacock &
   Valerie Maxfield) No. 8. Nov/Dec 2004
Curtis, Garniss; Swisher, Carl & Lewin, Roger : *Java Man.* Little, Brown & Co. 2001
Cruz-Uribe, Kathryn & Klein, Richard G.: *Faunal Remains from some Middle and Later Stone Age
   archaeological Sites in South West Africa.* Journal, SWA Scientific Society, 1983
Dalton, Rex : *Ancient footprints found in Mexico.* www.nature.com, 4 July 2005.
Darwin, Charles. *The Origin of Species.* Wordsworth Classics 1998
Davenport, T.R.H.: *South Africa, a Modern History.* Macmillan (S.A.), 1977
Dawkins, Richard : *The Blind Watchmaker.* Longman, 1986
-   - : *The Extended Phenotype.* Oxford 1999
de Gramont, Sanche: *The Strong Brown God.* Hart-Davis, 1975
Deacon, H.J. : *Guide to Klasies River 2001.* HJ Deacon, Stellenbosch 2001
Deacon, H.J & Deacon, Janette : *Human Beginnings in South Africa.* David Philip 1999
Delegorge, Adulphe : *Travels in Southern Africa,* University of Natal, 1990 (orig. 1847)

306

Delius, Peter; Maggs, Tim; Schoeman, Alex : *Forgotten World.* Wits University Press, 2014
Diamond, Jared: *The Rise and Fall of the Third Chimpanzee.* Radius, 1991
-        -   : *The Shape of Africa.* National Geographic, September 2005
Dugard, Martin : *Into Africa.* Bantam Press. 2003.
Duminy, Andrew & Guest, Bill: *Natal and Zululand, from Earliest Times to 1910.*
        University of Natal - Shuter & Shooter, 1989
Durrani, Nadia : *Flores: Human evolution rewritten.* Current World Archaeology. No 8. 2004
-        -   : *Çatalhöyük. The most ancient town in the world?* Current World Archaeology.
        No 8. 2004
Etler, Dennis: *Homo Erectus in East Asia : Human ancestor or Evolutionary Dead-end?*
        Athena Review, 2004
Evensberget, Snorre, *Thor Heyerdahl, the Explorer.* Stenersens Forlag, 1994
Farsi, Sheikh Abdalla Saleh: *Seyyid Said bin Sultan 1804-1856.* Lancers Books, 1986
Feely, J.M. & Bell-Cross, S.M. : *The Distribution of Early Iron Age Settlements in the Eastern Cape.*
        South African Archeological Bulletin, 2011.
Felgate, W.S.: *The Tembe Thonga of Natal and Mozambique.* African Studies, University of Natal, 1982
Ferguson, Niall : *Empire - How Britain Made the Modern World.* Allan Lane, 2003
Fock, G.J. & D.: *Felsbilder in Südafrika, Kinderdam und Kalahari.* Böhlau Verlag, 1984
Fynn, Henry Francis (Stuart & Malcolm eds.) *The Diary of Henry Francis Fynn.* Shuter & Shooter, 1969.
Franzen, Harald. : *Scientists track the origins of Malaria.* Scientific American, 25-6-2001
Gall, Sandy. *The Bushmen of Southern Africa, Slaughter of the Innocent.* Pimlico, 2002
Garlake, Peter S.: *Great Zimbabwe.* Thames & Hudson, 1973
Gerster, Georg: *Tsetse-Fly of the Deadly Sleep.* National Geographic, December 1986
Gibb, H.A.R.(ed.) : *The Travels of Ibn Batuta* vol II. Hakluyt Society, 1959
Gibert, J.; Gibert, Ll.; Iglesias.A. & Muestro,E. *Two 'Olduwan' assemblages in the Plio-Pleistocene*
        deposits of the Orce region, southeast Spain. Antiquity 72, 1998.
Gifford-Gonzales, Diane & Olivier, Henrietta : *Domesticating Animals in Africa.* The Oxford Handbook of
African Archeology (Mitchell & Lane eds.), Oxford University Press, 2013
Gleick, James: *Chaos, Making a New Science.* Heinemann, 1988
Goodall, Jane van Lawick: *In the Shadow of Man.* Collins, 1971
Goodman, Gurasira : *Apollo 11 and the Oldest Rock Art in Africa* . National Museums of Namibia, 1998
Gore, Rick: *Extinctions.* National Geographic, June 1989
-   : *The First Steps.* National Geographic, February 1997
Gray, John: *Straw Dogs.* Granta Books, 2002
Gray, Leslie C. & Moseley, William G. : *A geographical perspective on poverty-environment inetractions.*
        The Geographical Journal, March 2005
Grosset-Grange, H.: *La Côte Africaine dans les Routiers Nautiques Arabes au Moment des*
        Grandes Découvertes. Azania XIII, 1978.
Grün, R & Beaumont, P. *Border Cave Revisited, a revised ESR chronology.* Jounral of Human
        Evolution , 2001
Gupta, Sunil : *Piracy and trade on the western coast of India (AD1-250).* Azania XLII, 2007
Hakluyt, Richard; ed. Jack Beeching: *Voyages and Discoveries.* Penguin, 1972
Hall, Richard: *Empires of the Monsoon.* Harper Collins, 1996
Hall-Martin, Anthony: Walker, Clive & Bothma, J.du P.: *Kaokoveld, the Last Wilderness.*
        Southern Books, 1988
Harari, Yuval Noah : *Sapiens.* Penguin Random House, 2014
Heikell, Rod : *Indian Ocean Cruising Guide.* Imray Laurie Norie & Wilson, 1999
Heinz, Hans-Joachim & Lee, Marshall: *Namkwa, Life among the Bushmen.* Cape, 1978
Henshilwood, CS; Sealy,JC; Yates,R; Cruz-Uribe,K; Goldberg,P; Grine,FE; Klein,RG;
        Poggenpoel,C; van Niekerk,K; Watts,I; *Blombos Cave, Southern Cape, South Africa;*
        Preliminary Report on the 1992-1999 Excavations of the Middle Stone Age Levels.
        Journal of Archaeological Science , 2001.
Henshilwood, Christopher S., et al. : *Emergence of Modern Human Behavior: Middle Stone*
        Age Engravings from South Africa. Science, February 2002.
Henshilwood, Christopher S.; D'Errico, Francesco & Watts, Ian : *Engraved ochres from the Middle*
        Stone Age at Blombos Cave, South Africa. Journal of Human Evolution v 57, 2009.
Herodotus : (Trans. G.C.MaCauley) : *An Account of Egypt.* Gutenberg Etexts , 2000
Heyerdahl, Thor: *The Maldive Mystery.* Allen & Unwin, 1986
Highfield, Roger : *Links between humans' ancestors redrawn.* Daily Telegraph, London. 6 May 2008.
Himmelsbach, Dr. Thomas. *The Paleohydrogeology of the Okavango Basin and Makgadikgadi Pan*
        (Botswana) in the Light of Climate Change and Regional Tectonics.
        Bundesanstalt für Geowissenschaften und Rohstoffe, 2008
Horton, Mark: : *The Periplus and East Africa.* Azania XXV, 1990.
-        -   : *The Swahili Corridor* . Scientific American, September 1987

307

Kramer, Samuel Noah: *Cradle of Civilisation*. Time-Life Books, 1969
Hoste, Skipper. (ed. N.S. Davies) : *Gold Fever*. Pioneer Head, 1977
Huffman, Thomas N.   : *Archeaological Evidence and Conventional Explanations of*
                      Southern Bantu Settlement Patterns. Africa, 56 (3), 1986
    -               : *Broederstroom and the Origins of Cattle-keeping in South*
                      Africa. African Studies, University of Witwatersrand, 1991
    -               : *Ceramics, Settlements and Late Iron Age Migrations*.
                      African Archaeological Review 7, 1989
    -               : *Symbols in Stone*. University of Witwatersrand Press, 1987
    -               : *Snakes and Birds: Expressive Space at Great Zimbabwe*.
                      African Studies, University of the Witwatersrand, 1981
    -               : *Handbook to the Iron Age*. University of KwaZulu-Natal Press, 2007
    -               : *Mapungubwe*. Wits University Press, 2005
Humphrey, Nicholas: *The Inner Eye*. Faber & Faber, 1986
Huntingford, G.W.B. ed.: *The Periplus of the Erythraean Sea*. Hakluyt Society, 1980
Howells, William.: *Mankind in the Making*. Doubleday, 1967
Huxley, Elspeth: *Livingstone and his African Journeys*. Weidenfeld & Nicolson, 1974
Hydrographer of the Navy   : *Africa Pilot, vol I*. British Hydrographic Department, 1967
    -           -   : *Africa Pilot, vol II*. British Hydrographic Department, 1977
    -           -   : *Africa Pilot, vol III*. British Hydrographic Department, 1954
    -           -   : *Indonesia Pilot, vol II*. British Hydrographic Department, 1983
    -           -   ; *Mediterranean Pilot, Vol IV*. British Hydrographic Department, 1955
    -           -   : *Red Sea and Gulf of Aden Pilot*. British Hydrographic Department, 1980
    -           -   : *South America Pilot, Vol I*. British Hydrographic Department, 1975
    -           -   : *South Indian Ocean Pilot*. British Hydrographic Department, 1971
    -           -   : *West Coast of India Pilot*. British Hydrographic Department, 1975
    -           -   : *Ocean Passages for the World*. British Hydrographic Department, 1973
Ingman, Max : *Mitochondrial DNA Clarifies Human Evolution*. Bioscience Productions. 2001
Inskeep, Ray : *The Problem of Bantu Origins*. Duckworth 1973
Isaac, Glynn: *Visitors' Guide to the Olorgesaile Prehistoric Site*. Museums of Kenya, 1985
Jabavu, Noni : *The Ochre People*. John Murray, 1963
Jacobson, L.: *The Archaeology of the Kavango*. Journal, SWA Scientific Society, 1987
    -             : *The Brandberg*. Rössing Magazine, Dec., 1981
Johanson, Donald C. & Shreeve, James : *Lucy's Child*. Viking, 1990
Johanson, Donald C.: *The Dawn of Humans, Face to Face with Lucy's Family*.
                      National Geographic, March 1996.
Jakubowski, Peter. : *The Cosmic Carousel of Life* Naturics Foundation. 2003
Kaner, Simon : *The Oldest Pottery in the World*. Current World Archaeology. v 1., 2003.
Katanekwa, N.M.: *Some Early Iron Age sites from the Machili Valley of South Western*
                 Zambia, Azania XIII, 1978
Keller, Werner: *The Bible as History*. Hodder & Stoughton, 1956
Kinehan, J.: *The Stratigraphy and Lithic Assemblages of Falls Rock Shelter, Western Damaraland,*
             Namibia. Cimbebasia (B) 4 (2), 1984
Kingsley, Mary : *Travels in West Africa*. MacMillan. 1897
Kinver, Mark : *Tools unlock secrets of early man*. BBC News website, 14-12-2005
Kirkman, James: *The Early History of Oman in East Africa*. Journal of Oman Studies, 1983
    -           - : *Gedi*. Museums of Kenya, 1975
    -             : *Fort Jesus*. Museums of Kenya, 1981
Kislev, Mordechai; Hartmann, Anat; Bar Yosef, Ofer : *Early Domesticated Fig in the Jordan Valley*.
                 Science, 2-6-2006
Kislev, M.E.; Nadel, D.; Carmi, L. : *Epipaleolithic (19,000 BP) Cereal and Fruit Diet at Ohalo II,*
                 Sea of Galilee, Israel. Review of Paleobotany & Palymology. V.73 ,1992
Klein, Richard G., *Whither the Neanderthals?*. Science, v.299, 2003
    -        -   & Edgar, Blake. *The Dawn of Human Culture*. John Wiley & Sons, 2002
Knehtl. Irena.: *The Voyages of Zheng He*. Yemen Times, 8 September 2005
Lanfranchi, Raymond; Ndanga, Jean; Zana, Henri : *New Carbon 14C Datings of Iron Age Metallurgy*
                 in the Central African Dense Forest. Yale Bulletin 102, 1998
Larick, Roy; Ciochon, Russell & Zaim, Yahdi: *Homo erectus and the Emergence of Sunda in the*
                 Tethis Realm. Athena Review v 4, No 1. 2004
Latham, Ronald [translator]: *The Travels of Marco Polo*. Folio Society, 1968
LaViolette, Paul A.: *Earth under Fire*. Bear & Co, 2005
    -        -   . : *Evidence for a Global Warming at the Termination I Boundary and Its Possible*
                 Cosmic Dust Cause .The Starburst Foundation, Fresno, USA, 2005

308

Leakey, Mary: *Disclosing the Past.* Weidenfeld & Nicolson, 1984
- - : *Olduvai Gorge, my Search for Early Man.* Collins 1979.
Leakey, Meave: *The Dawn of Humans, The Farthest Horizon.* National Geographic, September 1995
Leakey, Richard E.: *Skull 1470.* National Geographic, June 1973
- - & Lewin, Roger: *Origins.* Macdonald & Jane's, 1977
- - & Walker, Alan: *Homo Erectus Unearthed.* National Geographic, November, 1985
- - & Lewin, Roger: *Origins Reconsidered.* Little, Brown, 1992
Lemonick, Michael & Dorfman, Andrea : *Father of us All?* Time Magazine 22-7-2002
Lewin, Roger: : *Complexity, Life at the Edge of Chaos.* Dent, 1993
Lewis, David. *We, the Navigators.* University of Hawaii Press, 1994
Lewis-Williams, J. D. : *The Economy and Social Context of Southern San Rock Art.* Current Anthropology v23.4., 1982
Lewis-Williams, David.: *Images of Mystery, Rock Art of the Drakensberg.* Double Storey Books, 2003
- - - & Pearce, David : *Inside the Neolithic Mind.* Thames & Hudson, 2005
- - - & Dowson : Thomas: *Images of Power*, Southern Books, 1989
Leyland, J.: *Adventures in the Far Interior of South Africa.* Routledge, 1866
Lhote, Henri: *Oasis of Art in the Sahara.* National Geographic, Aug. 1987
Liebenberg, Doyle P.: *The Drakensberg of Natal.* Bulpin, 1972
Liveing, Edward. *Across the Congo.* Witherby, 1962
Livingstone, David : *Missionary Travels and Researches in South Africa.* 1857. (Gutenberg Etexts 1997)
- - : *A Popular Account of Dr. David Livingstone's Expedition to the Zambesi and its Tributaries & the Discovery of Lakes Shirwa & Nyassa.* Johh Murray 1894
- - (Ed. Waller, Horace.) : *The Last Journals of David Livingstone in Central Africa from 1865 to his Death. (2 vols.)* John Murray 1874
Londhe, Sushama. *Seafaring in Ancient India.* A tribute to Hinduism - WWW, 2001
Lovelock, James: *The Ages of Gaia.* Oxford, 1988
- - : *The Revenge of Gaia.* Allen Lane, 2006
Lüthi, Dieter, *et al* : *High-resolution carbon dioxide concentration record 650,000-800,000 years before present.* Nature, 15 May 2008
Mabulla, Audax Z. P. : *The Rock Art of Mara Region, Tanzania.* Azania XL, 2005
Mack, John : *The Land Viewed from the Sea.* Azania XLII. 2007
Maclean, Charles Rawden: *The Natal Papers of John Ross.* Univ. of Natal, 1992
Maggs, Tim: *Mzonjani and the Beginning of the Iron Age in Natal.* Natal Museum 24(1), 1981
- - : *The Iron Age South of the Zambezi.* A.A.Balkema, 1984
Majid al-Najdi, Ahmad ibn (translator and editor : Tibbets, Gerald R.) : *Arab Navigation in the Indian Ocean before the coming of the Portuguese.* Royal Asiatic Society, 1971
Mana, Dembo *et al* : *The evolutionary relationships and age of Homo naledi. An assessment using detail Bayesian phylogenic methods.* Journal of Human Evolution v.97, 2016
Mas'udi (Translator Lunde, Paul & Stone, Caroline) : *The Meadows of Gold.* Penguin, London, 2007.
Manwell, Clyde & Baker: *Chemical Classification of Cattle.* Genet.11, University of Adelaide, 1980
Marais, Eugene: *The Soul of the Ape.* Human & Rousseau, 1969
Marean, Curtis W. : *Pinnacle Cave 13B (Western Cape, South Africa) in context.* Journal of Human Evolution v. 59, 2010
Marscher, Alan P. *et al* : *The inner jet of an active galactic nucleus as revealed by a radio-to-γ ray outburst.* Nature, vol 452. 24-4-2008
Marsh, David : *Waters Edge Man: the new paradigm currently displacing the Savannah Theory of Human Origins.* Nutrition & Health . v. 14.2
- - : *Role of the Essential Fatty Acids in the Evolution of the Modern Human Brain.* Positive Health Magazine, May 2001
- - : *The Origins of Diversity: Darwin's Conditions and Epigenetic Variations* Nutrition & Health, vol 19, 2007
Marshall, John & Ritchie, Claire: *Where are the JU/WASI of Nyae Nyae?.* African Studies, University of Cape Town 1984
Maslin, Mark; Trauth, Martin; Christensen, Beth : *A Changing Climate for Human Evolution.* Geotimes. Septermber 2005.
Mathews, Robert. *Meteor Clue to end of Middle East Civilisations.* Sunday Telegraph 4-11-2001
Matthews, Samuel W.: *Ice on the World.* National Geographic, Jan. 1987
Matthiessen, Peter: *The Tree where Man was Born.* Collins, 1972
Maylam, Paul: *A History of the African People of South Africa.* David Philip, 1986
McCrindle, J.W.: *The Christian Topography of Cosmas, an Egyptian Monk.* Hakluyt Society, 1897
McLaren, Angus: *Reproductive Rituals.* Methuen, 1984
McPhun, Delwyn : *East Africa Pilot.* Imray Laurie Norie & Wilson, 1998
Meier, David L, : *Exhaust Inspection,.* Nature, 24-4-2008

309

Meinel, Aden B.; Meinel. Marjorie P.; Meinel, B.; Drach-Meinel, D. : *Fingerprints in Ice: A Cosmic Encounter, a Cat's Eye, and Origin of Modern Humans.* Theoretical Archeological Group Conference, Sheffield University, December 2005.
Mendelssohn, Kurt: *Riddle of the Pyramids.* Praeger, 1974
Merfield, Fred G. & Miller, Harry: *Gorillas were my Neighbours.* Longmans, 1956
Merrick, H.V.: *Visitors Guide to the Hyrax Hill Site.* Museums of Kenya, 1983
Milliken, Sarah: *Out of Africa or Out of Asia? The colonization of Europe by Homo erectus.* Athena Review. V4, No 1. 2004
Monbiot, George : *No Man's Land.* Macmillan, 1994
Montgomery, Denis : *The Reflected Face of Africa.* African Insight, 1988
-           -   : *Two Shores of the Ocean.* Malvern Publishing, 1992
Moorehead, Alan: *The White Nile.* Hamish Hamilton, 1960
-     -   : *The Blue Nile.* Hamish Hamilton, 1962
Morais, João: *Mozambican Archaeology: Past and Present.* African Archaeological Review, 2, 1984
Morgan, Elaine: *The Descent of Woman.* Souvenir Press, 1972
-    -   : *The Aquatic Ape.* Souvenir Press, 1982
-    -   : *The Scars of Evolution.* Souvenir Press, 1990
-    -   : *The Aquatic Ape Hypothesis,* Souvenir Press.1997
Morgan, Elaine & Davies, Stephen. *Red Sea Pilot.* Imray, Laurie, Norie & Wilson, 2002.
Morris, Desmond: *The Naked Ape.* Cape, 1967
-    -   : *The Human Zoo.* Cape, 1969
-    -   : *Manwatching.* Cape, 1977
-    -   : *The Naked Woman.* Cape, 2004
Morris, Donald R.: *The Washing of the Spears.* Cape, 1966
Morwood, M.J., et al : *Archaeology and age of new hominin from Flores in eastern Indonesia.* Nature, 27-11-2004
NASA : *NASA Achieves Breakthrough In Black Hole Simulation* - News release 18/4/2006
National Geographic Society: *Where did Columbus Discover America?.* Nov. 1986
-              -   : *Does Living a Stone Age Life Cut Cancer Risk?.* August, 1993
Nature : Sundry original papers, including Dart, Johanson, Leakey etc : www.nature.com/nature/ancestor
Nicholson, Ward: *Longevity and Health in Ancient Palaeolithic v Neolithic Peoples.* www.beyondveg.com 1999
O'Brien, Frederick : *Mystic Isles of the South Seas.* Hodder & Stoughton, 1921
Oberholster, J.J.: *The Historical Monuments of South Africa.* Nat. Monuments Council, 1972
O'Connor, Anthony: *Poverty in Africa.* Belhaven Press, 1991
Oliver, Roland: *The African Experience.* Weidenfeld & Nicolson, 1991
-     -   & Fage, J.D.: *A Short History of Africa.* Penguin, 1962
Oppenheimer, Stephen : *Out of Eden, the Peopling of the World.* Constable. 2003
Owens, Mark & Delia: *Cry of the Kalahari.* Collins, 1985
Parfitt, Simon. *Pakefield: a weekend to remember.* British Archaeology. V 86. Jan-Feb 2006
Parkington, John : *The Mantis, the Eland & the Hunter.* Krakadouw Trust, 2002
-              : *Cederberg Rock Paintings.* Krakadouw Trust, 2003
-              : *Shorelines, Strandlopers and Shell Middens.* Krakadouw Trust 2006
Pearse, R.O.: *Barrier of Spears.* Howard Timmins, 1973
Pennisi, Elizabeth : *Genomes Throw Kinks in Timing of Chimp-Human Split.* Science, v 312. 19 May 2006
Phillipson, David W. *African Archaeology, 2nd Edition.* Cambridge, 1993
Phillipson, Laurel. *Ancient Gold Working at Aksum.* Azania XLI, 2006
Potts, Richard *et al* : *Small Mid-Pleistocene Hominin Associated with East Africa Acheulean Technology.* Science, 2 July 2004
Putnam, John J.: *The Search for Modern Humans.* National Geographic, Oct. 1988
Ransford, Oliver: *David Livingstone, the Dark Interior.* John Murray, 1978
Rasmussen, R.Kent: *Migrant Kingdom.* Rex Collings, 1978
Raven-Hart, R.: *Before van Riebeeck.* Struik, 1967
Ravenstein, E.G.: *The Voyages of Diogo Cão and Bartholomeu Dias 1482-1488.* The Royal Geographical Society Journal, 1900.
Reader, John : *Africa, a Biography of a Continent.* Penguin 1997
Redfield, T.F.: *A kinematic model for Afar Depression lithospheric thinning and its implications for hominid evolution : an exercise in plate tectonic paleoanthropology.* Geological Society of America, 2002
Redfield, T.F.; Wheeler. W.H.; Often, M. : *A kinematic model for the development of the Afar Depression and its paleogeographical implications.* Pre-publication paper. 2003
Reik, W., et al. : *Epigenic reprogramming in mammalian development.* Science, 2001.
Rigaud, Jean-Philippe: *Art Treasures from the Ice-Age, Lascaux Cave.* National Geographic, October, 1988

310

Rincon, Paul : *Footprints of 'First Americans'* . BBC News, 5 July 2005
    -   : *Hobbit was 'not a diseased human'* . BBC News 3 March 2005
Robertshaw, Peter : *Early Pastoralists of South-western Kenya*. BIEA, 1990
Roebroeks, Wil. *Archaeology: Life on the Costa del Cromer*. Nature, 15-12-2005
Roede, Machteld; Wind, Jan; Patrick, John & Reynolds, Vernon [eds.]: *The Aquatic Ape: Fact or Fiction*. Souvenir Press, 1991
Rosenblum, Mort & Williamson, Doug: *Squandering Eden*. Bodley Head, 1988
Sadr, Karim. *The First Herders at the Cape of Good Hope*. African Archaeological Review 15/2, 1998
Sample, Ian : *Neanderthal DNA reveals human divergence*. Guardian Unlimited. 16-11-2006
Sandelowsky, B.H.: *Archaeology in Namibia*. American Scientist v.71, 1983
Saugstad, Letten F. : *Are neurodegenerative disorder and psychotic manifestations avoidable brain dysfunctions with adequate dietary omega-3?* Nutrition & Health 18-2 (2006)
Schapera, I.: *Married Life in an African Tribe*. Faber, 1940
Schapera, I (ed.) *David Livingstone South African Papers 1849-1853*. Van Riebeeck Society, 1974
Schapera, I (ed.) *Bantu-Speaking Tribes of South Africa*. 1937
Schilling, Govert. : *Do Gamma Ray Bursts Always Line Up with Galaxies?* Science v 313 - 5788, 2006
Schoeman, P.J. (Prof.) : *Hunters of the Desert Land*. Howard Timmins, 1957
Schoff, William, H. : *The Periplus of the Erythraean Sea*. Longmans Green, NY. 1912
Schwandler, Jakob, et al. : *A tentative chronology for the EPICA Dome Concordia ice core*. Geophysical Rearch Letters. V.28 no.22, 2001
Segal, Ronald : *Islam's Black Slaves*. Atlantic Books, 2001
Selous, Frederick Courtney: *Travel and Adventure in South-East Africa*. Rowland Ward, 1893
Semino, Ornello ; Santachiara-Benerecetti, A.Silvano ; Falaschi, Francisco ; Cavalli-Sforza, L.Luca ; Underhill, Peter A. : *Ethiopians and Khoisan share the deepest Clades of the Human Y-chromosome Phylogeny*. American Journal of Human Genetics, 2002.
Shlovskii, I.S. & Sagan, Carl: *Intelligent Life in the Universe*. Holden-Day, 1966.
Sinclair, Paul : *Chibuene - An Early Trading Site in Southern Mozambique*. Paideuma 28, 1982
  -   -   : *Ethno-Archaeological Surveys of the Save River Valley, South Central Mozambique*. African Studies Programme, Uppsala. 1985
  -   -   : *Archeology in Eastern Africa, an Overview of Chronological Issues*. Journal of Asfrican History 32-01 1991.
Soderberg, A.M., et al. : *An extremely luminous X-ray outburst at the birth of a supernova*. Nature, 22-5-2008
Soper, Robert. *Nyanga, Ancient fields, settlements and agricultural history in Zimbabwe*. BIEA., 2002
Sparrman, Anders : *A Voyage to the Cape etc. and to the Country of the Hottentots and the Caffres from the year 1772-1776*. Robinson, London. 1785
Speke, John Hanning. *Journal of the Discovery of the Source of the Nile*. Blackwood, 1863
Spindler, Konrad: *The Man in the Ice*. Weidenfeld & Nicolson, 1994
Stanley, Henry Morton : *Through the Dark Continent*. Dover Publications. 1988 (orig1899)
Steyn, H.P. & du Pisani, E.: *Grass Seeds, Game and Goats: an Overview of Dama Subsistence*. Journal, SWA Scientific Society, 1985
Stone, Richard : *Java Man's First Tools*. Science magazine, 21 April 2006
Stringer, Chris : *Modern Human Origins*. The Royal Society, April 2002
  -   -   : *The First Humans North of the Alps*. British Archaeology v 86, Jan-Feb 2006
Stringer, Chris & McKie, Robin. *African Exodus, the Origins of Modern Humanity*. Jonathan Cape, 1996
Stringer, Chris & Gamble, Clive. *In Search of the Neanderthals*. Thames & Hudson, 1993
Stuart, James & Malcolm, D.McK. (Eds): *The Diary of Henry Francis Fynn*. Shuter and Shooter, 1969
Sutton, J.E.G: *A Thousand Years in East Africa*. British Institute in Eastern Africa, 1990
      -   : *Engaruka and its Waters*. Azania XIII, 1978
      -   : *Towards a History of Cultivating the Fields*. Azania XXIV, 1989
      -   [Ed]: *The Growth of Farming Communities in Africa from the Equator Southwards*. Azania [BIEA], 1996
Tavani, M. Et al : *Extreme particle accelerations in the microquasar Cynus X-3*. Nature v. 422, 2009
Templeton, Alan : *Recent finds in archaeology*. Nature. March 2002
Theal, George McCall: : *Records of South-Eastern Africa,*. Government of the Cape Colony, 1899
Theroux, Paul: *The Happy Isles of Oceania*. Hamish Hamilton, 1992
Thomas, Elizabeth Marshall: *The Harmless People*. Secker & Warburg, 1959
Thompson, George : *Travels and Adventures in Southern Africa*. Henry Colburn, 1827
Tishkoff, Sarah H., et al. : *History of Click-Speaking Populations of Africa Inferred from mtDNA and Y Chromosome Genetic Variation*. Molecular Biology and Evolution 24-10, 2007
Tobias, Phillip V .: *The Peoples of Africa South of the Sahara*. Clarendon Press, 1966
      -   : *On the Increasing Stature of the Bushmen*. Anthropos v 57, 1962
      -   : *Recent Human Biological Studies in Southern Africa with Special Reference to Negroes and Khoisans*. Royal Society of South Africa. 40-3, 1972
      -   : *Into the Past*. Picador Africa, 2005.

Trauth, Martin; Maslin, Mark; Delno, Alan; Streckner, Manfred : *Late Cenezoic Moisture History of East Africa*. Science v.309. September 2005.

Uhlig, Robert: *Mega-Neutron blast 'killed off dinosaurs'*. The Daily Telegraph, December 1996

Uyanker,B., Reich, W., Yar, A., Kothes, R., Fürst, E. : *Is the Cygnus Loop two supernova remnants?* Astronomy and Astrophysics, 2002.

van Grunderbeek, Marie-Claude. *Chronologie de l'Age du Fer Ancien au Burundi, au Rwanda et dans le Région des Grands Lacs,* AZANIA XXVII, 1992

van Schalkwyk, Len: *Settlement Shifts and Socio-economic Transformations in Early Agriculturalist Economies in the Lower Thukela Basin.* AZANIA XXIX-XXX, 1996

-            -   & Greenfield, Haskel J. *Intra-settlement Social and Economic Organisation of Early Iron Age Farming Communities in Southern Africa: a view from Ndondwane.* Azani XXXVIII, 2003

Vansina, Jan: *Western Bantu Expansion.* Journal of African History v 25, 1984

-            -   : *A Slow Revolution : Farming in sub-Tropical Africa.* AZANIA XXIX-XXX ,1996

Verhagen, Marc & Puesch, Peirre-Francois : *Hominid Lifestyle and Diet Reconsidered: Paleo-Environmental and Comparative Data.* Human Evolution 15, 2000

Vernet, Thomas. *Le commerce des eclaves sur le côte swahili,* 1500 - 1750. Azania XXXVIII, 2003

Wainwright, G.A. : *Cosmas and the Gold Trade of Fazogli.* Man, vol 42, no. 30. June 1942

Walker, Iain : *Hadramis, Shimalis and Muwalladim: Negotiating Cosmopolitan Identities between the Swahili Coast and Southern Yemen.* Journal of Eastern African Studies, March 2008

Wandibba, Simiyu: *Ancient and Modern Ceramic Traditions in the Lake Victoria Basin of Kenya.* Azania XXV 1990

Watson, Lyall : *Earthworks.* Hodder & Stoughton, 1986

-            -   : *Dark Nature,* Hodder & Stoughton, 1995

-            -   : *Lightning Bird,* Hodder & Stoughton, 1982

-            -   : *Elephantoms,* Norton & Co., 2002

Weinberg, Paul : *Once We were Hunters.* David Philip, 2000

Wendt, C.E.: *'Art Mobilier' from the Apollo 11 Cave, South West Africa.* South African Archaeological Bulletin 31, 1976

Werz, B.E.J.S. & Flemming, N.C. *Discovery in Table Bay of the oldest handaxes yet found demonstrates preservation of hominid artefacts on the continental shelf.* South African Journal of Science, May/June 2001.

Wheeler, Sir Mortimer: *The Indus Civilisation.* Cambridge, 1968

White, Randall. *Personal Ornaments from the Grotte du Rennes at Arcy-sur-Cure.* Athena Review 2001

White, Tim D. *et al : Pleistocene Homo sapiens from Middle Awash, Ethiopia.* Nature, 12 June 2003

Whitelaw, Gavin & Moon, Michael : *The ceramics and distribution of pioneer agriculturalists in KwaZulu-Natal.* Natal Museum Journal of Humanities, 1996

Whitelaw, Gavin : *Economy and cosmology in the Iron Age of KwaZulu-Natal.* PhD. thesis in the University of Witwatersrand, (unpublished) 2015

-            -   : *An Iron Age fishing tale.* Southern African Humanities 21:195-212, 2009

Wilding, Richard: *The Shorefolk.* Fort Jesus Museum, 1987

Willcox, A.R.: *The Drakensberg Bushmen and their Art.* Drakensberg Publications, 1984

Wilfiord, John Noble : *Mutation Cited in Evolution.* New York Times, 24 March 2004

Wills, A.J.: *An Introduction to the History of Central Africa.* Oxford, 1973

Wilson, Ian: *The Exodus Enigma.* Weidenfeld & Nicolson, 1985

Wilson, Monica & Thompson, Leonard (eds.): *Oxford History of South Africa.* Oxford, 1969

Withnell, Allan. *The Nature and Importance of Our Prehistoric Diet.* Nurition & Health v.17 No.4, 2004

Wong, Kate : *The Littlest Human.* Scientific American, Feb. 2005

Wood, Bernard : *Hominid Revelations from Chad :* Nature 418, 2002

Wright, John & Hamilton, Carolyn : *Traditions and Transformations* included in *Natal and Zululand from the Earliest Times to 1910.* University of Natal Press, 1989/

Wrigley, C.C.: *Bananas in Buganda.* Azania XXIV, 1989

Züchner, Christian : *Grotte Chauvet Archaeololically Dated.* IRAC Conference papers. 1998.

312

GENERAL INDEX

313

314

315

316

317

318

319